CW01653528

BBC

Speak out

3RD EDITION

B2

Split 1

Units 1–4

Student's Book and Workbook with eBook

LISTENING/VIDEO	SPEAKING	WRITING
Listen to a podcast about identity	Use a diagram to explain your identity	Write a blog post describing yourself
	Describe a memory **FUTURE SKILLS** Communication	
	Agree on an itinerary for a day in a city **FUTURE SKILLS** Collaboration **MEDIATION SKILLS** create tourist recommendations for your town/area	
BBC Street Interviews about personality	Discuss personality traits	Write a letter of recommendation
	Make predictions **FUTURE SKILLS** Critical thinking	
BBC Radio *Why we should listen to trees*	Suggest ways to encourage people to spend time in nature **FUTURE SKILLS** Leadership	Write a for-and-against essay on the pros and cons of living in the countryside
Listen to a conversation about unusual lifestyles	Speculate about the lives of famous people	**MEDIATION SKILLS** summarise an informal interview
BBC Programme *Doctor Who*	Talk about an imaginary trip back in time	Write a competition entry
	Plan an eco-friendly festival **FUTURE SKILLS** Collaboration	Write a formal email proposing a new festival
Listen to a podcast about stage fright	Practise speaking in public **FUTURE SKILLS** Self-management	
Listen to a conversation about binge-worthy TV shows	Describe your favourite film or TV series	**MEDIATION SKILLS** describe a film
BBC Street Interviews about music	Ask and answer questions about the importance of music in your life	Write a forum comment
	Talk about how your life will be different in five years' time **FUTURE SKILLS** Communication	
BBC Radio *The science of sleep*	Discuss statements about sleep	Write an article about how to get a good night's sleep
Listen to a conversation about the benefits of exercise	Hold short debates on sports and exercise **MEDIATION SKILLS** decide how to contribute to an event	
BBC Programme *Earth from Space*	A discussion about traditional vs. modern lifestyles	Write a cause-and-effect essay

LISTENING/VIDEO	SPEAKING	WRITING
	Tell an anecdote about the first time you did something **FUTURE SKILLS** Communication	
BBC Radio *Is one career in your life enough?*	Discuss a time when your life plans changed	Write a report about broadening young people's career aspirations
Listen to three problematic video conference calls **MEDIATION SKILLS** agree on a course of action	Practise describing problems and suggesting solutions	
BBC Street Interviews about working in a team	A discussion about working alone vs. in a team	A thank-you message
	Discuss your top three ways to avoid distraction **FUTURE SKILLS** Self-management	Edit notes to make them more concise
Listen to a conversation about introverts	Take a quiz about introverts and extroverts	
Listen to someone asking for advice	Practise giving advice tactfully	**MEDIATION SKILLS** add to posts in a thread, building on the advice of other people
BBC Programme *Would I Lie to You?*	A true or false story	An email giving news
	Speculate about a series of chance events	
Listen to people talking about missed opportunities	Discuss your regrets	Write a personal essay
Listen to someone explaining a recipe	Explain your way of doing something **FUTURE SKILLS** Communication **MEDIATION SKILLS** make a concept easier for someone else to understand	
BBC Street Interviews about talent and hard work	A discussion about talents	A social media post
	Discuss co-living spaces **FUTURE SKILLS** Collaboration	Write a job application letter/email
Listen to a talk about world issues	Discuss hypothetical situations **FUTURE SKILLS** Creative and critical thinking	
Listen to part of a debate about online communities	Hold a debate about online communities	**MEDIATION SKILLS** make a discursive argument on a topic
BBC Programme *Amazing Humans*	A presentation on a project	A mission statement

GRAMMAR

1 A Read the text. Who is it? Look on page 142 to find out.

Who am I?

I'm one of the most famous British men who ever lived, but my family wasn't famous. My father made gloves! I got married at eighteen and became an actor. My career took off rapidly when I moved to London, but it wasn't acting. If the printing press hadn't been invented, you probably wouldn't have heard of me. People have been reading and watching my works for over four centuries, and some of my plays have been made into well-known films. In 2116, I will have been dead for 500 years.

B Read the text again and find examples of the following.

1 a relative clause
2 a conditional sentence
3 a verb in the present perfect continuous form
4 a verb in the future perfect form
5 a verb in the past perfect passive form
6 a phrasal verb
7 an adverb

COMMON ERRORS

2 A Correct the mistakes in the questions.

1 How long you have been studying English?
2 Do you enjoy listening music in English?
3 When was the last time you watch a film in English?
4 Do you like discussing about current affairs?
5 Are you looking forward to learn more English?
6 What would you do if you would have unlimited time and money?

B Which mistakes in Ex 2A feature:

1 a verb pattern?
2 a conditional form?
3 word order?
4 a verb tense?
5 a missing preposition?
6 an extra preposition?

C Work in pairs. Ask and answer the questions in Ex 2A.

PRONUNCIATION

3 A Match the sentence beginnings (1–10) with the endings (a–j) that rhyme.

1 I thought I could	a back on my farm.
2 I stayed although	b and I feel great.
3 She felt so calm	c while in the queue.
4 All that stuff	d the pot of gold.
5 I watch my weight	e they'd all find out.
6 We read the review	f escape this wood.
7 He had no doubt	g felt so rough.
8 When you cough	h I wanted to go.
9 The girl controlled	i that bit of earth.
10 It was worth	j it puts me off.

B Work in pairs. Think of other words in English that have the same rhymes as 1–10.

VOCABULARY

4 A Look at the nouns and noun phrases in the boxes. Which verb do they go with?

***do* or *make*?**

a choice a fortune a profit business me a favour notes the laundry your best

***take* or *have*?**

a chat a course a dream a good time a relationship an important step charge your time

B Work in pairs. Say a noun or noun phrase from Ex 4A. Your partner says the correct verb, without looking at the book.

5 A Choose the correct prepositions to complete the sentences.

1 I get **on** / **in** / **up** well with my dad.
2 He gave **on** / **up** / **in** eating fast food.
3 This machine is out **of** / **in** / **to** order.
4 We'll always keep **in** / **on** / **to** touch.
5 We arrived **to** / **by** / **at** the stadium early.
6 We may be late. It depends **of** / **by** / **on** the traffic.
7 Ken is married **to** / **with** / **on** Jan.
8 Congratulations **on** / **for** / **of** your success!

B Complete the sentences with the correct form of the phrasal verbs in Ex 5A.

1 Who do you .... well with in your family? Why?
2 Have you ever .... anything .... ? What and why?
3 How do you .... with your friends and family?

C Work in pairs. Discuss the questions.

identity 1

VLOGS

Q: Who do you take after in your family?

1 Watch the video. Note down the family members that people mention and the characteristics they share.

2 Work in pairs. Discuss who you take after in your family. Give examples.

Global Scale of English

LEARNING OBJECTIVES

1A LISTENING | Understand a podcast about identity: personality adjectives; suffixes

Talk about your identity: present perfect simple and continuous

Pronunciation: weak forms of *have* and *been*

Write a blog post about yourself

1B READING | Read an article about people who never forget: infinitive and *-ing* forms; collocations about memory; idioms: memory

Pronunciation: chunking: two-part collocations

Describe a memory

1C HOW TO ... | express personal preferences; emotions and feelings

Pronunciation: word stress: dependent prepositions

1D BBC STREET INTERVIEWS | Understand street interviews about people's personalities

Talk about personality traits: *while*, *whereas* and *whilst*

Write a letter of recommendation

1A My ID

GRAMMAR | present perfect simple and continuous
VOCABULARY | personality adjectives; suffixes
PRONUNCIATION | weak forms of *have* and *been*

VOCABULARY

personality adjectives

1 A Work in pairs and discuss the questions.

1 How would you usually describe yourself to someone you have never met before?
2 How do you think the factors in the box might influence someone's personality?

| the language you speak | where you live |
| your family | your life experiences |

B Read the article. Does it include any of your ideas?

C Work in pairs and discuss the questions.

1 Which ideas in the article do you agree or disagree with? Which do you find surprising?
2 Do you feel your personality changes when you speak a different language? In what way?
3 What other things do you think can influence your personality?

2 A Complete the meanings with the adjectives in bold in the article.

1 If someone doesn't follow the rules, you can say they are being ....
2 When you are interested in learning about new things, you are ....
3 When you have big plans to achieve a lot of things, you are ....
4 If you like to go out with a lot of people and enjoy yourself, you are ....
5 If you smile a lot and feel happy most of the time, you are ....
6 People who often disagree with other people are ....
7 If you're not afraid of going to new places and taking risks, you are ....
8 If you refuse to change your mind about something, you are ....

B Work in pairs. Describe three people you know using words from Ex 2A. Explain why you chose each word.

C Learn and practise. Go to the Vocabulary Bank.

page 136 **VOCABULARY BANK** suffixes

What shapes our personality?

Sarah Logan | Wed 6th Jan | 22.18 GMT

Our experiences have a huge impact on our personalities. The jobs we do, the people we meet, our achievements and disappointments all contribute to the kind of person we are. What other factors might also be important?

Family

A lot of people think that our personality is shaped by the size of our family and our position in it. Some argue that first-born children are more likely to be **ambitious** achievers. Younger children, on the other hand, might be more **rebellious** and willing to break rules. The youngest child of a family is often fun-loving and **adventurous** – always keen to try new things. We can inherit personality characteristics, too, like being **argumentative** or **stubborn**.

Language

Research suggests that the language we speak influences our personality and the way we think. In a recent survey of international students, Gosia, a Polish-born immigrant in the USA, says that when she speaks English, she feels 'more **curious** about the world'. Natasha, who speaks several languages, says that she feels more romantic when she's speaking in Portuguese, more **cheerful** and likely to smile when speaking Italian and more relaxed when speaking in Greek.

Geography

Other studies show that where we live or were born might also influence our lifestyle, our personality and the way that we interact with others socially. People living in warmer climates often see themselves as more sociable and **outgoing**, whilst people from mountainous areas seem to be more open to new experiences.

LISTENING

3 A 🔊 1.01 | Listen to a podcast on what makes us who we are. Who mentions the following topics? Matteo, Hana or both?

1 living in different countries
2 enjoying food from a particular country or area
3 having a mixed identity
4 identifying with a particular type of music
5 work experience
6 family influence

B 🔊 1.01 | Listen again and answer the questions.

1 How was Matteo able to get an Italian passport?
2 How has Matteo's Italian background influenced his lifestyle?
3 Does Matteo feel British? Why/Why not?
4 How does Hana feel about the different countries she has lived in?
5 Which part of her personality does Hana think she gets from a parent?
6 Why does Hana think she is so ambitious and focused on her career?

C Work in pairs. Look at the quotes from the podcast. Are the comments true for you? Can you think of examples?

1 '… everything I grew up with – the food, the language, the people – all of that forms a big part of who I am.'
2 '… all of these different places [where I've lived] play a part in who I am, far beyond the idea of nationality or belonging to one single place.'
3 'Everyone is an individual with different life experiences and different stories to tell.'

GRAMMAR

present perfect simple and continuous

4 A Work in pairs. Read each pair of sentences (a and b) and answer the questions (1–6).

a We've been interviewing people out on the street.
b We've had some really interesting replies.
1 Which tense focuses on the result of an activity?
2 Which tense focuses on the activity itself?

a I've lived in lots of different places around the world.
b I've been living in the UK for over five years now.
3 Which tense answers the question: How many?
4 Which tense answers the question: How long?

a I've learnt that hard work always pays off.
b I've been learning Dutch, but it's really hard!
5 Which tense describes a completed action?
6 Which tense describes an activity which is unfinished?

B Learn and practise. Go to the Grammar Bank.

▶▶ page 108 **GRAMMAR BANK**

PRONUNCIATION

5 A 🔊 1.02 | *weak forms of have and been* | Listen and complete the questions.

1 How long .... living here?
2 .... lived in another country?
3 What .... doing recently?
4 How long .... studying English?

B 🔊 1.02 | Listen again. Does the speaker use the strong forms of *have* and *been* (/hæv/ and /biːn/) or the weak forms (/həv/ and /bɪn/)?

C Work in pairs. Ask and answer the questions in Ex 5A.

SPEAKING

6 A Draw a pie chart like the one below to explain what makes you who you are. Make notes about why each part is important.

B Work in groups. Show your charts to each other and talk about the different parts of your personal identity. Whose ideas are similar to yours?

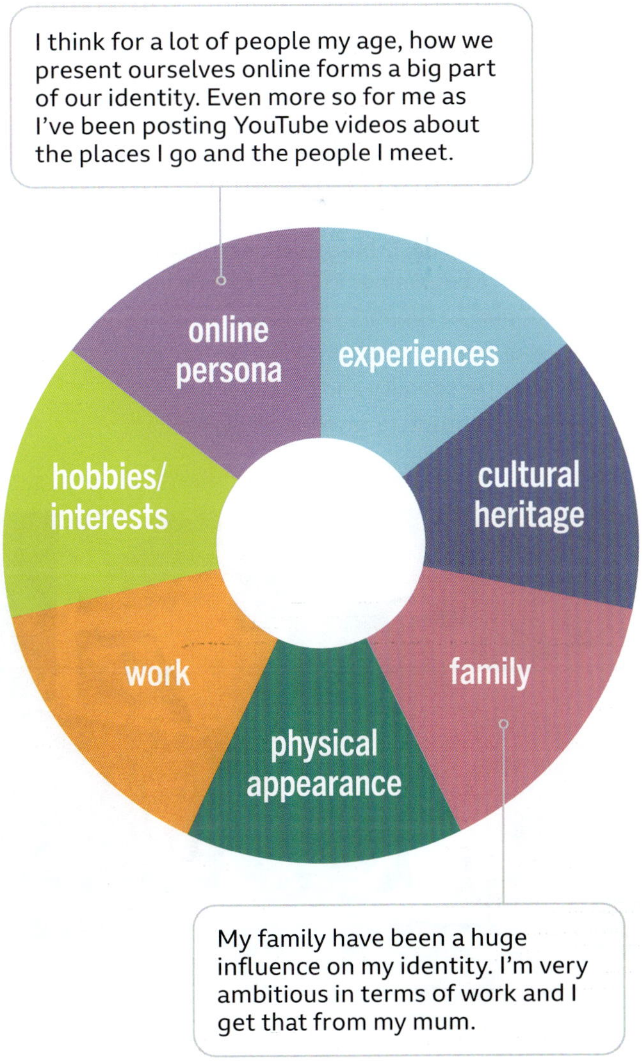

WRITING

a blog post

7 A Read the blog post. What do you learn about Sydney's family background, personality and attitude to work?

B Complete the blog post with Sydney's examples to support her ideas.

a Recently, I've taken up rock climbing and surfing.
b I love nothing more than getting together with a big group of friends!
c I love the Chinese New Year celebrations, and I'm crazy about Asian food!
d You will often find me working late at night to get the job done.

C Match the sentence beginnings (1–7) with the endings (a–g).

1 I would say that I
2 In my work, I'm very
3 You will often find me
4 In my personal life,
5 I would like to think
6 I love nothing more than
7 Recently I've taken up

a at my desk before anyone else arrives at work.
b I like to be sociable.
c that I'm cheerful and friendly.
d reliable. I will always complete a job I'm given.
e doing a job to the best of my abilities.
f work harder than most people I know.
g skateboarding and I'm really enjoying it.

D Write a *Who am I?* blog post describing yourself. Use the sentence beginnings in Ex 7C to help you, and include examples to support your ideas. Write about:

- your family background and identity.
- your personality and personal life.
- your attitude to work or studying.

Who am I?

My name is Sydney and I was born in Sacramento, in the USA. My parents are immigrants from China, so I've grown up speaking Mandarin at home but English at school and with my friends. We have family in China so we have always visited regularly. As well as my U.S. identity, I would say that I identify quite strongly with my Asian roots. [1] ....

In my personal life, I would like to think that I'm quite adventurous. I love trying out new experiences. [2] .... I'm not particularly good at either, but I'm quite stubborn, so I plan to keep going. I'm also outgoing and sociable. [3] ....

In my work, I'm very ambitious. I never settle for anything less than the best and always work hard. [4] .... In terms of my experience, I've been designing websites for over seven years. I co-founded WebDesignSY, an award-winning creative studio. I've designed websites for businesses, charities and individuals. I've also taught several courses in design at the California Institute of Arts and Technology. I love nothing more than thinking of interesting ways to represent you and your brand, so please get in touch.

1B Memory

GRAMMAR | infinitive and *-ing* forms
VOCABULARY | collocations about memory; idioms: memory
PRONUNCIATION | chunking: two-part collocations

GRAMMAR

infinitive and *-ing* forms

1 **Work in pairs. Ask and answer the questions.**

1 Can you remember …
- what you were doing on Sunday two weeks ago?
- the birthdays of all your family members?
- the last film you saw at the cinema?
- how you celebrated your birthday two years ago?
- what your first teacher looked like?

2 Do you generally have a good memory or are you forgetful?

3 Do you know any special techniques to improve your memory?

2 A **Work in pairs. Read about seven different ways to remember things. Which do you do already? Which would you like to try? Why?**

B **Match the phrases in bold in Ex 2A with the rules (1–4).**

1 We can use an infinitive after the verb *be*.
to write

2 We can use an infinitive to express a purpose.

3 We use the *-ing* form after prepositions.

4 We can use some verbs followed by an infinitive or an *-ing* form, with a change in meaning (four phrases).

C **Learn and practise. Go to the Grammar Bank.**

page 109 **GRAMMAR BANK**

1 When I have to **remember to do** things, I write notes to myself.

2 I like using visualisation – connecting facts to images. It works well for me. I **remember visualising** facts for a test last month and I passed!

3 Before a presentation, I **try to practise** in front of a mirror to make sure I don't forget what I'm going to say.

4 **To keep** a list in my head, I invent songs, which I sing to myself.

5 I heard sleep is good for your memory, so I **tried taking** naps after class.

6 I remember facts **by imagining** I'm in a building. Everything on the list is in a different room and I walk through the rooms.

7 My technique is **to write** a story that uses everything I need to remember.

READING

3 A Work in pairs. Think about your family and friends. Who has the best memory? What kinds of things can they remember well?

B Read the article and answer the questions.

1 What kinds of things do Funes, Veiseh and Price remember?
2 What kinds of people are more likely to have HSAM?
3 What is the connection between emotions and memory?

C Scan the article again and find the information.

1 the author of the book *Funes the Memorius*
2 the significance of the date 15 December 2000
3 the age at which Jill Price first contacted Dr McGaugh
4 the date when Elvis Presley died
5 what the abbreviation HSAM stands for
6 the amount of time Dr McGaugh has spent researching memory

D Work in groups. Discuss the questions.

1 What do you think are the advantages and disadvantages of having abilities like Veiseh and Price?
2 Why do you think some people are better at remembering things than others?

VOCABULARY

collocations about memory

4 A Scan the article again. Complete the sentences with the correct form of the collocations in bold.

1 Your .... are things you can remember from when you were very young.
2 If you have a good .... , you can remember things for an extended period of time.
3 If you have .... , you can remember things exactly as they are, without making mistakes.
4 If something .... , it makes you think of something from the past.
5 If you are generally able to remember things well, you ....
6 When you .... , you learn them in such a way that you can repeat them from memory.
7 If you .... of something, you remember every small part and moment of it.
8 You have a good .... if you can remember things from a few moments ago.

B Work in pairs. Find the idiom *go in one ear and out the other* in paragraph five of the article. What do you think it means?

C Learn and practise. Go to the Vocabulary Bank.

▶▶ page 136 **VOCABULARY BANK** idioms: memory

The people who never forget

What research is telling us about people with amazing memories

Ayodele Odetoyinbo
Mon 18th June

In Jorge Luis Borges's story *Funes the Memorius*, the title character falls off his horse, bangs his head, and suddenly remembers everything he's ever experienced. He remembers the changing shapes of clouds and the exact position of a dog at different times of day. He remembers every leaf on every tree he's ever seen and reconstructs his dreams at will.

Some people say that truth is stranger than fiction, and sure enough, there are real people with similar abilities to Funes. The designer, artist and entrepreneur Nima Veiseh can **remember every detail** of his late teenage years: the clothes he was wearing on any given day, what he ate at every meal, every painting on every wall of every art gallery he's ever visited. He can even remember the day he started to remember everything: 15th December, 2000.

But Veiseh wasn't the first. Before him was Jill Price. When Price was thirty-four, she contacted Dr James McGaugh, director of the Center for the Neurobiology of Learning and Memory at the University of California, Irvine. She explained that she had a problem: whenever she saw a date on TV, it **brought back memories** and she began reliving everything that had happened on that day. McGaugh invited her to the centre.

To test her memory, McGaugh used a book which contained summaries of the major news stories from every day of the twentieth century. He quizzed her. What happened on 16th August, 1977? Price told him Elvis Presley died that day and it was a Tuesday. When did the singer Bing Crosby die? 14th October, 1977. It was a Friday, and Price heard the news on the car radio on her way to football practice. Asked about the date of one major international event, she got the answer wrong. McGaugh corrected her, but she insisted. He checked another source and found that the book was wrong.

Jill Price was the first person to be diagnosed with HSAM (Highly Superior Autobiographical Memory), a condition which enables someone to remember the events of their life in great detail. Jill doesn't make the effort to **learn things by heart** – it just happens. However, her ability only functions with things she is interested in. When asked to recall a long series of numbers or other general information, she loses her **perfect recall**. Like the rest of us, things go in one ear and out the other. Her memory is connected to her individual identity and things that are important to her.

Dr McGaugh has spent half a century researching memory. He has led numerous experiments on **long-term memory** and **short-term memory**. One conclusion from the research is that people who have HSAM are more likely to enjoy daydreaming, creating fantasies and imagining different worlds. This may mean they have greater ability to create memorable pictures in their minds, which helps them remember things. Another conclusion is that **having a good memory** is aided by the ability to focus completely on what we are doing. Immersing ourselves deeply in a task means we are more likely to remember the details. A third finding is the importance of emotional connections. When we are engaged emotionally in something, we are less likely to forget it. That's why our **childhood memories** are often very powerful.

People in many walks of life – students, teachers, lawyers – need to remember information to be successful. Even if we can't recall details in the way Price, Veiseh and Borges's Funes can, maybe there *are* things we can learn from McGaugh's research. For example, we're more likely to remember information if we focus deeply on it, or if we can find an emotional connection with it. Understanding these things might benefit all of us.

PRONUNCIATION

5 A 1.03 | **chunking: two-part collocations** | **Listen to the sentences. Is there a pause between the words in bold, or are they said as one chunk?**

1 I definitely don't have **perfect recall** when it comes to remembering appointments!
2 My **long-term memory** is pretty good.
3 There are lots of techniques for improving your **short-term memory**.
4 We love sharing our **childhood memories**.

B 1.03 | **Listen to the sentences again. Then practise saying the collocations in bold as one chunk.**

C Work in pairs and discuss the questions.

1 Which is better – your short-term memory or your long-term memory?
2 Are you good or bad at learning things by heart?
3 Do you enjoy talking about childhood memories with your family?
4 Are there any sounds or smells that bring back memories for you?

SPEAKING

6 A You are going to describe a memory. Think of something interesting or funny that happened to you recently or in your childhood. Use the prompts below to make notes.

- When did it happen?
- Where were you?
- Who was there?
- What happened?

B Read the Future Skills box and do the task.

FUTURE SKILLS
Communication

When we tell a story, we need to maintain our listeners' interest. One way to do this is by describing details that are unusual, funny or interesting.

Look at your notes in Ex 6A and add interesting details. Think about the place, the weather, the people, the sights, sounds and smells, etc.

C Work in groups. Tell your story. Remember to describe details to keep your listeners interested.

I'm going to tell you about a memory from when I was about ten. I remember meeting …

1C I'd much rather ...

HOW TO ... | express personal preferences
VOCABULARY | emotions and feelings
PRONUNCIATION | word stress: dependent prepositions

VOCABULARY

emotions and feelings

1 A Work in groups. Discuss the questions.

1. What kind of things do you like doing when you visit a new city?
2. When was the last time you visited a new place? Where was it and what did you do?

B Work in pairs. Read the travel guide entry about Lagos, Nigeria. Which of the activities would you like or not like to do? Why?

C Scan the guide again. Complete the sentences with the words in bold.

1. If you're passionate about something, you love it.
2. If you're .... of something, you like it.
3. If you're .... something, you feel worried about doing it.
4. If you're .... something, it frightens you a lot.
5. If you're .... the idea of something, you find it very exciting.
6. If you're really .... something, you like it a lot.
7. If you're not .... something, you don't like it much.
8. If you are .... something, you don't want to do it anymore.

PRONUNCIATION

2 A 1.04 | word stress: dependent prepositions | Listen to the sentences and look at the phrases in bold. Which word is stressed, the adjective or the preposition?

1. I'm **terrified of** the traffic.
2. I'm **passionate about** trying local food.
3. I get **nervous about** taking taxis.
4. I'm not **keen on** museums.
5. I'm **fond of** the street markets.
6. I was **thrilled by** the chance to explore.

B Work in pairs. Discuss the activities in the box using the phrases in Ex 1C.

driving in foreign countries getting lost in a new city going on boat rides learning about new cultures trying unusual foods visiting museums watching dance performances

A: I'm really into trying new or unusual foods.
B: Me too!

AFRICA > NIGERIA

Lagos

Welcome to Lagos

Are you **passionate about** fashion? **Thrilled by** the idea of discovering new and interesting art? Maybe you're **fond of** street markets? Or are you **really into** cities by the ocean? If you like any of these, Lagos might be the place for you.

The most populous city in Africa, Lagos is full of life: loud chatter, the smells of delicious street food, and non-stop music. Because it's so big, you may be **nervous about** getting lost or **terrified of** the crazy traffic. Never fear! Use tour buses or rent a private car with a driver. And plan ahead. It can take a while to get around.

For a perfect day in Lagos, start at Bogobiri House, a wonderful hotel with striking artworks on the walls. Next, go to Freedom Park to learn about Nigerian history and culture, and watch dancers and musicians performing. If you're **not keen on** culture but like shopping, go to Victoria Island, Lagos's equivalent of Manhattan, with stylish designer shops and great restaurants. By now, you may be **fed up of** the city centre, so head to Tarkwa Bay Beach and go for a relaxing boat ride. End the day with a meal of pepper soup followed by jollof rice and chicken. Perfection on a plate!

How to …

express personal preferences

3 A 🔊 **1.05 | Listen to two businesspeople discussing what to do on their day off in Lagos. What do they decide to do?**

B 🔊 **1.05 | Complete the sentences from the conversation. Then listen again and check.**

1 The .... about it is the street life.
2 I'd be happy to go there .... , but maybe not more than a couple of hours.
3 I'm not a big .... shopping generally.
4 I'd .... to a park and just wander about for a bit.
5 I think I'd .... do that than to go wandering around the shops.
6 You know, ... really like doing is surfing.

C Complete the table with the phrases in the box. Use the sentences in Exercise 3B to help you.

I'd be happy I'd prefer
I'd rather I'm (not) a big fan of
What I love about

expressing personal preferences	
expressing likes and dislikes	I'm really into/I'm passionate about … I'm (not) keen on [1] .... … [2] .... /The thing I love/like about … is …
discussing options	[3] .... (to do that) because … [4] .... (do that) because … I'd much rather …
compromising	[5] .... to … , but …

D Learn and practise. Go to the Grammar Bank.

⏩ page 110 **GRAMMAR BANK**

4 A Read the list of things to do in Prague. Which activities would you choose to do? Why?

Top 5 Things to do in Prague

1 Charles Bridge – walk across this famous, historical stone bridge with its thirty statues.
2 Farmers' Market, Náplavka – visit this great street market and try meat, fish, baked goods, etc.
3 Prague Castle – visit the historical castle, over 1,000 years old, with halls, towers, gates and gardens.
4 Gallery of Steel Figures – see amazing metal sculptures of superheroes, cars, bicycles, etc.
5 Westfield Chodov – spend time in this modern shopping centre with designer stores, restaurants and an eighteen-screen cinema.

B Work in pairs. Imagine you have a day to spend in Prague together. Take turns making suggestions and responding using the phrases in Ex 3C.

A: Why don't we go to the Farmers' Market? I'm really into trying new kinds of food.
B: Great idea! I'm passionate about food, too.

SPEAKING

5 A Work in groups. Brainstorm some cities you would like to visit, and choose one you are all interested in.

B Work alone. Imagine you are going to spend a day in the city you chose in Ex 5A. Make notes about:

- places to visit (e.g. famous sites, museums, green spaces, etc.).
- activities (e.g. shopping, concerts, city tours, etc.).
- how you'll get around.
- meals (e.g. what to eat, when, where, etc.).
- what to do in the evening.

C Read the Future Skills box and do the task.

FUTURE SKILLS
Collaboration

When we collaborate, we sometimes have to compromise, to find a solution that everyone can accept.

Look at your notes in Ex 5B. What ideas might you need to compromise on? Why? What other ideas would be acceptable to you, as a compromise?

D In your groups, try to agree on an itinerary for a day in the city. Use your notes in Ex 5B to help you. Then present your ideas to the class.

MEDIATION SKILLS
organising a group task

create tourist recommendations for your town/area

⏩ page 146 **MEDIATION BANK**

Speak anywhere Go to the interactive speaking practice

1D BBC Street Interviews

Personality

Collin

GRAMMAR | *while*, *whereas* and *whilst*
SPEAKING | discuss personality traits
WRITING | a letter of recommendation

Anna

PREVIEW

1 A Work in groups. Take turns describing the personality of someone in the group without saying their name. Try to guess who is being described.

B Match the sentence beginnings (1–8) with the endings (a–h).

1 Camille is really **bubbly** – she's always
2 Ali is very **committed** to
3 My sister loves trying new things. She's always **enthusiastic**
4 You should try to be more cheerful
5 I always seem to worry about things – I'd love to
6 My grandma is a very kind
7 I always try to stay
8 Everyone was very **welcoming** to

a when I suggest doing something different.
b and **loving** person.
c laughing and full of life.
d be more happy-go-lucky.
e **positive** when things go wrong.
f and less **grumpy**!
g the new club members.
h his job – he takes it very seriously.

C Work in pairs. Take turns using the adjectives in Ex 1B to describe your friends and family.

Q1: How would you describe your personality?

Q2: How does your personality change in different situations?

VIEW

2 A Work in pairs. Watch the interviews. Which of the speakers is similar to you? In what ways?

B Watch the first part of the interviews again. Note down at least one adjective each speaker uses to describe themselves. Which of the adjectives can describe you?

C Watch the second part of the interviews again. Choose the correct words to complete the sentences.

1 Elaine's personality changes when she is **in other countries** / **at work**.
2 Anna thinks she is more **serious** / **stressed** at work.
3 Valeria is more **direct** / **compassionate** at work.
4 Elijah talks more when he is with his **friends** / **mother**.
5 Gwen sometimes has the feeling she doesn't want to be at **work** / **a party**.
6 Roisin is less confident **with new people** / **at work**.
7 Collin says that his personality **changes a lot** / **never changes**.

D Choose the correct meanings (a or b).

1 Elaine: I try to make the best that I can out of life.
  a She tries to think positively even in bad situations.
  b She feels sad in many situations.
2 Anna: I'm a people person.
  a She thinks she is similar to many other people.
  b She likes people and gets on well with them.
3 Collin: I never give up.
  a He keeps trying even in difficult situations.
  b He is always generous to others.
4 Elaine: I'll need to be a little bit more professional.
  a She has to speak more.
  b She has to be more serious.
5 Gwen: It varies.
  a It always stays the same.
  b It changes, depending on the situation.

BBC

GRAMMAR

while, *whereas* and *whilst*

3 A Read the sentences from the interviews and choose the correct option to complete the rule.

1 At work, maybe I'm more serious, **whereas** when I go to, like, a café with my friends, er, I'm a lot more relaxed.

2 I'm probably less confident when I meet new people, **whilst** when I'm with my friends, I'm a bit more confident, a bit more chatty, a bit more comfortable.

We use *while*, *whereas* and *whilst* to introduce a second idea that is **similar to** / **different from** the first idea in the sentence.

B Learn and practise. Go to the Grammar Bank.

page 111 **GRAMMAR BANK**

SPEAKING

discuss personality traits

4 A Make notes on the following questions.

1 How would you describe your personality?

2 How does your personality change in different situations (e.g. when you're hanging out with friends, with family, at work or when you meet new people, etc.)?

3 Has your personality changed as you've got older? If so, how?

4 In what ways is your personality similar to and different from other people in your family?

5 What personality traits are important in a friend?

6 What personality traits are important for the roles or jobs in the box? Why?

comedian	hairdresser	lawyer
manager	parent	police officer
sales representative	teacher	

B Work in pairs. Discuss the questions in Ex 4A. Use your notes to help you.

C Work with a different partner. Describe your first partner's personality. What job do you think they would be good at? Why?

WRITING

a letter of recommendation

5 A Work in pairs. Discuss the questions.

1 Who would you ask to write a letter of recommendation for you? Why?

2 What do you think they might say about you?

B Write a letter of recommendation. Go to the Writing Bank.

page 104 **WRITING BANK**

GRAMMAR

present perfect simple and continuous

1 A Use the prompts to write questions in the present perfect simple or continuous.

1 How long / you / learn / English?
2 How many teachers / you / have?
3 What / you / do / improve your English recently?
4 you / finish / today's homework?
5 you / study / a lot / recently?
6 you / watch / any films in English recently?

B Work in pairs. Ask and answer the questions.

infinitive and *-ing* forms

2 Complete the sentences (1–8) with the correct ending, a or b.

1 I stopped to call Omar because
2 I stopped calling Omar because
a I needed his help.
b he never wanted to talk to me.

3 Do you remember to send
4 Do you remember sending
a those funny letters when we were children?
b your mum a birthday message every year?

5 I forgot to take
6 I forgot taking
a that photo. We were so young then!
b a photo, so I can't show you where we went.

7 Sarita tried to take the medicine,
8 Sarita tried taking the medicine,
a but it didn't help.
b but she couldn't – it was too disgusting.

VOCABULARY

3 A Choose the correct words to complete the sentences.

1 I think this person is really **into** / **about** music.
2 I don't think they're very **keen** / **curious** on sport.
3 They're passionate **about** / **for** the environment.
4 This person seems to **have** / **keep** a good memory.
5 This person enjoys doing exciting things. They are very **adventurous** / **stubborn**.
6 They enjoy being with people – they're very **ambitious** / **outgoing**.
7 This person might be **nervous** / **terrified** about taking exams.
8 They are good at learning things by **memory** / **heart**.

B Work in pairs. Name someone in your class who you think matches each sentence in Ex 3A. Then talk to that student. Were you right?

A: Are you really into music?
B: No, not really. I listen to it at work, but that's about it. How about you?

4 A Choose the correct options (A–C) to complete the anecdote.

Stormy weather

Since I was very young, I [1]........ the outdoors. As a ten-year-old, I read lots of books about explorers and I was extremely [2]........ . I was happy wandering into the woods on my own, or exploring abandoned houses. [3]........ most children are [4]........ about the natural world, I was obsessed. I have one particular childhood [5]........ of a day with my grandfather. He was really [6]........ hiking and one day, when I was ten, he took me with him. The idea was [7]........ up a hill called Gomez Peak, and we needed to go at a good pace so [8]........ back by dinnertime. Unfortunately, we got caught in a storm. There was no escape. We tried [9]........ under a pine tree to stay dry, but it didn't work; we got soaked. As we stood there, he kept trying [10]........ me, saying, 'It's going to be OK.' He thought I'd be [11]........ of all the noise and wind. But I wasn't scared – I loved it. I'll never forget [12]........ to the rain falling like drumbeats. To this day, I have never had so much fun in my life!

	A	B	C
1	have always been loving	always love	have always loved
2	adventurous	ambitious	nervous
3	While	Because	However
4	terrified	keen	curious
5	recall	memory	detail
6	keen	passionate	into
7	to go	going	by going
8	as we were	that we are	as to be
9	standing	stand	to stand
10	comfort	comforting	to comfort
11	fed up	terrified	not keen
12	listen	to listen	listening

B R1.01 | Listen and check your answers.

different worlds 2

VLOGS

Q: What impact does social media have on your life?

1 ▶ Watch the video. What impacts of social media do the people mention?

2 Work in pairs. Discuss the impact that social media has on your lives.

Global Scale of English

LEARNING OBJECTIVES

2A READING | Read an article about virtual reality: science and technology; word families
Discuss possible future uses of virtual reality: future probability
Pronunciation: connected speech: future probability

2B LISTENING | Understand a radio programme about spending time in nature: nature; quantifiers
Talk about ways to encourage people to spend time in nature
Pronunciation: connected speech: quantifiers
Write a for-and-against essay on living in the countryside

2C HOW TO ... | speculate: lifestyle adjectives
Pronunciation: stress to show certainty

2D BBC PROGRAMME | Understand a TV drama about time travel: extreme adjectives
Talk about an imaginary trip back in time
Write a competition entry

2A Real or virtual?

GRAMMAR | future probability
VOCABULARY | science and technology; word families
PRONUNCIATION | connected speech: future probability

READING

1 A Work in pairs. Discuss the questions.

1 Have you ever used a virtual reality headset like the one in the photo? Would you like to?
2 What do you know about how VR is used now? How do you think it might be used in the future?

B Read the article. Which topics in the box do the people mention?

education gaming health shopping sport training for work travel

C Read the article again. Complete the table with the main points and supporting details it includes.

main point	supporting detail
People in the tech industry expect VR to be used more in the future.	1 Microsoft and Google are spending a lot of money on it.
VR will be useful in schools.	2 ....
3	Using VR can help reduce stress.
VR can help surgeons.	4 ....
5	Firefighters need practice in real situations.
VR will never replace real travel.	6 ....

D Work in pairs. Discuss the questions.

1 Which arguments in the article do you find the most convincing? Why?
2 Which uses of VR do you think will be the most useful? Why?
3 Which events in other countries would you most like to attend using VR? Why?

VOCABULARY

science and technology

2 A Scan the article again. Complete the sentences with the correct form of the words in bold.

1 I work as a researcher. I find out information by reading and speaking to people.
2 When you play a video game with ...., you actually feel as if you are in the gaming world.
3 .... technology is controlled by computers and seems to make some decisions for itself.
4 After arranging scientific tests, we publish the .... so people can learn from them.
5 In 2020, two of the biggest brands in the .... were Facebook and Apple.
6 Many people now don't need to go into an office, but can work ...., from anywhere in the world.
7 We .... information: we read it, test it, and explain the results.
8 Technology helps us to .... many things, like tomorrow's weather or the future of financial markets.

B Work in pairs. Discuss the questions.

1 Do you have to analyse anything in your work or studies? What do you do with the findings?
2 Name one thing you have to predict or research in your daily life.
3 When's the last time you did something remotely? How did it go?
4 What's your favourite smart device? Why?
5 Do you think the tech industry has too much influence? Why/Why not?

C Learn and practise. Go to the Vocabulary Bank.

page 137 **VOCABULARY BANK** word families

Is virtual reality the future?

Many of us have experience of **virtual reality** in gaming, but does the technology have other, more serious uses? Many people in the **tech industry** certainly think so. Microsoft and Google have spent hundreds of millions of dollars developing VR projects, and when Facebook bought a company called Oculus VR for $2.3 billion, Facebook's CEO, Mark Zuckerberg, **predicted** that VR is going to become a part of daily life for billions of people. So, is VR really the future? We hear two different views.

YES

Yulia Ivanovich

VR has huge potential in education and training. Several studies have compared the performance of students taught traditionally to those taught using VR. The **findings** showed that students who used VR tended to perform better. It makes sense. Imagine you're learning about the Amazon rainforest. What's more effective: reading about it or going there? VR also helps in training for dangerous jobs like firefighting and mountain rescue, allowing people to practise dealing with difficult situations in a safe environment.

Another possible use for VR is in health. In one study that looked at using VR to relieve stress, participants spent time in a virtual forest. They reported feeling more positive afterwards, and the **researchers** concluded that spending time in a virtual forest can decrease stress as much as being in a real one. It could also help surgeons as they can practise their skills in a safe, virtual environment. This use is certain to become more common because it can save lives.

VR is also likely to be used more in the travel industry. People are becoming aware of the environmental costs of travel and tourism, so VR could provide a virtual alternative. Instead of flying halfway around the world to attend a festival or watch a sports event, people could experience it **remotely** without causing environmental damage.

NO

Noor El-Basany

When it comes to education and training, everyone says VR has potential, but it probably won't be used widely in schools. Why not? Firstly, it's too expensive, and secondly, when you **analyse** the research in detail, you realise there isn't much evidence that it works. Similarly, VR has some applications in training, but it will never replace real-life training. If you're a firefighter, fighting a fire in a virtual environment just isn't the same – you need real practice.

In health, VR may be useful in a few situations, but it's unlikely to be used as a serious treatment. Does anyone really believe that putting on a VR headset and visiting a virtual world is any kind of long-term solution to anything? It sounds more like escapism to me, rather than a serious solution to a problem.

Some people have said VR might replace some kinds of tourism, but it'll never work. The whole point of going to a festival or sporting event is to be part of the crowd. And travelling is about having experiences: seeing new sights, getting to know other cultures, and trying different food. No **smart** machine can ever replace that. Travel is also about showing off your photos and bragging to your friends about the amazing things you have seen. You can't do that if your trip consists of you sitting in your living room wearing a headset!

GRAMMAR

future probability

3 A Read the sentences (1–8). Complete the uses (a–e) with the correct modal verbs and the phrases in bold.

1 VR **is going to** become a part of daily life for billions of people.
2 Surgeons who **are due to** operate on patients could practise their skills.
3 This use **is certain to** become more common because it can save lives.
4 VR **is likely to** be used in the travel industry.
5 People **could** experience it remotely.
6 It **will** never replace real-life training.
7 VR **is unlikely to** be used as a serious treatment.
8 VR **might** replace some kinds of tourism.

a We use <u>will</u> .... and .... to make general predictions.
b We use .... to say we are sure something will happen.
c We use .... to say we think something will probably happen. The opposite is ....
d We use .... and .... to say we think something is possible.
e We use .... to say something is scheduled to happen, e.g. a train to arrive.

B Learn and practise. Go to the Grammar Bank.

page 112 **GRAMMAR BANK**

PRONUNCIATION

4 A 2.01 | connected speech: future probability | Listen and complete the sentences with the correct phrases.

1 VR .... be used more in the future.
2 The new headsets .... go on sale next week.
3 This game .... be a big hit!
4 VR .... replace our summer holidays.

B 2.01 | Listen again. Notice how the phrases are pronounced in connected speech. Practise saying the full sentences.

C Work in pairs. Take turns completing the sentences with your own ideas.

1 Video games are certain to …
2 New technology is going to …
3 In the future, people are unlikely to …
4 The next football World Cup is due to …
5 In future, medical professionals could ...
6 Teachers of the future might …
7 By 2030, tourists are likely to …
8 In the future, firefighters might …

SPEAKING

5 A Work alone. Read the predictions. Decide which ones you agree with, and which you disagree with.

By 2040 …

- offices will not exist. Former office workers will meet and socialise in virtual spaces.
- virtual university professors will give virtual lectures in the environments they are teaching about.
- most people will go to virtual concerts and sporting events instead of real ones.
- doctors will use VR to predict health issues. They will analyse findings based on VR simulations.

B Read the Future Skills box and do the task.

FUTURE SKILLS
Critical thinking

Being accurate is an important part of critical thinking. For example, 'By 2040, nobody will eat meat.' is a big claim. It seems unlikely that every single person in the world will give up meat in the future. Something like, 'By 2040, the majority of people in the UK will have reduced the amount of meat in their diet.' is far more accurate and easier to evaluate.

Think again about your responses to the predictions in Ex 5A. Think about how you can express your opinions accurately, to show how sure you feel about each one.

C Work in groups. Discuss the predictions in Ex 5A and answer the questions.

1 Which of the predictions:
   - will happen?
   - might happen?
   - is unlikely to happen?
   - definitely won't happen?
2 What do you think of the predictions? How would they affect our day-to-day lives?
3 What other uses do you think there will be for virtual reality in the future? What other predictions would you make about life in 2040?

2B Closer to nature

GRAMMAR | quantifiers
VOCABULARY | nature
PRONUNCIATION | connected speech: quantifiers

LISTENING

1 A Work in pairs. Read the information about the BBC Radio programme and discuss the questions.

> **Why we should listen to trees** BBC
>
> Most of the world's population live in big, noisy cities, where we don't have many opportunities to get close to nature. For many of us, this means we miss out on some of the positive effects of spending time in nature. Alex Smalley explains.

1 Do you spend time out in nature? Why/Why not?
2 What kinds of natural places do you enjoy visiting?
3 Why do you think spending time in nature is good for us?

B 2.02 | Listen to the programme. Tick the ideas that are mentioned.

1 People have known for a long time that we benefit from spending time in nature.
2 In the past, doctors didn't recognise the benefits of spending time in nature.
3 In recent centuries, we seem to have forgotten the health benefits of being in nature.
4 The excitement of city life brings health benefits.
5 Spending time in or near nature helps restore balance.
6 Studies have indicated that listening to the sounds of nature can improve your well-being.

C Work in pairs and answer the questions.

1 According to the programme, how would most people describe their idea of paradise?
2 What did doctors in the 1700s recommend for their patients?
3 What has helped improve people's quality of life in the last 200 years?
4 What problems does living in 'big, busy and noisy cities' cause us?
5 How does spending time in a natural environment help us?
6 Why did some hospital patients in the 1980s recover faster than others?

D 2.02 | Listen again and check your answers.

GRAMMAR

quantifiers

2 A Work in pairs. Read the comments about the radio programme. Which do you agree with? Which do you disagree with? Why?

Rodrigo
07:56 | 13 June

Alex is right! **The majority of** the world's population now live in cities, and there is **a lack of** green public spaces where people can relax.

Fumi
08:20 | 13 June

I work in an office where most people spend **a good deal of** time stuck at a computer screen, and **very little** time outdoors. **Several** of us try to find time in the day to go out and enjoy nature, but we're definitely **in a minority**.

Alexis
10:47 | 13 June

I agree! There are ways to get closer to nature even if you live in a city, and have **no** time to spare. **Every** day, take **a few** moments to notice the nature around you. Sit outside with your morning coffee, grow **a handful of** plants on your desk, or take **a little** time to enjoy the view from your office window. **Each** time you do this, you'll feel more relaxed.

B Read the comments again. Match the quantifiers in bold with the meanings (1–4).

1 a large number or amount
2 a small number or amount
3 one individual person or thing
4 none

C Complete the rules with the type of noun: *singular*, *plural* or *uncountable*.

1 Use *several, few, a few, a handful of* + ... nouns.
2 Use *the majority of, a lack of, no* + ... nouns or .... nouns.
3 Use *each, every* + ... nouns.
4 Use *very little, a little, a good deal of* + ... nouns.

D Learn and practise. Go to the Grammar Bank.

page 113 **GRAMMAR BANK**

PRONUNCIATION

3 A 2.03 | connected speech: quantifiers | Listen to the sentence. Look at the quantifier in bold and draw (‿) between any words that link together.

The majority of the world's population now lives in cities.

B 2.04 | Draw (‿) to show connected speech in the quantifiers. Then listen and check.

1 **A good deal of** my time is spent commuting.
2 There's **a lack of** green public spaces.
3 **Several of us** walk along the beach in the morning.
4 People who live in the countryside are definitely **in a minority**.
5 I grow **a handful of** herbs on my balcony.

C Work in pairs. Take turns to complete the sentences with your own ideas.

1 A good deal of my time is spent …
2 There's a lack of …
3 Several of us …
4 People who … are definitely in a minority.

VOCABULARY

nature

4 A Complete the article with the words and phrases in the box.

coastline	deserted	open space	river bank
scenery	sunlight	track	woodland

Did you know?

New research has found that spending just two hours a week in nature is enough to improve your health and well-being.

For some people, this might mean sitting by the sea on a [1] deserted beach somewhere on a wild [2] coastline, looking up at a clear blue sky and listening to the sound of the waves crashing onto the sand. Or perhaps enjoying a wide [3] open sp where the [4] scenery is spectacular. For others, it might be walking through [5] woodland near where they live and watching the morning [6] sunlight through the trees. Or maybe walking along a narrow [7] track to a [8] river bank, to sit and watch the water flowing past.

B Read the article again. Which word or phrase:

1 means that there is no one else around?
2 refers to the land by the side of a river?
3 refers to a rough path or road?
4 is the opposite of a small, contained area?
5 refers to an area with a lot of trees?
6 is another word for landscape?
7 refers to the area of land near the sea?
8 refers to light from the sun?

C Work in pairs. Describe a natural place that you know or enjoy spending time in.

SPEAKING

5 A Work in groups. Imagine your school or college wants to encourage people to spend more time in nature to improve their well-being. Make notes about:

- green spaces nearby and how you could use them.
- changes you could make to the building (e.g. creating a rooftop garden).
- one-off events or activities you could do (e.g. a tree-planting event).
- changes you could make to ways of working or schedules.
- posters, leaflets, etc. you could create.

B Read the Future Skills box and answer the question.

FUTURE SKILLS
Leadership

When you are working in a group, a discussion can sometimes get stuck on one topic for too long. When this happens, it is important to refocus the group by suggesting what you should discuss next.

What expressions can you use to move the discussion on to a new topic?

C Work in your groups. Try to agree on five suggestions for your college or school. Remember to refocus the discussion if you get stuck on one topic for too long.

WRITING

a for-and-against essay

6 A Work in pairs. Write down five advantages of living in a city and five advantages of living in the countryside.

B Read the essay. Does it mention your ideas? Do you agree with the writer's point of view?

C Read the essay again. Then choose the correct words to complete the sentences.

1 The introductory paragraph **explains what the topic is and why we might be interested / gives the writer's opinion on the topic**.

2 Paragraph two gives points **for / for and against** the idea.

3 Paragraph three gives points **against / for and against** the idea.

4 The conclusion **asks the reader's / gives the writer's** opinion.

7 A Look at the sentences in bold in the essay. Find linkers which are used to show a contrasting idea. The first one has been done for you.

B Work in pairs and answer the questions.

1 What punctuation follows *However*?

2 Which verb form follows *despite*?

3 Which linker is used in the phrase '.......................... the fact that ...'?

4 Which linker is used to start a sentence which contrasts with the previous ideas?

C Connect the ideas in two different ways using the linkers in brackets.

1 Some young people love living in the city / others don't like it at all. (although / however)

Although some young people love living in the city, others don't like it at all.

Some young people love living in the city. **However,** others don't like it at all.

2 Public transport can be very overcrowded / people still use it (despite the fact / while)

3 Life in the city is exciting / it can be stressful (while / however)

4 Pollution and crime are problems / many young people prefer living in the city (although / despite)

D Write notes for the four paragraphs of a for-and-against essay on living in the countryside. Then write the essay (180–200 words).

City living – pros and cons

Rural and urban living have always held a different appeal for different people. [1]**While some people love living in the countryside, others find it boring and can't wait to get back to the excitement of the city. So, what are the pros and cons of living in the city?**

For many people the city offers plenty of advantages. Firstly, cities are much more exciting. There are lots of things to do, from shopping and eating out to going to the theatre or the cinema. In a city, all of these things are easy to access on public transport, which makes life a lot easier. Secondly, there are a great number of professional opportunities available in the city which are not available if you live in the countryside. Many big businesses have their headquarters in the city. Therefore, there are more businesses to choose from and more jobs available. Also, you're likely to get a higher salary. Lastly, when you live in a city, you get the opportunity to meet a huge number of diverse people. [2]**Although you can build a network of friends and professional contacts anywhere you live, being in a city makes this easier.**

[3]**However, there are some downsides to living in the city.** It's a lot noisier and more crowded than the countryside. The pace of life is very busy and this can feel stressful. [4]**Despite having efficient public transport, life in the city means you often have to spend a lot of your time commuting to work.** Also, the cost of living is often higher in the city. In addition to this, you have to consider that pollution and levels of crime are likely to be worse than in the countryside.

On balance, I think the advantages of being in a city outweigh the disadvantages, especially for younger people. [5]**Despite the fact that there are benefits to living a peaceful life in the countryside, it's no surprise that so many people choose to give this up in order to find more excitement and opportunities in the city.**

2C Amazing lives

HOW TO ... | speculate
VOCABULARY | lifestyle adjectives
PRONUNCIATION | stress to show certainty

VOCABULARY

lifestyle adjectives

1 A Work in pairs. Look at the photos and answer the questions.

1 Where are the people?
2 What are they doing?
3 What is unusual about their lives?

B Read the article. What do you think is the hardest thing about each lifestyle?

2 A Scan the article. Complete the sentences (1–7) with the adjectives in bold.

1 My life is so busy and tiring – it's ....
2 My job is so .... – I do exactly the same thing every day, so I'm always bored.
3 My job gives me a lot of personal satisfaction, as well as a good income – it's very ....
4 My life is very ...., like everyone else's. There's nothing unusual about it.
5 I don't think anybody else lives like me. I have a(n) .... lifestyle.
6 My lifestyle is very .... I don't spend a lot of money on myself.
7 Life here is very ...., with very cold weather and a lot of snow in the winter.

B Work in pairs. Do any of the statements in Ex 2A apply to your life? Why/Why not?

Life at the extreme

This week, we continue our profiles of some of the world's most amazing people, by looking at three women with extreme lives.

Life at sea

Diana Botutihe's lifestyle is definitely **unique**. She has lived her entire life at sea. Born at sea, she has spent her whole life on boats that are typically 5 m long and 1.5 m wide. She visits land only to trade fish for other essentials such as rice and water. It's a simple, **modest** life. Her boat looks homely: filled with water cans, cooking pots, plastic utensils, a kerosene lamp and a couple of pot plants. Diana is one of the world's last marine nomads, a member of the Sama-Bajau ethnic group, a group of Malay people who have lived a traditional life at sea for centuries.

Life in space

Astronauts have been living on the International Space Station for more than a decade. Whilst floating in the air without gravity may sound like fun, there are plenty of challenges which make doing even **ordinary** things like washing your hair difficult. Karen Nyberg spent more than twenty years in a hugely fulfilling career working as an astronaut. While she was on the Space Station, Karen, who enjoys running and has run nine marathons, would typically spend at least two hours a day training on a running machine or an exercise bicycle. Life in space can be **tedious** at times, so as well as dealing with technical and practical problems on the Space Station, Karen also enjoyed creative pursuits like sewing and sketching.

Life around the world

Rosie Swale-Pope is the only person in history to have undertaken a solo, unsupported run around the world. Over nearly five years, she has travelled over 32,000 km, facing extreme danger, **harsh** Siberian winters, wolves and loneliness. Rosie runs pulling a trailer, which she then uses to camp inside. Life on the road can be **exhausting**, but also incredibly **rewarding**. She says she is happiest when sleeping alone in remote forests and meeting people as she runs by day, often starting before dawn to avoid the traffic.

How to ...
speculate

3 A 2.05 | **Listen to a conversation about a TV series. What factual information do you learn about Karen Nyberg and Rosie Swale-Pope?**

B 2.05 | **Read the sentences from the conversation. Are they talking about Karen (K) or Rosie (R)? Then listen again to check.**

1 **I'd guess** it must be so inspiring to see the world like that.
2 **I'd have thought** it would be exhausting to live like that all the time.
3 **I'd imagine** that was really hard.
4 **I reckon** it must be pretty lonely at times.
5 She's **clearly** the kind of person who just has to keep moving.
6 **I suppose** they had video chats.
7 **There's no way** I would ever consider doing that.
8 She's **bound to** feel scared sometimes.

C Work in pairs. Look at the words and phrases in bold in Ex 3B. Which can you use:

1 instead of saying 'I think … '?
2 to talk about what you think as a result of the evidence you see?
3 to talk about something you think is not possible?

D Learn and practise. Go to the Grammar Bank.

page 114 **GRAMMAR BANK**

PRONUNCIATION

4 A 2.06 | **stress to show certainty | Listen to the sentences and underline the words with the main stress.**

1 There's no way I would ever consider doing that.
2 She's clearly the kind of person who just has to keep moving.
3 She's bound to feel scared sometimes.

B Write sentences about the lives of the people in the article in Ex 1B using the phrases in Ex 3B. Write about the topics in the box or your own ideas.

entertainment food friends and family sleep

C Work in pairs. Take turns to read your sentences. Do you agree with each other's ideas? Why/Why not?

SPEAKING

5 A Work in groups. You are going to talk about the lives of some famous people. Agree on four people you all know about from the categories below.

actor businessperson fashion model
influencer singer sports star

B Work alone. Think about the people you have chosen. Prepare to discuss the questions.

1 What do they enjoy about their life?
2 How do they feel about being famous?
3 Why might they feel unhappy sometimes?

C Discuss your opinions and assumptions about the people you chose in Ex 5A. Which person do you think has the best life? Why?

MEDIATION SKILLS
note taking and summarising
summarise an informal interview

page 147 **MEDIATION BANK**

Speak anywhere Go to the interactive speaking practice

2D BBC Entertainment

The time traveller

VOCABULARY | extreme adjectives
SPEAKING | an imaginary trip back in time
WRITING | a competition entry

PREVIEW

1 A Work in groups. Discuss the questions.

1. Which famous artists can you name? What do you know about their lives?
2. What do you know about Vincent van Gogh?

B Read the programme information. What did you learn about Vincent van Gogh?

Doctor Who

Doctor Who is a BBC science-fiction series about a character called the Doctor who can travel backwards or forwards in time. In this episode he and his companion, Amy, go to France to visit the artist Vincent van Gogh. Van Gogh was a 19th-century painter from the Netherlands. During his lifetime, he was unsuccessful and had a difficult life. He was often unhappy because no one recognised his talent. After he died, his work became popular and he is now one of the most famous artists in history.

VIEW

2 A ▶ Watch the video. What does van Gogh learn about his paintings by the end of the episode?

B ▶ Number the events in order. Then watch the video again and check.

- **a** Van Gogh talks about the wonders of the universe.
- **b** Van Gogh hears a tour guide speaking about his work.
- **c** Van Gogh takes the Doctor and Amy to his cluttered home.
- **d** The Doctor and Amy go back in time and meet van Gogh in a café.
- **e** A guide in a museum tells visitors about van Gogh. 1
- **f** The Doctor has an idea.
- **g** Van Gogh tries to give the Doctor a gift.
- **h** The group go to a museum called the Musée d'Orsay.

C Work in groups. Discuss the questions.

1. Why do you think the Doctor took van Gogh to the Musée d'Orsay?
2. How do you think van Gogh feels by the end of the episode? How has his life changed?

VOCABULARY

extreme adjectives

3A Read the sentences from the programme. Choose the correct meanings for the adjectives in bold.

1. Those final months of his life were probably the most **astonishing** artistic outpouring in history.
   a sad and dark **b** very surprising or amazing
2. That's **incredible**, don't you think, Amy?
   a extremely good or great **b** not believable
3. You know, you should be careful with these [paintings]. They're **precious**.
   a valuable and important **b** very large
4. This is the **mighty** Musée d'Orsay, home to many of the greatest paintings in history.
   a very large and important **b** extremely old
5. Van Gogh is the **finest** painter of them all.
   a most famous **b** best
6. His command of colour, the most **magnificent**.
   a extremely good **b** very bright or shiny

B Which of the adjectives in Ex 3A can you use with *very*? Which are extreme adjectives?

C Work in groups. Try to name the following:

- a magnificent work of art.
- an astonishing scientific achievement.
- a very fine film or piece of music.
- something precious in your country.
- a mighty person.
- an incredible time to be alive in history.

D Compare your ideas with other groups.

SPEAKING

an imaginary trip back in time

4A 2.07 | Listen to someone explaining where they would go if they could travel back in time. Where do they choose and why?

B 2.07 | Listen again. Tick the phrases that you hear.

> **KEY PHRASES**
>
> To start with, …
> So, what would I do?
> With that in mind, I'd …
> What else?
> Another possibility would be to …
> And last but not least, I'd …

C Read the Key phrases again and answer the questions.

1. Which two phrases introduce a new topic?
2. Which phrase refers to something just mentioned earlier?
3. Which two phrases can we use to show a sequence of events?

5A Imagine you could travel back in time. Make notes about:

- where you would go (e.g., which area, city, country, etc.).
- which time you would go back to.
- who you would like to meet.
- what you would do.

B Work in groups. Take turns to explain which time periods you would visit and why. Whose trip sounds the most exciting?

WRITING

a competition entry

6A Work in pairs. Discuss the questions.

1. Have you ever won a competition? What was the prize?
2. Have you ever entered a creative competition (e.g., with a piece of writing, art, music, etc.)? Did you win?

B Write a competition entry. Go to the Writing Bank.

page 104 **WRITING BANK**

GRAMMAR

future probability

1 A Write as many predictions as you can using the topics in Box A and structures in Box B.

A

future holidays | the weather | your future career | your plans for the weekend

B

be going to | certain to | could | due to | likely to | may | may not | might | might not | unlikely to | will + certainly/definitely/possibly/probably | won't

I might go the cinema at the weekend. I'll definitely speak to my parents.

B Work in pairs. Take turns reading your predictions. Are any of them similar?

quantifiers

2 A Read the results of a survey about a group of language learners. Then choose the correct words to complete the sentences.

LANGUAGE LEARNING SURVEY
Participants: 20 students, aged 18–52, average age 26

use a book to learn the language	**18**
use online resources	**20**
use some kind of dictionary	**13**
use a pronunciation app	**5**
don't have enough time to study	**16**
review the lesson for ten minutes or more afterwards	**10**
read in the target language for more than four hours a week	**2**
prefer to learn with others	**16**

1 **Few / Several / The majority** use a book to learn the language.
2 **Every student / Several / A handful** use(s) the internet to get input.
3 **A minority of / Few / Plenty of** students use a dictionary.
4 **The majority / A handful / Plenty** of students use a pronunciation app.
5 Most students mention having **a lack of / a bit of / plenty of** time to study.
6 Half say they do **all / a little / a good deal of** revision outside class.
7 **Very few / No / The majority of** students read a lot in the target language.
8 **A large number of / A lack of / Few** students prefer learning with others.

B Work in pairs. Guess which of the sentences are true for your class.

VOCABULARY

3 Complete the sentences with the words in the box. There are two words you don't need.

coastline | deserted | findings | predict | scenery | smart | sunlight | track | virtual reality

1 It's impossible to .... the future.
2 Researchers should publish their ....
3 .... is almost as realistic as real life.
4 You should go up into the mountains because the .... is amazing!
5 After midnight the town is ....
6 The .... is very wild and dramatic.
7 Open the curtains! We need some .... !

4 A Choose the correct options (A–C) to complete the text.

Another world: Finding solitude

Anyone looking for solitude [1]........ find it in a 21st-century city, but there are still [2]........ of places one can be alone. In the 19th century, the American writer Henry Thoreau did an experiment in solitary living. He went to live on a patch of [3]........ owned by his friend Ralph Waldo Emerson. Thoreau built a hut on the [4]........ of Walden Pond. He spent over two years there and wrote a book, *Walden*, about his experiences.

More recently, the Italian writer Paolo Cognetti left Milan and rented a shepherd's hut near the mountains of Valle d'Aosta. There he lived for [5]........ months, surrounded by [6]........ scenery and [7]........ noise besides the wind. While there, he took time to [8]........ his life and think about what he [9]........ do next. Like Thoreau, he wrote a book: *The Wild Boy*.

[10]........ people are able to escape like Thoreau and Cognetti. [11]........ of us are lucky if we get a few days on a [12]........ beach. But there will always be quiet places for those with the desire and resources to find them.

	A	B	C
1	is due to	will definitely	is unlikely to
2	plenty	good deal	a lack
3	track	woodland	scenery
4	coastline	open space	banks
5	a good deal of	few	several
6	incredible	precious	mighty
7	the majority of	each	very little
8	research	analyse	predict
9	might	is going to	was due to
10	Few	Little	Enough
11	Several	The minority	The majority
12	coastline	deserted	woodland

B R2.01 | Listen and check your answers.

showtime 3

VLOGS

Q: What live events or performances do you enjoy and why?

1 Watch the video. Which events are mentioned and why?

2 Work in pairs. Which live events or performances you do enjoy? Why?

Global Scale of English

LEARNING OBJECTIVES

3A READING | Read an article about a sustainable music festival: festivals; the environment; relative clauses
Plan an eco-friendly festival
Pronunciation: pitch in non-defining relative clauses
Write a formal email about an event

3B LISTENING | Understand a podcast about stage fright: phrasal verbs: performing; phrasal verbs: communication; cleft sentences
Speak in public
Pronunciation: emphatic stress

3C HOW TO ... | use vague language: film and TV
Pronunciation: linking and elision

3D BBC STREET INTERVIEWS | Understand people talking about music
Talk about a music questionnaire: *do* and *did* for emphasis
Write a forum comment about music

3A Festival

GRAMMAR | relative clauses
VOCABULARY | festivals; the environment
PRONUNCIATION | pitch in non-defining relative clauses

VOCABULARY

festivals

1 A **Work in pairs. Which music festivals have you been to? Which would you like to go to? Why?**

B **Read *Festivals: The good, the bad and the ugly*. What problems associated with festivals does the writer mention?**

C **Scan the article again. Complete the sentences with the words in bold.**

1 People who attend a festival can be called ....
2 Another word for places where events take place is ....
3 The people who plan an event are the ....
4 An actor, musician or performer who entertains people on stage is a(n) ....
5 Instead of 'go to' an event we can say people .... an event.
6 The list of performers for an event is the ....
7 If you make people want to come to an event, you .... them.
8 When we talk about the feeling that a place or event gives you, we call it the ....

2 A **Work in groups. Discuss the questions.**

1 What kinds of things create a good festival atmosphere and attract large crowds?
2 How important is it for event organisers to think about their impact on the environment?
3 How can festival-goers reduce their impact on the environment when they attend events?

B **Find words in the text related to the environment.**

C **Learn and practise. Go to the Vocabulary Bank.**

page 137 **VOCABULARY BANK** the environment

Festivals: The good, the bad and the ugly

Everybody loves a good music festival, right? Sleeping in a tent for days to catch a glimpse of your favourite **act** on stage, and being outside with old friends and people you've only just met. Festivals are one of the highlights of summer, which is why they **attract** millions of people each year. Often set in **venues** in some of the most stunning locations, with a fantastic **line-up** of performers, they're a great place for people to get together and enjoy a few days of arts and live music in a truly relaxed **atmosphere**.

However, festival **organisers** are becoming increasingly aware that events like these can have a hugely negative impact on the environment. They generate a lot of waste and carbon emissions. It's estimated that in the UK alone, over 100 million plastic cups are used at festivals and live events. And then there's the rubbish that gets left behind by **festival-goers** – each of the major festivals in the USA generates 100 tonnes of waste per day, and after Glastonbury Festival in the UK, more than 5,000 tents and 6,500 sleeping bags are often left behind.

Luckily, if you want to **attend** a festival but also want to keep a clear conscience, there are plenty of great sustainable festivals happening all over the world.

Encourage – заохочувати
Profitable – вигідний
Sort out rubbish –

READING

3 A Work in groups of three. You are each going to read about a festival, before telling your classmates about it. Read about your festival. Student A: Read the text below. Student B: Read the text on page 142. Student C: Read the text on page 144. Makes notes.

- Name of the festival • Venue • Dates
- Activities, events and features of the festival
- Eco-friendly ideas

B Summarise the information about your festival to your group. Use your notes from Ex 3A to help you.

C Discuss and comment on all three festivals. Use the questions below to help you.

1 Which of the festivals would you choose to go to? Why?
2 Which one do you think has the best eco-friendly ideas? Why?

A

Burning Man

Where: USA When: August/September

Burning Man is unique. Held every summer in Nevada's Black Rock Desert, this famous festival attracts travellers from all over the globe. It's officially an art festival and as you wander around the desert you will find all types of amazing art installations. But there is much more to the festival than just art. The desert location becomes a temporary city, filled with people wearing costumes and enjoying complete freedom and creative expression. Nobody uses money – people give each other gifts of food and drink. The week-long event (they don't like the word 'festival') is dedicated to art and community. There's no fixed line-up as such – things just 'happen'. At the end of the festival everyone gets together to watch the burning of a huge statue of a man.

Despite the name, the iconic Burning Man event operates with the aim of 'leaving no trace'. Throughout the festival, people are encouraged to pick up any rubbish they find and put it in their pocket to dispose of later. Festival-goers are also encouraged not to buy things which will later be thrown away. The organisers aim to be carbon negative and to sustainably manage their waste by 2030. They are keen to use the city as an example of how a sustainable city of the future could work. They use solar power for electricity and electric cars to get around the desert. Every year, they create Black Rock City in the middle of the Nevada desert, and every year they take it down, pack up and leave the area without a trace.

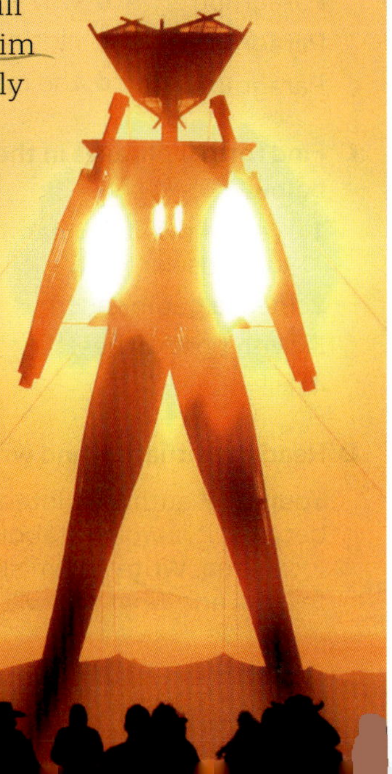

GRAMMAR

relative clauses

4 A Complete the sentences about the festivals with *who*, *which* or *where*.

1 Burning Man festival, ... takes place at the end of August, attracts huge crowds.
2 Fuji Rock Paper reuses wood .... would otherwise go to waste.
3 People .... attend the festival are encouraged to arrive by bus.
4 The festival appointed Damon Gameau, ... is a world-renowned filmmaker, as their Eco Ambassador.
5 Fuji Rock offers hot springs .... festival-goers can relax.
6 These are the eco-initiatives .... the festival encourages.

B Work in pairs. Answer the questions.

1 Which sentences contain defining relative clauses? Which sentences contain non-defining relative clauses?
2 In which sentences can you replace the pronoun with *that*?
3 In which sentence can you omit the relative pronoun?
4 Are commas used with defining or non-defining relative clauses?

C Learn and practise. Go to the Grammar Bank.

page 115 **GRAMMAR BANK**

PRONUNCIATION

5 A 3.01 | pitch in non-defining relative clauses | Listen to sentences 1 and 4 from Ex 4A. Does the speaker use a high or low pitch in the non-defining relative clause? Why?

B Add commas to the text where there are non-defining relative clauses. Then practise reading it.

The Green Man festival which is held annually in Wales is an independent arts and music festival. Being environmentally friendly is fundamental to Green Man whose organisers encourage festival-goers to bring their own water bottles and take home all their waste. They also send any tents which have been left unwanted at the site to refugee charities. Green Man which started with just a few hundred people in 2003 is now one of the UK's best-loved festivals.

C 3.02 | Listen and compare your pronunciation with the recording.

SPEAKING

6 A **You are going to work in a group to plan a new eco-friendly festival. Think of your own ideas first and make notes.**

B **Work in pairs. Read the Future Skills box and do the task.**

> **FUTURE SKILLS**
> **Collaboration**
>
> When you discuss a plan with others, use language to suggest ideas, ask for people's opinions and check that everyone agrees. For example: 'One idea we could consider is … What do you reckon? Don't you think it would be better to … ? Is everyone agreed that … ?'
>
> Make a list of other useful phrases to help you encourage discussion, invite others to join in and say what they think, etc.

C **Work in groups and plan your festival. Use the questions to help you.**

1. When will the festival be held? What will it be called? What is the venue for your festival?
2. How will you attract festival-goers and ensure a good atmosphere? What acts are in the line-up? How much will it cost? Will there be any special food or events?
3. How will you make the festival sustainable and protect the local environment?

D **Present your festival to the class. Which do you think is the best? Why?**

WRITING

a formal email

7 A **Work in pairs. Read the email and answer the questions.**

1. What is the purpose of the email?
2. What are the main features of the proposed festival?
3. How will the festival be sustainable?
4. What do you think of the ideas suggested?
5. Is the email formal or informal? How do you know?

To M.Drapers@council.org
From T.Stubbings@ecofest.net
Subject Ecofest – Festival Proposal

Dear Ms Draper,

[1]We are writing to you with a proposal for a new family- and eco-friendly music festival, which we would like you to consider. Ecofest would be held annually in Riverside Park on the last weekend in June.

[2]The festival would feature local artists and musicians as well as a line-up of popular acts. Music to suit all tastes would be provided, and there would also be plenty of entertainment for children on offer, such as drumming workshops and arts and crafts activities.

[3]The festival would have a strong eco-theme which encourages families to move towards a more sustainable way of living through recycling and reducing our dependence on natural resources. Ecofest itself aims to keep a low carbon footprint by using solar power to run the festival and banning single-use plastic on site. We would like to assure you that there would be no mess left in the park. A team of volunteers will organise a clean-up at the end of the festival and dispose of any waste that is left by festival-goers.

[4]I hope you will consider our proposal. If you require any further information about Ecofest, please feel free to contact us. We look forward to hearing your response.

Kind regards,
Toni Stubbings
Manager of Ecofest

B **Read the email again. Match the paragraphs (1–4) with their functions (a–d).**

Paragraph 1	**a** eco-friendly initiatives
Paragraph 2	**b** why you are writing and the name of the festival
Paragraph 3	**c** closing sentences and future steps
Paragraph 4	**d** the main features/activities of the festival

C **Find formal phrases in the email which match the informal phrases below.**

1. We can't wait to hear your answer
2. Please get in touch
3. With best wishes
4. Hi!
5. If you need to know anything else …
6. Please think about our ideas.
7. You can be sure that …

D **Read the situation and write a formal email with your proposal.**

Your local authority intends to allow only one festival this summer because it is worried about the environmental impact on the local area. Write an email explaining why they should choose your festival and what you will do to make it sustainable.

3B Performers

GRAMMAR | cleft sentences
VOCABULARY | phrasal verbs: performing; phrasal verbs: communication
PRONUNCIATION | emphatic stress

VOCABULARY

phrasal verbs: performing

1 **Work in pairs. Rank the following from 1 (the most frightening) to 4 (the least frightening).**

- giving a presentation in English
- making a speech in public
- performing in front of an audience
- competing in a live sporting event

2 A **Read the social media thread. Have any of these things ever happened to you?**

B **Read the thread again and match the phrasal verbs in bold with the definitions below.**

1. to use a method or plan after other options have failed fall back on
2. to continue doing something
3. to think of an idea, plan, or solution
4. to make a mistake or do something badly
5. to be as good as people expect or hope
6. to accept a bad situation without complaining
7. to make it difficult for someone to focus
8. to finally do something

C **Choose four topics below and write your answers.**

- one thing I never mess up
- an event that lived up to my expectations
- a good idea I came up with recently
- something I ended up doing by accident
- a hobby I started as a child and carried on doing
- something I have to put up with every day

D **Work in pairs. Take turns to read your answers and guess which topic they match.**

B: Is it a hobby you started as a child and carried on doing?
A: Yes.
B: When did you start?

E **Learn and practise. Go to the Vocabulary Bank.**

▶▶ page 138 **VOCABULARY BANK** phrasal verbs: communication

Jaxfunnyguy_123
1 hour ago
Like | Comment | Share

Advice needed!

Does anyone have any advice for performing in public? I just did my first stand-up comedy act and, let's just say, it didn't quite **live up to** my expectations. Actually, it was a complete disaster. The worst thing is, I thought I was well prepared. I **came up with** loads of jokes beforehand and learnt them all, and I thought they were pretty funny. I was determined not to **mess up**. So I went up on stage and the lights were in my eyes and it was really hot. I started telling a joke and then someone in the crowd shouted something. It completely **put me off** and I forgot everything. I **ended up** running off stage and hiding for the rest for the evening.

Strawby_King2
55 minutes ago
Like | Comment | Share

Urgh! I'm sorry you had to **put up with** a heckler. As an actor, what puts me off is when people in the audience start coughing or looking at their phones! My advice is to ignore them. You just have to **carry on** and hope they stop!

SamiraPRS
47 minutes ago
Like | Comment | Share

Try again. I remember being told I had to give a huge presentation at work once. I was so nervous I felt sick. But once you've done it a few times, it gets easier because you have more experience to **fall back on**. So when things go wrong, you know how to cope.

LISTENING

3 A Work in pairs. What do you think are the best ways to prepare for a public performance?

B Read the information about a podcast. Who do you think it is mainly aimed at?

Up in lights

Entertainment

★★★★

Up in lights is a weekly radio podcast in which Pauline Hazany talks to performers about everything from getting your foot in the door and auditioning, to writing your own material and finding an agent.

29 Jan

Stage fright

In this episode, Pauline discusses stage fright with a musician, an actor and a motivational speaker.

4 A 3.03 | Listen to an extract from the episode on stage fright. What do all three performers discuss in their interview?

1. They talk about their experiences and give advice.
2. They explain why stage fright means they no longer enjoy performing.
3. They discuss the differences between performing in a studio and performing in public.

B 3.03 | Answer the questions. Then listen again and check.

Which speaker, Katherine (K), Rufus (R) or Mahmoud (M) …

1. received advice from someone with the same job?
2. imagines performing in front of familiar people?
3. imagines the consequences if things go wrong?
4. prepares less than in the past?
5. imagines they are a different person?
6. tries to remember why the audience is there?

C Work in groups. Discuss the questions.

1. Which pieces of advice from the recording do you think are the most useful? Why?
2. What is 'visualisation'? In what situations do you think it might be effective?

5 A Read the extract from the recording. Does the example of hyperbole in bold make the sentence sound more or less dramatic?

You've practised **a thousand times**.

B Read the sentences and underline the examples of hyperbole.

1. My time on stage seemed to go on forever!
2. Every time I had to go on stage, I could hardly stand up, I was shaking so much.
3. You feel as if you're going to die of fright.
4. I used to get incredibly nervous before giving my talks. I mean like a total disaster.
5. Every day I had to go on stage, it was like the worst day of my life!

GRAMMAR

cleft sentences

6 A Read sentences a–d from the podcast. Then complete the rules (1 and 2).

a. What I needed to do was prepare both physically and mentally.
b. It's the character that's important, not me.
c. It was the build-up beforehand that scared me.
d. What worked for me was approaching the presentation differently.

We can use a cleft sentence to add emphasis or focus attention on one part of the sentence.

1. We start the cleft sentence with *it* or ....
2. We use the correct form of the verb ....

B Learn and practise. Go to the Grammar Bank.

page 116 **GRAMMAR BANK**

PRONUNCIATION

7 A | emphatic stress | Work in pairs. Read the sentences (1–4). Which words do you think are stressed? Why?

1. What helped me was breathing deeply.
2. What works for me is to prepare well.
3. It was a friend who made this suggestion.
4. It's the music that's important.

B 3.04 | Listen and check. Which words are stressed? Choose a or b.

a. the verb *be*.
b. the words or phrase that are/is the main focus of the cleft structure.

C Work in pairs. Take turns to complete the sentences with your own ideas. Focus on putting the stress in the correct place.

- When I needed advice, it was … who (taught/told me) …
- When I'm nervous, what helps me …
- When I want to have fun, it's … who I call.
- When I need to relax, what I do is …
- When I have a lot of work to do, what works for me is …
- It's … who/that always cheers me up when I'm feeling sad.

SPEAKING

8 A You are going to practise speaking in public. Follow the instructions below.

- You have to get from A to B across the grid.
- You can move straight across or diagonally, one square at a time.
- When you move to a square, you have to talk about the topic for thirty seconds.
- First, look at the topics and plan your way from A to B.
- Then take turns to speak.
- Time each other to make sure you speak for thirty seconds.

Talk about:

A ⟶ **B**

a type of food you've never eaten	the first time you did something	a number or date that's important to you	two favourite books	something funny
which animal makes the best pet	something in the news	a photo	something you always carry with you	sport
a place you want to visit	a musician or singer	an app	coffee	a great actor
something you hear every morning	two pieces of technology	two favourite items of clothing	one thing that would make your life easier	smells you love
video games	someone who should be (more) famous	your favourite moment of the week	the last thing you watched on TV	something you did yesterday

B How did you perform in the speaking activity in Ex 8? Read the Future Skills box and discuss the questions.

1 What did you find difficult about the task?
2 Which topics did you find it easy and difficult to talk about?
3 What techniques do you think might help you cope better in the future?
4 What advice would you give to someone who is preparing for a speaking exam in English?

FUTURE SKILLS
Self-management

Many people feel nervous or experience some difficulties when they have to speak in front of other people. After you have spoken in public, it is a good idea to reflect on what you did well and what you can improve next time.

3C Binge-watch

HOW TO… | use vague language
VOCABULARY | film and TV
PRONUNCIATION | linking and elision

VOCABULARY

film and TV

1 **Work in pairs. Look at the infographic and discuss the questions.**

1. Which facts surprise you most?
2. Do you ever binge-watch? How many hours have you binge-watched in one go? Which programmes?
3. Which of these things have you done in order to continue watching your favourite show?

called in sick at work	cancelled social plans
stayed at home all day	stayed up all night

2A **Work in pairs. Match the sentence beginnings (1–9) with the endings (a–i). Then discuss the meaning of the words in bold.**

1. I had to watch the whole series so that
2. I love that film, especially the **scene**
3. Ela's dress was beautiful! In fact,
4. That's the film with brilliant actors. It's got
5. I enjoy watching films in other languages
6. The film is **based** on
7. Have you watched the last episode? It's got
8. I loved the music so much that
9. It's a detective drama which is **set** in

a. the true story of a famous scientist.
b. and learning a few words by reading the **subtitles**.
c. all the **costumes** were amazing.
d. Sweden.
e. I've downloaded the **soundtrack**.
f. I could see the **ending** and find out what happened.
g. a brilliant **twist** at the end.
h. where she finally tells him she loves him.
i. a fantastic **cast**.

B **Work in groups. Discuss the questions.**

1. What films have you seen that were based on true stories?
2. How do you feel about watching films with subtitles?
3. What's your favourite film soundtrack?
4. What films or series have you watched recently with a good cast?

BINGE! The stats behind our viewing obsession

The average American watches 2.8 hours of TV per day or nearly 20 hours each week. Much of that time is spent binge-watching. 38% of people surveyed said they binge-watched weekly for an average of 4.2 hours per session.

In the UK, 18–34-year-olds watch an average of **1 hour of Netflix per day.**

37% of Netflix users binge-watch at work.

24% of Americans have cancelled social plans in order to watch a show.

94 hours The world record for the longest binge watch – set by New York resident, Alejandro 'AJ' Fragoso.

76% of 18–29-year-olds in the USA have stayed up all night to watch a TV show.

7.1% of men worldwide reported spending between five and seven hours watching an online series in one sitting, and just under 2% said that they did so for more than ten hours at a time.

One in five British workers admits to calling in sick at work so they can stay at home and binge-watch TV shows.

How to ...

use vague language

3 A Work in pairs. What kinds of TV programme do you enjoy most? Why?

B 3.05 | Listen to three friends talking about two shows they have binge-watched. What did they enjoy about them? Tick the points they mention.

- the acting
- the cast
- where it's set
- who/what the story is based on
- the soundtrack
- plot twists
- interesting characters
- costumes
- the ending

C 3.05 | Work in pairs. What did the speakers say about each topic? Listen again and check.

4 A 3.06 | Complete the extracts from the conversation with the words and phrases in the box. Then listen and check.

and that kind of thing	around the 1950s

Alice: So, it's about a woman, Beth Harmon, who is a chess prodigy. It's set in the USA [1] .... and it shows her rise to becoming, like, a world-class chess player, you know, beating all the grand masters [2] ....

and stuff	bit

Alice: Yes, I loved that [3] .... at the end when … well, I won't spoil it for you, but it's really good. And it's beautiful to watch, too, you know, the costumes [4] .... It's done really well.

or something	young-ish	what's her name

Alice: It's like a murder mystery [5] ....

Sam: That's right. Oh, it's brilliant. It's based on a book by um, [6] ....? You know, that Australian author … Liane Moriarty. It tells the story of five [7] .... women …

sort of	that kind of thing

Sam: Every episode is [8] .... incredibly tense and gripping to watch. You get really caught up in the drama and [9] ...., all the plot twists.

about	something like that

Alice: The show I'm watching at the moment has got [10] .... ten seasons, or [11] ....

B Work in pairs. Read the examples of vague language (a–f) and answer the questions.

- **a** It's sort of like *Groundhog Day*, but set in the future.
- **b** It's a book by what's his name? You know, that …
- **c** I watched for a couple of hours or so.
- **d** It's a kind of detective drama.
- **e** He's tall-ish and very good looking.
- **f** I watch a lot of action films, crime drama and that kind of thing.

1. Which sentence refers to people without saying their name?
2. Which refer to approximate numbers?
3. How can we change adjectives to make them more vague?
4. How do you say something is similar, but not exactly the same?
5. How can we avoid giving a long list at the end of a sentence?

C Find more examples of the different types of vague language in Ex 4A.

D Learn and practise. Go to the Grammar Bank.

page 117 **GRAMMAR BANK**

PRONUNCIATION

5 A 3.07 | linking and elision | Listen to the sentences and look at the parts joined by a ‿. Which show:

- **a** linking between words which end in a consonant sound and words which begin with a vowel sound?
- **b** elision (when a consonant sound disappears before another consonant sound)?

1. It's based‿on‿a book by what's her name?
2. Every episode is sort‿of incredibly tense.
3. You get‿caught‿up in the drama and that‿kind‿of‿thing.
4. It's got‿about ten seasons‿or something like‿that.

B Practise saying the sentences.

SPEAKING

6 Work in groups. Take turns telling each other about a film or TV programme you would recommend. Ask questions to find out if you would enjoy it.

A: You really should watch *Stranger Things*. It's a really gripping story!

B: What's it about?

C: Is it scary?

MEDIATION SKILLS

giving general and personal views

describe a film

page 148 **MEDIATION BANK**

3D BBC Street Interviews

Music lover?

GRAMMAR | *do* and *did* for emphasis
SPEAKING | a music questionnaire
WRITING | a forum comment

PREVIEW

1 **Work in groups. Discuss the questions.**

1 Which types of music in the box do you like and why?

classical	contemporary R&B	film scores	folk	hip hop	jazz	opera	rap	rock	soul

2 Who are your favourite artists in these genres?
3 What other types of music do you like?
4 Do you ever go to gigs or concerts? If so, who was the last act you saw? If not, which bands or singers would you most like to see live?
5 How important is music in your life?

Q1: What kind of music do you like and why?

Q2: How important is music in your life?

VIEW

2A ▶ **Watch the video. Which genres does each speaker like? How many speakers say that music is really or very important to them?**

B ▶ **Watch the first part of the video again. Match the speakers (1–8) with what they say about music (a–h).**

1 Kaelan — **a** I enjoy music from films.
2 Roisin — **b** I enjoy singing along while I'm listening.
3 Ryan — **c** I listen to songs that are quite relaxed.
4 Aslan — **d** I like music that is good to dance to.
5 Oby — **e** I like the lyrics and the beat behind the music.
6 Leanne — **f** I can express myself freely and improvise when I play.
7 Sophia — **g** I listen to rap while I'm doing exercise.
8 Lucy — **h** I like music with guitars and drums in it.

C ▶ **Watch the second part of the video again. Are the statements True (T) or False (F)?**

1 Kaelan is a professional musician.
2 Roisin likes going to live music performances.
3 Ryan only listens to music at home.
4 Aslan always listens to music while he's working.
5 Oby played an instrument in the past.
6 Leanne listens to music to help her relax.
7 Sophia listens to music for most of the day.
8 Lucy often goes to festivals.

D **Work in pairs. Discuss the questions.**

1 What do you think Ryan means when he says that music is the soundtrack to his life?
2 Leanne likes to put music on in the background when she's doing things. Do you do this? If so, what do you listen to?

GRAMMAR

do and *did* for emphasis

3 A Work in pairs. Read the extracts from the interviews. Why do the speakers use *do* and *don't*?

1 I **do** listen to music on Spotify, like, public platforms, but I **don't** play any instruments.

2 There's certain bits of work where I **do** listen to music while I'm working and there's certain bits of work where I **don't**, where I can't, if it's very technical, or if I'm trying to be very creative, then I can and **do** listen to music.

3 I have to say I **don't** like orchestra music so much, but I **do** like background music, listening to relaxing things.

4 Although I **don't** go to festivals, I **do** listen to it a lot at home and I play the piano as an instrument.

B Learn and practise. Go to the Grammar Bank.

page 118 **GRAMMAR BANK**

SPEAKING

a music questionnaire

4 A Read the questionnaire and make notes on your answers.

How important is music in your life?

1 Have your music tastes changed since you were younger? How?
2 Can you play an instrument? If so, how long have you been playing it? If not, which instrument would you most like to learn?
3 Are you a good singer? Have you ever sung karaoke? If so, what did you think of the experience?
4 Do you listen to music to motivate yourself and/or to help you concentrate? If so, what type of music?
5 What is your favourite band or song?
6 Do you listen to a lot of music in English?
7 Who is the most famous musician from your country? What do you think of them?
8 What is the first song you ever remember?

B Work in groups. Ask and answer the questions in the questionnaire. Use your notes and the Key phrases to help you.

KEY PHRASES

I absolutely love …
I'm really into …
I'm a big fan of …
I couldn't live without …
I'm not very keen on …
I don't like … , but I do like …
I can't stand …

WRITING

a forum comment

5 A Work in pairs. Discuss the questions

1 Which online discussion forums have you used in the past?
2 Do you prefer to read online discussions or take part in them?
3 What are the main advantages and disadvantages of forums?

B Write a forum comment. Go to the Writing Bank.

page 105 **WRITING BANK**

GRAMMAR

relative clauses

1 A Complete the relative clauses in the sentences. Add commas where necessary.

1 I met a woman yesterday. She was Aki's mother.
The woman .... Aki's mother.
2 He wrote his books with this pen.
This is the pen ....
3 That girl's father predicted the disaster.
She's the girl .... disaster.
4 The event first took place in 1923.
1923 is the year .... place.
5 Jan is a circus performer. He's Lia's boyfriend.
Jan .... a circus performer.
6 He's famous for this book.
This is the book ....

B Which relative clause in Ex 1A is non-defining? In which sentences can the relative pronoun be omitted?

C Work in pairs. Take turns defining the things in the box using relative clauses. Guess who or what your partner is describing.

a city · a famous person · an object in your bag · a person you both know · a TV series or film · something you use every day

She's the politician who …

cleft sentences

2 A Put the words into the correct order to make cleft sentences.

1 What / about / we / scenery / the / New Zealand / is / like
2 The / is / thing / that / about / I'm / my / nervous / exam
3 It / arrive / on / was / that / she / Monday / was / to / due
4 What / learning / difficult / heart / is / I / things / find / by
5 The / was / grandmother / who / me / person / my / taught
6 The / about / passionate / is / thing / location / she's / the

B Work in pairs. Take turns completing the sentences with your own ideas.

- It was … who taught me …
- It was in the year … that I …
- What I'd like to do next weekend …
- What I've always liked about …

VOCABULARY

3 A Choose the correct words to complete the sentences.

1 When someone corrects me while I'm speaking English, it puts me **on** / **off**.
2 I love the lively **atmosphere** / **venue** you get when you're in a big festival crowd!
3 I know which bands and singers would be in my perfect festival **act** / **line-up**!
4 When I speak in public, I think I come **across** / **back** as too formal.
5 I love films that are **based on** / **set in** true stories.
6 I don't study at home because I can't put **up to** / **up with** the noise.
7 I don't enjoy watching films where I have to read the **soundtrack** / **subtitles**.
8 I sometimes find it hard to get my message **across** / **up** in English.

B Work in pairs. Which sentences in Ex 3A are true for you?

4 A Choose the correct options (A–C) to complete the story.

The show goes on

I once took on the challenge of trying to put on a show with people who had never performed on stage before. At first it seemed impossible. People kept [1] .... their lines. After a few weeks, I really didn't want to continue, but everyone was so enthusiastic that in the end, I [2] .... agree to carry on. But then I realised that we were trying to rehearse in the evenings, [3] .... everyone was tired. So I [4] .... the idea of rehearsing early in the mornings instead, [5] .... was much more successful because everyone was fresh. [6] .... I liked about working with people new to acting was that they were completely free – they had no expectations to [7] ....

As the day of the performance approached, I must admit I became more nervous. We had put up posters to [8] .... an audience, but I wasn't sure how many would [9] .... Thankfully, the theatre was full. My amateur cast [10] .... giving an incredible performance, and the audience loved it!

	A	B	C
1	ending up	messing up	speaking up
2	did	have	do
3	which	what	when
4	put up with	came up with	got on with
5	where	who	which
6	What	Which	This
7	live with	live for	live up to
8	attract	act	come
9	set	attend	attract
10	came up	put up	ended up

B R3.01 | Listen and check your answers.

lifestyle 4

VLOGS

Q: Name one change you could make to your life to improve your health.

1 Watch the video. What changes do they mention?

2 Work in pairs. Discuss one change you could make to your health.

Global Scale of English

LEARNING OBJECTIVES

4A READING | Read an article about healthy lifestyle choices: health and lifestyle; illness and treatment

Discuss your future lifestyle: future continuous and future perfect

Pronunciation: connected speech: future perfect

4B LISTENING | Understand a radio programme about sleep: sleep

Discuss sleep: passives

Pronunciation: sentence stress: content and function words

Write an article about sleep

4C HOW TO ... | express agreement and disagreement: exercise; sport: motivation and benefits

Pronunciation: stress in phrases for partial agreement

4D BBC PROGRAMME | Understand a documentary about beekeeping: phrases related to time

Talk about traditional vs. modern lifestyles

Write a cause-and-effect essay

4A Making changes

GRAMMAR | future continuous and future perfect
VOCABULARY | health and lifestyle; illness and treatment
PRONUNCIATION | connected speech: future perfect

READING

1 A Work in groups. Which of the following are important for a healthy lifestyle? In what ways?

exercise food money sleep stress where you live

B Read *How to live well: the thinker, the bather and the eater*. Answer the questions.

1 What change did each person make?
2 Why did they make the change?
3 What are their goals for the future?

C Choose the correct option (a or b) for each question (1–3).

1 How does Felipe feel about the other students on his course?
a astonished that they are so young
b pleased that they have accepted him
2 How does Fiona feel about swimming in the Okavango Delta?
a excited that it might happen
b concerned that it might be dangerous
3 How does Derek feel when he thinks about his diet in the past?
a ashamed at how unhealthy it was
b surprised that he didn't realise it was harming him

D Work in groups. Discuss the questions.

1 What do you think of the changes the people in the text are making?
2 What other positive changes could they make?
3 Do you know anyone who has made similar lifestyle changes?

VOCABULARY

health and lifestyle

2 A Complete the sentences with the correct form of the phrases in the box. Use the phrases in bold in the article to help you.

cut down on ~~do a regular workout~~ do a sedentary job expand your horizons keep mentally active keep up my progress stay in shape transform my lifestyle vary my diet work long hours

1 I do a regular workout in the gym once or twice a week.
2 I'd hate to .... where I have to sit in an office all day.
3 I try to .... and eat lots of different foods, to get a balance of all the things my body needs.
4 I think travelling is a great way to .... and help you understand other people's lives.
5 I exercise because I enjoy it, not because I want to ....
6 I'd like to .... my screen time; I spend too long in front of a computer.
7 I don't need to .... I'm already very healthy and happy.
8 In my job I have to .... , sometimes up to ten hours a day!
9 I like doing puzzles as a way to ....
10 Starting an exercise programme is easy. I'm fine for a few weeks, but I find it hard to ....

B Work in pairs. Are the sentences in Ex 2A true for you? Why/Why not?

C Learn and practise. Go to the Vocabulary Bank.

page 138 **VOCABULARY BANK** illness and treatment

How to live well

Life is full of turning points, when either we decide to make a change ourselves, or change is forced upon us. This month, we speak to three people who recently reached a turning point in their lives and decided it was time to **transform their lifestyle**. We ask them: Why did you make a change and where do you see yourself in two years' time?

the thinker

'I worked until the age of seventy in a job that was both interesting and intellectually stimulating. When I retired two years ago, I decided I needed to **keep mentally active**, so I signed up for a university degree in sociology. I'm the oldest student by a long way, but luckily the others on my course don't see that as a problem. I also started going to French classes because I'd always wanted to learn another language. I'm really enjoying both things, and I've made loads of new friends. Doing this degree has really helped me to **expand my horizons** and think about society and my place in it.

Personally, I think it's really important to **stay in shape** both mentally and physically. I hope it will help me fight off illnesses like Alzheimer's, and it also motivates me and gives me something to aim for. Where do I see myself in two years? Well, I'll have graduated, so I'll have a degree, and hopefully my French will have improved, too. There are lots of volunteer roles related to social issues, so maybe I'll be working as a volunteer two or three days a week. I guess it's also possible I'll be travelling around France and using my new language skills.'

Felipe Ortega

the bather

'For years I **did a sedentary job** and **worked long hours** in a corporate office. It was well paid, but high stress, and it was definitely having a damaging effect on my health. I didn't sleep well and had no time to exercise. I reached a point where I knew that I needed to change, so I started going to the gym and **doing regular workouts**. Then I saw a TV programme about wild swimming and I decided to give it a go. I loved it from the start, and now I swim 365 days a year in rivers, oceans and the occasional waterfall. It doesn't matter what time of year it is, or how cold the water is – I'll be there. I feel much happier and healthier now. There's a huge wild-swimming community worldwide, so I'm starting to plan a few trips abroad to places like the fjords in Iceland, where the water is beautiful, but apparently extremely cold. What will I be doing in two years' time? Well, I definitely want to **keep up my progress** and if I'm lucky, I'll be swimming in the Okavango Delta in Botswana – one of my dreams! I hope there won't be any crocodiles, but I doubt it will stop me even if there are! I've also started posting blogs about my experiences, and I'm getting quite a few followers, so who knows, maybe I'll have given up my job and I'll be earning a living as a wild-swimming influencer.'

Fiona Karlsson

the eater

'I was never particularly interested in healthy eating when I was younger – I would always choose a burger and chips over a salad! Then a few years ago, I started noticing that I didn't have much energy, and I was having a few health issues. I came across an article online about the effects of junk food on the body, and I suddenly realised how unhealthy my diet was – full of sugar and salt. So, I made the decision to **vary my diet** more and **cut down on** processed foods. And it worked. I started to feel better almost immediately, so I've since made more changes to the way I eat. I've started buying a lot of my food directly from local producers – butter and cheese from farmers and seafood from local fishermen. I've also started growing a few vegetables in my garden. When I look back, it seems really strange that it took me so long to work out what my diet was doing to me. The difference in my energy levels now is incredible. So, in two years' time? I'll have given up meat completely, and I'll have transformed my whole garden into a mini farm! Hopefully, I'll be growing most of my own fruit and vegetables, and I'll be eating fresh, seasonal produce all year round.'

Derek Mankham

GRAMMAR

future continuous and future perfect

3 A Read the sentences (a–d) and answer the questions (1–2).

a In two years I'll have graduated.
b I'll have transformed my whole garden into a mini farm.
c If I'm lucky, I'll be swimming in the Okavango Delta in Botswana.
d I'll be growing most of my own fruit and vegetables.

1 Which sentences are about things that will be completed before a specific time in the future?
2 Which sentences are about things that will be in progress at a specific time in the future?

B Learn and practise. Go to the Grammar Bank.

page 119 **GRAMMAR BANK**

PRONUNCIATION

4 A 4.01 | connected speech: future perfect | Listen and complete the sentences. Which words link together? Do we use the strong or weak form of *have*?

1 This time next year, ... graduated from university.
2 I hope .... cut down on junk food by then.
3 When you next see me, ... started working out.
4 I hope .... found a new job by the summer.

B Complete the sentences with your own ideas, using the future perfect. Then read your sentences to a partner. Make sure you link the words and pronounce *have* correctly.

- By the end of today, I'll have …
- By next weekend, I'll have …
- By next summer, I'll have …

SPEAKING

5 A Think about your lifestyle in five years' time. Do you have any goals? How might your life be different? Choose two topics from the box and make notes on your goals and predictions.

achievements	activities/experiences	
English	health and lifestyle	home
studies and/or work	travel	

B Read the Future Skills box and do the task.

FUTURE SKILLS
Communication

When you talk about your goals and predictions, it is a good idea to add examples and reasons, to make your answers more interesting.

'I want to vary my diet more. **For example**, I hope I'll be cooking dishes from different countries.'

'I hope I'll have transformed my lifestyle **because** I'm too stressed at the moment.'

Look at your notes in Ex 5A. What examples and reasons can you add?

C Work in pairs. Discuss what you will be doing in five years' time, and how your life will have changed. Ask your partner questions to learn more details.

A: In five years' time, I'll have graduated from university and hopefully have found a good job!
B: What kind of job would you like to do?

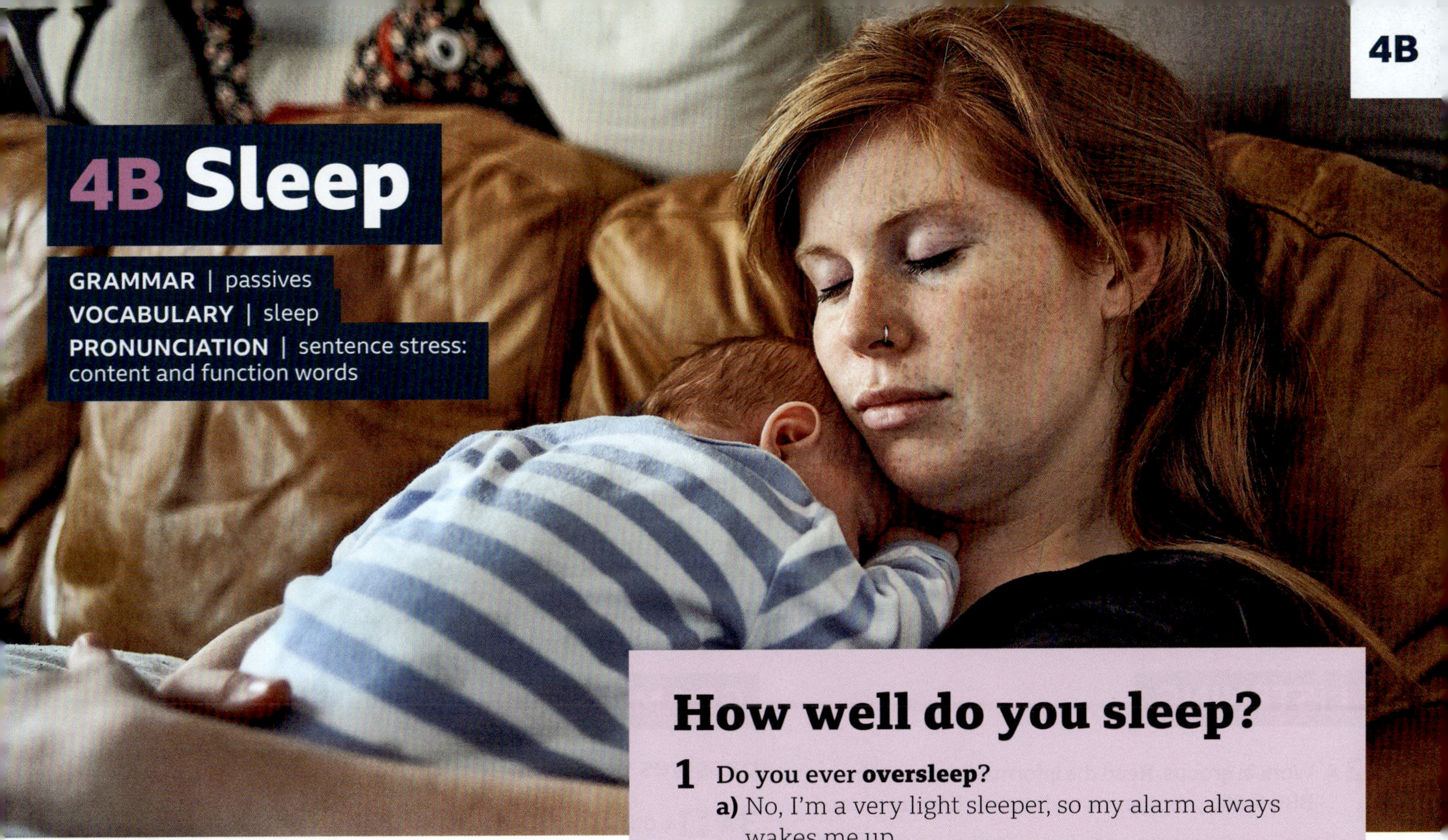

4B Sleep

GRAMMAR | passives
VOCABULARY | sleep
PRONUNCIATION | sentence stress: content and function words

VOCABULARY

sleep

1 A **Work in pairs. How many hours' sleep did you get last night? Was it a normal amount for you?**

B **Read the quiz. Then complete the sentences (1–10) with the words and phrases in bold.**

1 You can say that you .... to mean that you fall asleep.
2 A short sleep during the day is called a ....
3 Someone who often or always has trouble sleeping is a(n) ....
4 When you are very tired, you are ....
5 If you do not wake up easily, even when it's noisy, then you're a .... , and you usually go into a very ....
6 If you make a rough breathing noise when you sleep, then you ....
7 A dream where something bad happens is a ....
8 If you deliberately stay in bed later than normal, you ....
9 If you stop other people from sleeping, you .... them ....
10 If you don't wake up when you are supposed to, then you ....

C **Work in pairs. Ask and answer the questions in the quiz. How similar are your sleep habits?**

How well do you sleep?

1 **Do you ever oversleep?**
a) No, I'm a very light sleeper, so my alarm always wakes me up.
b) Yes, I'm a **heavy sleeper**, so I often sleep through the alarm.
c) Yes, but I don't mind. Sometimes it's good to **have a lie-in**.

2 **How long does it usually take you to fall asleep?**
a) Not long at all. I **drop off** as soon as my head hits the pillow.
b) Quite a long time. I usually read for an hour. It helps me to switch off.
c) It depends. I sometimes lie awake in bed thinking about work or family problems.

3 **Do you do anything to help you get to sleep?**
a) Yes, I sometimes do relaxation exercises.
b) If I can't sleep, I count or do maths problems in my head.
c) I listen to podcasts or check my phone until I feel tired.

4 **How often do you have trouble going to sleep?**
a) Never.
b) Occasionally. It's usually because I'm worried about something.
c) All the time. I'm an **insomniac**, so I often have a **nap** in the afternoon to try and catch up on sleep.

5 **Do you usually remember your dreams?**
a) I sometimes remember my dreams, especially if I've been in a **deep sleep**.
b) I never remember my dreams.
c) I don't usually remember dreams except when I wake up after having a **nightmare**.

6 **Do you ever snore?**
a) Sometimes when I'm really **exhausted**.
b) Only if I have a cold.
c) Yes, I'm very noisy. I sleep in a room on my own so that I don't **keep** my partner **awake**.

LISTENING

2 A **Work in groups. Read the information about the BBC Radio programme and answer the questions.**

> **The science of sleep** BBC
>
> We spend around a third of our lives asleep, but the reason we sleep is still a mystery. Could it be the biggest mistake the evolutionary process has ever made? What does sleep actually do for us? David Edmonds meets Matthew Walker, one of the world's leading sleep scientists, to find out.

1 On average, how many hours a night do you think people in the developed world sleep?
2 Why do you think humans sleep? Is it just a waste of time?

B **4.02 | Listen to the programme. Number the topics in the order they are mentioned.**

a sleep and the brain
b the number of hours people sleep on average
c why sleep seems an odd thing for humans to do
d the effects of changing the clocks twice a year

C **4.02 | Work in pairs. Answer the questions. Then listen again and check.**

1 Why does the presenter say that sleep seems 'a monumental waste of time'?
2 What do you learn about sleep in the 1940s, compared to now?
3 What happens to people's health when the clocks change in the spring and the autumn?
4 Why is sleep important for making decisions?

D **Work in groups. Discuss the questions.**

1 What happens to you if you don't get enough sleep?
2 Do you have an expression in your language meaning 'to sleep on a problem'?

GRAMMAR

passives

3 A **4.03 | Listen and complete the extract from the programme.**

.... if sleep doesn't serve an absolutely vital function, then it's the biggest mistake the evolutionary process has ever made.

B **Read the sentences (1–3) about sleep and look at the verbs in bold. Then choose the correct words to complete the rule.**

1 **It is believed that** most people need eight hours' sleep.
2 In ancient cultures, **it was thought that** dreams could predict the future.
3 **It is expected that** if we sleep less, we can be more productive.

We can use passive structures with *it* to talk about **general ideas or beliefs / our own ideas or beliefs**.

C **Learn and practise. Go to the Grammar Bank.**

page 120 **GRAMMAR BANK**

PRONUNCIATION

4 A **4.04 | sentence stress: content and function words | Listen to the sentence and underline the stressed words.**

It's believed that most people need eight hours' sleep.

B **Look at the sentence in Ex 4A again. Do we stress the content words (verbs, nouns, adjectives, etc.) or the function words (pronouns, articles, auxiliaries, etc.)? Why?**

C **4.05 | Work in pairs. Read the sentences and predict which words will be stressed. Then listen and check.**

1 It's expected that as we get older, we need less sleep.
2 It has been suggested that our use of technology affects our sleep.
3 It was thought a hot drink would help you to sleep better.
4 It's believed that if we sleep less, we can be more productive.

5 **Work in pairs. You are going to guess whether some statements about sleep are true or false. Student A: Go to page 142. Student B: Go to page 144.**

SPEAKING

6 A Work in groups. Discuss the statements about sleep (1–9). Do you think they are true, or are they myths? Can you give examples from your own experience?

Reality or myth?

1 It is believed that some adults only need five or fewer hours of sleep a night.

2 It's been suggested that, in health terms, it doesn't matter whether you sleep during the day or at night.

3 It is known that some people walk around in their sleep and can carry out complex activities, such as driving and cooking.

4 It's thought that boredom can make you sleepy.

5 It's been suggested that adults need less sleep as they get older.

6 It's been suggested that it is fine to sleep very little during the week, then catch up at the weekend.

7 It's thought that watching TV in bed is a good way to relax before going to sleep.

8 It's been suggested that doing exercise before going to bed will stop you from going to sleep.

9 It's believed that scrolling on your phone before you go to sleep or during the night makes it more difficult for you to wake up the next day.

A: I think it's a myth that some adults only need five hours of sleep.

B: I agree. I know that if I get less than seven hours, I feel terrible!

B Go to page 142 and find out which of the statements are true.

WRITING

an article

7 A Work in pairs. Read the article. Then discuss the questions.

1 What is the main argument being made by the writer? Do you agree with it? Why/Why not?

2 What reasons does the writer give for people sleeping less?

Why we're just not getting enough sleep

Kirsty Whitall | Wednesday 26 May

It is thought that the average adult requires seven to nine hours of sleep per night. However, we know that many people in the developed world are **not only** sleeping much less than this, **but also** suffering health problems as a result. In the USA, it has been suggested that people are sleeping at least one hour less than they did thirty years ago. There are many reasons why people might be sleeping less.

To start with, there is a problem with modern expectations of work since consumers expect information, entertainment **and** food to be available 24 hours a day. **Furthermore**, this 24/7 culture means that **as well as** consumers staying awake for longer than they used to, workers who provide us with these goods and services are expected to work longer hours or night shifts in order for companies to meet the demand.

In addition to this, in a fast-paced and competitive world of business, employees are often expected to work long hours, with more work to do and less time to do it. As a result, many employees are willing to sleep less in order to progress their careers. **Moreover**, with increased pressure at work, many employees find it difficult to find time to take holidays, with stress and burnout as likely consequences.

B Look at the linking words and phrases in bold in the article. Can you think of any more words and phrases we use to present additional ideas?

C Rewrite the sentences. Use the prompts in brackets to connect the ideas.

1 It's been suggested that people don't sleep well because they consume more caffeine than in the past. Another reason is that they spend a lot of time on screens. (not only … , but also …)

2 Many people sleep fewer than six hours a night and always feel tired. They are more likely to develop health problems. (Furthermore)

3 One problem is that people are required to travel long distances to get to work. Another problem is that people are working longer hours than before. (In addition to this, …)

4 Lack of sleep increases your risk of heart attacks. It also means that you are more likely to be in an accident. (As well as …)

D Write an article with the title *How to get a good night's sleep*. Use some of the ideas you discussed in Ex 7A. Use linking words to present additional ideas.

4C Keep moving

HOW TO ... | express agreement and disagreement
VOCABULARY | exercise; sport: motivation and benefits
PRONUNCIATION | stress in phrases for partial agreement

VOCABULARY

exercise

1 A Work in groups. Discuss the questions.

1 How much exercise do you do in a typical week?
2 What kinds of exercise do you do?
3 How easy or difficult do you find it to make yourself do exercise?

B Read the article. How much exercise is recommended per week? Do the majority of people manage this amount?

C Work in pairs. Look at the words and phrases in bold in the article and answer the questions.

1 Which involves more effort: moderate exercise or vigorous exercise?
2 Which quality allows you to lift heavy objects?
3 Which quality allows you to continue to run or cycle for a long time without getting tired?
4 Is skipping with a rope high-impact or low-impact exercise?
5 Is yoga an aerobic exercise?
6 Which quality allows you to bend and move your body easily?

D Complete the statements with the correct words and phrases from the article.

1 My .... is quite good. I can touch my toes easily.
2 I try to avoid ....-impact exercises such as running.
3 I think I need to do some training with weights to improve my ....
4 I can run a short distance, but I don't have much .... , so I can't go more than a few kilometres.
5 I don't like getting too out of breath, so I prefer .... exercise.

2 A Work in pairs. Discuss which statements in Ex 1D are true for you.

B Learn and practise. Go to the Vocabulary Bank.

page 139 **VOCABULARY BANK** sport: motivation and benefits

Getting and staying fit

Salim Rashid | Wednesday 27 May | 17.01 GMT

The world's strongest men pull twenty-tonne trucks on a rope. Ultra-marathon runners run 100-kilometre races, sometimes through the desert in forty-degree heat. Top surfers routinely surf six-metre waves. That's the crazy end of exercise. What about normal people? We all know it's important to exercise, but how much exercise should we do? And how can we stick at it even when we're tired or bored and it's raining outside?

According to one study from the UK, adults should be doing 150 minutes of **moderate exercise** or seventy-five minutes of **vigorous exercise** each week. This includes **strength** exercises such as lifting weights and **aerobic** exercises that make your heart beat faster, like jogging and cycling, which improve **stamina**. Experts recommend a mixture of **low-impact** exercise (where you keep at least one foot on the ground at all times) and **high-impact** activities such as running and jumping. Another recommendation is exercises that improve **flexibility**, for example yoga.

While such recommendations have been well known for a number of years, one report reveals that less than half the world's population does enough exercise. The key is motivation. People need to find an exercise type that they enjoy and then make it part of their daily routine, like having their morning cup of coffee.

How to ...
express agreement and disagreement

3 A 4.06 | Listen to two people discussing exercise. Who does more exercise – Martin or Leah?

B 4.06 | Read the statements. Do Martin and Leah agree, disagree, or partially agree about each one? Listen again and check.

1 Everyone should do 150 minutes of moderate exercise each week.
2 Everyone should do an hour of exercise every day.
3 Martin doesn't need to do any exercise because he has a physical job.
4 Yoga is the best way to relax.
5 Martin should do some kind of exercise occasionally.

4 A Work in pairs. Complete the table with the words and phrases in the box. Then check your answers in the audioscript on page 162.

agree more | although | fair point | see your point | the other hand | up to a point

expressing agreement and disagreement

agreeing/ disagreeing	I couldn't [1] .... That's a good/[2] .... , although it could also be argued that ... I completely disagree. I take/[3] .... But on [4] ....
partially agreeing	I know what you mean, but ... I agree [5] .... , but ... That's a fair point, [6] .... it could also be argued that ...

B Learn and practise. Go to the Grammar Bank.

page 121 **GRAMMAR BANK**

PRONUNCIATION

5 A 4.07 | stress in phrases for partial agreement | Listen to the sentences. Which word in the phrases in bold do we stress?

1 **I agree with you up to a point**, but not everyone has time to exercise every day.
2 **That's a fair point, although** strength training doesn't suit everyone.
3 **I take your point, but** it's important to make an effort to keep fit.
4 **I see your point, but** you can't expect everyone to enjoy going to the gym.

B 4.07 | Listen again and repeat the sentences.

6 A Choose the correct words to complete the conversations.

1 A: As far as I'm concerned, all sport is a waste of time and shouldn't be on TV.
B: I **couldn't** / **can't** agree more. It's just a distraction from serious issues.

2 A: If you ask me, football is the best sport because anyone can play it.
B: I **am** / **completely** disagree with you. I find football totally boring.

3 A: Personally, I believe sport is good for your character.
B: I agree with you **for** / **up to** a point, but not if it teaches you to cheat.

4 A: In my view, countries spend too much money on the Olympic Games.
B: True, but on **the other** / **another** hand, don't you think it's fun to watch?

B Work in pairs. Which of the ideas in Ex 6A do you agree with? Why?

SPEAKING

7 A Read the statements. Do you agree, partially agree or disagree? Why? Think of as many reasons as you can and make notes.

- 'All children should do sport at school at least once a day.'
- 'Some sports such as rugby and boxing are too dangerous and should be banned.'
- 'It's the government's duty to provide free gyms and sports equipment for everyone.'

B Work in groups. Discuss the statements in Ex 7A. Explain why you agree or disagree.

MEDIATION SKILLS
making group decisions
decide how to contribute to an event

page 150 **MEDIATION BANK**

Speak anywhere Go to the interactive speaking practice

4D BBC Documentary

Ancient traditions

VOCABULARY | phrases related to time
SPEAKING | a discussion about traditional vs. modern lifestyles
WRITING | a cause-and-effect essay

PREVIEW

1 A Work in pairs. Look at the photos and answer the questions.

1 What ancient tradition is shown in the photos?
2 What do you know about this tradition?

B Read about the programme. What do you think you might learn about the beekeepers' lives? What problems might they face?

Earth from Space

Earth from Space is a BBC series that uses cameras in space to tell stories about life on our planet from a different perspective. In this episode, we watch a group of nomadic beekeepers who travel across China to harvest honey. But they've run into a problem and time is not on their side.

VIEW

2 A ▶ Watch the video. Check your answers to Ex 1B.

B ▶ Watch the video again. Complete the sentences with one word or a number.

1 Nearly .... percent of the world's rapeseed oil comes from this part of China.
2 The thick cloud makes it too .... for the bees to fly.
3 The fields will be sprayed with pesticides in .... weeks' time.
4 Mr Dai waits .... days for the weather to change.
5 The bees need to visit two .... flowers to make a single jar of honey.
6 Bees play an essential part in .... production.
7 The total number of .... is falling each year.
8 Mr Dai has .... of honey and is happy to move on.

BBC

VOCABULARY

phrases related to time

3 A Work in pairs. Read the sentences from the video. What do you think the phrases in bold mean?

1 They've travelled across China **just in time** for the bloom.
2 These bees aren't going anywhere and **time is running out**.
3 Pesticides are contributing to a worldwide decline in the number of honeybees and their **future is under threat**.
4 Mr Dai's **window of opportunity** is short.
5 Mr Dai has plenty of honey. And **not a moment too soon**.
6 The fields will be sprayed in two days. **It's time to** move on.

B Work in groups. Take turns to complete the sentences with your own ideas.

1 The future of the planet is under threat from …
2 Time is running out for …
3 We have a small window of opportunity to …
4 If we manage to … , it will be not a moment too soon.
5 It's time to …

SPEAKING

a discussion about traditional vs. modern lifestyles

4 A 4.08 | Listen to someone talking about how lifestyles have changed in her community. Make notes about the differences she mentions between traditional and modern lifestyles.

B 4.08 | Listen again. Tick the phrases you hear.

KEY PHRASES

I would say that (my modern lifestyle) is different from …
Nowadays, … , whereas in the past …
Traditionally/In the old days, …
He/She/They used to/would … (get up early)
We still have … , but it's … (smaller/more difficult)
These days, it seems like …/it appears that …
Our modern-day lifestyle is much more … than in the past.

C Make notes about traditions in your community. Use the questions to help you.

1 What traditions do your family or community preserve?
2 How do you think lifestyles have changed between the generations?
3 Which older traditions are under threat? Why?
4 Which older traditions do you think the next generation may be interested in?

D Work in groups. Discuss how traditions have changed in your communities. Whose community is the most traditional? Whose is the most modern?

WRITING

a cause-and-effect essay

5 A Work in pairs. How might the following affect people's lifestyles?

- larger populations in cities
- increased pollution
- better access to technology

B Write a cause-and-effect essay. Go to the Writing Bank.

page 105 **WRITING BANK**

GRAMMAR

future continuous and future perfect

1 A Complete the sentences with the correct future continuous or future perfect form of the verbs in brackets.

1 Two years from now, I .... in the same place. (not live)
2 By the time I'm old, I hope I .... at least fifty countries. (visit)
3 A year from now, I expect I .... with all the friends I have now. (still communicate)
4 In five years' time, I .... (working) in the tech industry.
5 In five years, I .... my degree. (complete)

B Work in pairs. Are any of the sentences true for you? Change some of the sentences so that they are true.

passives

2 A Complete the second sentence using an appropriate passive verb and *it*.

1 The media has reported that drinking coffee stops you from growing.
.... in the media that drinking coffee stops you from growing.
2 People expect that in the future more people will choose a vegetarian diet.
.... in the future, more people will choose a vegetarian diet.
3 In the past, people suggested that walking 10,000 steps a day would keep you fit.
In the past, ... walking 10,000 steps a day would keep you fit.
4 People believe that natural sugar is better for you than processed sugar.
.... natural sugar is better for you than processed sugar.

B Work in pairs. Are the statements in Ex 2A true or myths? Check your answers on page 142.

VOCABULARY

3 Complete the sentences with the words in the box.

asthma cut down keep up long hours medication run-down sedentary shape transform vary workout

1 I try to do a regular .... , but recently I've been feeling a bit .... and I haven't been able to.
2 I work .... so I don't have much time for cooking. I should .... my diet more, and I should also .... on the amount of fast food I eat.
3 I have been thinking of ways I could .... my lifestyle.
4 I do a .... job which sometimes makes it hard for me to stay in ....
5 I've started running in the morning, and now I'm up to 7 km. I hope I can .... my progress.
6 I suffer from .... , so I take regular ....

4 Choose the correct words to complete the sentences.

1 I don't sleep very well at night because my husband **snores** / **naps** so loudly!
2 I get so tired during the week that at the weekend I like to **have a lie-in** / **keep me awake**.
3 My son is a very **heavy** / **exhausted** sleeper – nothing wakes him up.
4 I have some very noisy neighbours and they **keep me awake** / **drop off** some nights.
5 I **snored** / **overslept** and very nearly missed my connecting flight.
6 Jack is a(n) **insomniac** / **heavy sleeper** so he's always tired!

5 A Choose the correct options (A–C) to complete the text.

Health is the new wealth

Tara Williams | Monday 25 Feb | 13.00 GMT

In recent years, health and fitness has grown into a multi-billion-dollar industry as many of us strive to eat healthily and [1]........ in shape. With modern technology, the average lifestyle has become increasingly [2]........ . We are also busier and in general work [3]........ hours than in the past. So, to make up for it, we follow healthy-eating gurus on Instagram and try to [4]........ our diet by drinking fresh vegetable juice and eating superfood salads. We join gyms, buy fitness technology, take online yoga classes and [5]........ regular workouts. It is [6]........ that Americans spend more than $40 billion trying to improve their health and fitness every year.

And future trends look even more extreme. Some are predicting that within the next ten years, a lot of fitness training [7]........ moved outside. The [8]........ of training outdoors include exposure to the sun and fresh air, and running where the ground isn't flat. In addition, it's likely that more of us [9]........ personal tracking devices, which will offer us computer-generated personal training programmes based on our individual health metrics.

	A	B	C
1	stay	go	make
2	exhausted	sedentary	vigorous
3	higher	bigger	longer
4	vary	cut down	maintain
5	make	do	keep
6	thought	thinking	think
7	has	will have	won't be
8	motivations	incentives	benefits
9	will have worn	will be wearing	wear

B R4.01 | Listen and check your answers.

1D a letter of recommendation

1 A Read the letter of recommendation. Do you think Jenna would be suitable for the job? Why/Why not?

To Gómez, Natalia
From Hillstock, Martin
Subject Jenna Davison?

Dear Natalia,

You asked for my opinion about whether Jenna Davison would be a good manager. I have known Jenna for ten years. We met when she was a volunteer teacher in our school. As principal of St Mark's School, I have enjoyed working with Jenna for the last eight years. I would say she is a kind, friendly and enthusiastic teacher. I would also add that she's very passionate about her work. She has led several professional development workshops this term and has been mentoring one of our teaching assistants for the past year. In my opinion, whilst she has good communication skills with both students and teachers, Jenna can sometimes be shy or lack confidence when talking in public, or when making leadership decisions. I believe that while Jenna could make a good manager, she will need training and support to take on the role independently.

If you have any further questions with regard to her experience or qualifications, please do not hesitate to contact me.

Kind regards,
Martin Hillstock

B Work in pairs. Answer the questions.

1 What facts does Martin include about Jenna?
2 What opinions does he express about her?
3 Which phrases does he use to introduce his opinions?

C Work in pairs. Read the job advert. Who do you know that would be suitable for the job?

The Rock Café
4 hours ago

We're looking to recruit a new person to join our friendly team. We need someone to work in the café greeting customers, making coffees and serving at tables. The ideal candidate will need to be friendly and welcoming with a chatty personality to engage with customers as well as being organised and reliable. Flexible working hours.

No experience required – full training will be provided.

D Write a letter of recommendation. Include both facts and opinions about the person.

2D a competition entry

1 A Read the information about a writing competition. Answer the questions.

1 What happens to the best entries?
2 What do you have to write about?
3 What's the maximum number of words?
4 What do you have to include?

Get your article published!

If you could meet any person from the past, who would you meet, why and what would you do? Tell us in no more than 200 words and make sure you give it an attention-grabbing title!

The three winning entries will be published in next month's issue.

B Read the competition entry. Which is the best title?

a The biography of Jules Verne
b A visit with Verne
c A sailing trip to the Bay of Biscay

If I could go back in time and meet anyone I wanted, I'd go back to the 1800s and meet Jules Verne. Jules Verne was a French author who is famous for his revolutionary science-fiction and adventure novels like *Around the World in Eighty Days* and *Twenty Thousand Leagues Under the Sea*.

I'd take him for coffee and pastries in a café in Paris, where he lived, and ask him where he got his ideas from. Verne wrote about space travel and underwater travel before air travel and submarines were common, and before space travel existed. I would ask him what life was like for a writer in those times.

Although Verne wrote about travel adventures, he hadn't travelled much himself until the 1860s when he bought a small sailing boat. So, after our coffee, we would take a trip on his boat, perhaps to the Bay of Biscay, and I would ask him to read to me from his books.

C Choose the best tips (1–4) for writing engaging titles.

A good title:
1 shouldn't be too long.
2 should describe everything mentioned in the text.
3 will make someone want to find out more.
4 uses poetic devices like alliteration (words beginning with the same letter) or metaphors.

D Read the competition information in Ex 1A again. Plan your answer and think of a good title.

E Write your competition entry.

3D a forum comment

1 A Work in pairs. Read the main post and comments on a music forum. Whose opinion do you agree with? Why?

B Look at the highlighted phrases. Which express a general opinion and which express an opinion that the writer feels very sure about?

C Write your own comment for the forum. Use some of the opinion phrases in Ex 1B.

Music_Man 1 hour ago

How important do you think music is to society in general?

Big question I know, but I'm working on an essay for college on this topic and wanted to get a few opinions to help get me started.

289 Comments | Share

DJ Mikey 58m

I think that music is hugely important. I couldn't live without it. While every country has its own language, there's one language that we all understand, and that's the language of music. We don't need the words to understand what the music is saying – we can feel it. I go to festivals all over the world and one thing I know is that when the music starts, everyone understands and they just start dancing.

Reply | Share

Dannygirl 41m

I don't think music is that important. It's nice and I do enjoy listening to music sometimes, but it's definitely not as important as food, water and shelter, or even education. I'd say it's a luxury.

Reply | Share

Banodrums 40m

Music has the power to connect people. People can enjoy playing musical instruments together, share an interest in a particular kind of music, dance to the rhythm of a drum beat or sing aloud with friends to a favourite song. One thing is for certain, music brings us enjoyment.

Reply | Share

Adidreams64 39m

Music is essential for society. It gives us a way to relax and enjoy ourselves so that we don't feel too stressed all the time. It can improve our mood, so if we're feeling a bit down, we can listen to music and feel better. I don't play an instrument myself, but I do think music – playing it, listening to it and dancing to it – is really important for society.

Reply | Share

4D a cause-and-effect essay

1 A Read the extract from an essay about changing lifestyles. What reasons does the writer give for the changes?

The effect of urbanisation on modern lifestyles

William Crane | Wednesday 10 October

Over the last fifty years, there has been a huge shift from rural to urban living, which has resulted in some big changes to our lifestyles. Because cities have grown and developed, they have offered work opportunities to people living in rural environments, who previously had little access to this kind of labour.

In addition, there have been many changes due to improvements in education. More people have access to educational programmes than ever before, resulting in younger people growing up with higher ambitions than those of previous generations. Young people have flocked to the city and have had to adapt to a very different lifestyle, often working in a factory or an office, rather than out in the fields. Working long hours, they have little time for home cooking, which has led to poorer diets. As a result, many people now rely on fast food, which is more easily available in the city. Because of this, there has been an increase in health problems, such as …

B Scan the extract and find the phrases (1–5). Which introduce a cause, and which introduce an effect?

1 Resulting in …/which has resulted in …
2 Because … ,
3 Due to …
4 This has led to …/which has led to …
5 As a result, …/Because of this, …

C Plan a short cause-and-effect essay about how modern lifestyles are changing. Make notes about:

- what you see as the biggest changes.
- possible causes (e.g. better technology, changes to work patterns, etc.).
- possible effects of each change.

D Write your essay.

1A present perfect simple and continuous

REFERENCE

page 9

We use both the present perfect simple and the present perfect continuous to talk about situations or actions which started in the past and continue into the present.

Sometimes there is no important difference between the two tenses, particularly with verbs such as *work*, *live* and *study*.

Mauro **has lived/has been living** in Bologna since 2010.

However, there are also some important differences between the two.

Focusing on the result of the activity

We use the present perfect simple to focus on the result of a completed activity.

He's **passed** all of his exams. (Focuses on the result – passing the exams)

We use the present perfect continuous to focus on the activity itself.

He's **been studying** for his exams. (Focuses on the activity of studying)

How many? vs. *How long?*

We use the present perfect simple to answer the questions: 'How many?', 'How much?' or 'How far?'

We**'ve interviewed** more than 100 applicants (How many?)

He**'s raised** €1,000 for charity. (How much?)

They**'ve driven** over 3,000 kilometres. (How far?)

We use the present perfect continuous to answer the question: 'How long?' and to emphasise that an action has continued for a long time (using *for* and *since* to describe the duration), or is repeated. We often use the present perfect continuous with verbs that describe long actions, such as *wait*, *stay*, *play*, *sit*, *stand*, *write*, etc.

We**'ve been waiting** for over forty minutes now!

He**'s been sitting** on that bench since this morning.

Completed vs. unfinished actions

We use the present perfect simple to describe completed actions.

We use the present perfect continuous to describe actions that are unfinished or in progress.

Oh no, I**'ve missed** the bus!
(The bus has gone, so the action is completed.)

I'm afraid she**'s left** the office.
(She isn't here now, so the action is completed.)

I**'ve been learning** Mandarin.
(I'm still learning, so the action is not completed.)

She**'s been trying** to speak to you.
(She still hasn't spoken to you, so she's still trying.)

State verbs, experiences and habits

We use the present perfect simple, NOT the present perfect continuous, with state verbs, to talk about states or situations that started in the past and are in progress.

How long **have you known** Jessica?

I**'ve owned** this car since 2009.

We also use the present perfect simple with the words *always*, *ever* and *never* to talk about experiences and habits.

He**'s never driven** to work, he always goes by bike.

I**'ve always baked** my own bread.

PRACTICE

1 Choose the correct word(s) to complete the sentences.

1 I've **watched** / **been watching** this amazing series recently.
2 I've **been** / **been going** to the gym twice already this week.
3 We've **known** / **been knowing** them for about ten years.
4 You've **worked** / **been working** on that report all morning!
5 He's **stayed** / **been staying** with me whilst they finish repainting his flat.
6 I've probably **seen** / **been seeing** that film about twenty-five times!

2 Complete the sentences with the correct present perfect simple or continuous form of the verb in brackets.

1 Oh, no! I think he .... (break) his foot.
2 I .... (cook) all morning, but I've still got a lot to do!
3 I .... never .... (try) skiing.
4 How many invitations .... you .... (send) so far?
5 .... all the guests .... (arrive) yet?
6 I'm worried about Piotr. He .... (work) so hard recently.
7 How long .... you .... (know) Natasha?
8 She .... (study) for her exams for weeks.

3 Use the answers and the verbs in bold to write questions in the present perfect simple or continuous. If both forms are possible, use the continuous form.

1 I **teach** at the university.
How long .... there?
2 I **know** Johanna really well.
How long .... her?
3 I'm **developing** a new website.
How long .... it?
4 I **play** golf on Saturdays.
How long .... ?
5 I **live** in Krakow.
How long .... there?
6 He **wins** a lot of awards.
How many .... ?

1B infinitive and *-ing* forms

REFERENCE

page 11

Some verbs can be followed by a *to* infinitive or an *-ing* form, but with a change in meaning.

If you *try to do* something, you make an attempt to do it.

If you *try doing* something, you test it to see if it is suitable, useful or works.

I **tried to fix** the roof.
(I attempted it, but I failed.)

Try drinking green tea if you have a stomachache. (Test it to see if it works.)

If you *remember to do* something, you remember it and then do it.

If you *remember doing* something, you have a memory of doing it in the past.

Remember to feed the dog! (Don't forget!)

I **remember going** to school for the first time when I was five.

If you *forget to do* something, you don't do it because you don't remember.

If you *forget doing* something, you have no memory of it.

I **forgot to feed** the dog! (I didn't remember.)

If you *stop to do* something, you pause what you are doing in order to do something else.

If you *stop doing* something, you finish, and no longer do it.

I **stopped to call** my mother. (I stopped doing something so I could call her.)

I **stopped watching** TV two years ago.
(I no longer watch TV.)

Infinitive after the verb *be*

We can use a *to* infinitive after the verb *be*.

My idea is **to build** an app.

The purpose of the call was **to choose** a design.

Infinitive to express a purpose

We can use a *to* infinitive to express a purpose.

To make the perfect cup of tea, leave the bag in the water for three minutes.

You should practise every day **to get** better.

We can use *so as (not) to* as a formal alternative to a *to* infinitive, to express a purpose.

The house was built with big windows **so as to let** in lots of light.

She ran to school **so as not to be** late.

-ing form after a preposition

We use an *-ing* form, not a *to* infinitive, after a preposition.

I passed my exams **by working** hard.

PRACTICE

1 Find the mistakes and correct them. One sentence is correct.

1 For improve your memory, you need to make emotional connections with the subject.
2 The purpose of this article is show how memory is connected to our personalities.
3 She prepared for her exam by revise every day with a friend.
4 I try to remember all my students' names, but it's difficult.
5 He worked all morning except for when he stopped taking a coffee break.
6 If your computer freezes, try to switch it off and on again.
7 I remember to play in the back garden when I was six years old.
8 Don't forget buying snacks for the party tomorrow!

2 Complete the second sentence using the correct form of the verb in brackets and an *-ing* form or a *to* infinitive.

1 Oh no! I didn't switch on the alarm before we left.
Oh no! I .... the alarm on before we left. (forget)
2 I experimented with drinking more water, but I still get headaches.
I .... more water, but I still get headaches. (try)
3 It's important that we take our medicine tomorrow.
We must .... our medicine tomorrow. (remember)
4 I took a break from my work because I wanted to talk to Jack.
I .... because I wanted to talk to Jack. (stop)
5 The memory of singing on TV will always be with her!
She'll never .... on TV! (forget)
6 Because of his injury, he doesn't cycle anymore.
Because of his injury, he .... (stop)

3 Choose the correct verb forms to complete the text.

When professional chess players play against amateurs, they sometimes make it more challenging for themselves by playing several games at once, while blindfolded, so they can't see the boards. Their opponents have to tell them where they are moving their pieces, and the professionals play by [1]**remember / remembering** where everything is on the board. Of course, it's not only chess players who need good memories. Some judges have to remember thousands of laws. Actors must learn their lines but also remember [2]**to take / taking** a step to the left, turn around, and take a pace to the right. How can people like this prepare so as not [3]**to forget / forgetting** the information they need? One technique is [4]**by create / to create** a memory palace. [5]**Remembering / To remember** lists of objects, you can imagine a huge building. Inside it, you put each imaginary object in its special place. [6]**So as not to forget / Not forgetting** the location, you imagine the objects somewhere meaningful. So a hat might hang above a door, a book might be placed by a bed. [7]**Recalling / To recall** the objects, you enter the imaginary building and walk around 'seeing' the objects in the places where you have put them.

Occasionally, teachers ask students to [8]**try creating / try for creating** memory palaces to help them remember important facts. My advice? Try [9]**put / to put** the objects somewhere significant to you. And don't forget [10]**closing / to close** the door to the building. Opening it is a vital part of the remembering process.

1C How to ... express personal preferences

REFERENCE

page 15

We use *really into* something to say we like something a lot.

I'm really into Polish films.

We use *passionate about* something to talk about something we really love.

I'm passionate about Mexican music.

We can use the idiom *It's not my cup of tea* to say that we generally don't like something.

Sorry, football just **isn't** really **my cup of tea**.

Expressing likes and dislikes

I'm really into/I'm passionate about + noun/*-ing* form
I'm (not) keen on/I'm (not) a big fan of + noun/*-ing* form
I love/hate/can't stand + noun/*-ing* form
It's not my cup of tea.
What I like/love about ... is ...
The thing I love about ... is ...

We use *would rather* to express a preference. Notice that it is followed by the infinitive without *to*.

I'd rather have rice than pasta.

Would prefer is an alternative to *would rather*. Notice that it is followed by the infinitive with *to*.

We'**d prefer to** travel on Tuesday.

We can use *given the choice* to talk about hypothetical options, to say that you would like to do something, if it was possible.

Given the choice, I'd go to Malawi for my holiday.

Discussing options

I'd rather (not) + infinitive without *to* ...
I'd (much) rather + infinitive without *to* ...
I'd prefer (not) + infinitive with *to* ...
Given the choice, I'd ...

When we can't agree completely on what to do, we compromise. This means we agree to do some things that the other person wants to do and some things that we want to do. This keeps both sides happy.

We can use *I'd be happy to ... , but I don't want to ...* to compromise.

We'd be happy to visit the gallery, **but we don't want to** go to the museum.

We can also use *how about if we .../what if we ... , then we can ...* to compromise.

How about we spend the morning shopping, **then we can** go to the castle in the afternoon?

Compromising

I'd be happy to ... , but I don't want to ...
How about if we ... (do your idea), **then we can ...** (do my idea)?

PRACTICE

1 Choose the correct words to complete the conversations.

1 A: I **can't stand** / **rather not** getting caught in traffic jams in big cities. It's awful.
B: Me neither! **What** / **Thing** I like about going by bicycle is you can avoid them.

2 A: I'm not a big **passionate** / **fan** of museums and art galleries.
B: Oh, I'm the opposite. I'm really **keen** / **into** modern art.

3 A: How **about** / **to** if we go to the beach first, then go shopping?
B: I'd much **prefer** / **rather** spend all day on the beach.

4 A: **Thing** / **The thing** I love about this city is the historical monuments.
B: Really? I'm not keen **on** / **about** all those statues myself.

5 A: **If** / **Given** the choice, I'd just wander around the city centre.
B: Oh no. I'd prefer **not to** / **don't** do that because it's too tiring.

6 A: I'm so **keen** / **passionate** about the food! Shall we try the jollof rice?
B: Sorry, I'd rather **not** / **no**.

2 Complete the email with the words in the box.

about	choice	into	keen
passionate	prefer	rather	stand

Hi Mostafa,

Thank you for the suggested itinerary for my upcoming trip to Cairo. Given the [1] ...., I'd spend several days with you, but unfortunately I only have twenty-four hours!

I'm [2] .... about history and ancient monuments, so I'm really looking forward to seeing the pyramids. I'm also really [3] .... trying new experiences, so I'd love to sail down the Nile in a felucca! I love all kinds of boats, so that should be interesting.

Normally, I'd much [4] .... walk around the city because you see more when you walk, but if it's going to be really hot, as you suggest, I'd [5] .... to be driven. How [6] .... we see how hot it is on the day?

I agree it would be nice to spend the late afternoon buying souvenirs. I can't [7] .... modern shopping centres, so I like your idea of going to Khan el-Khalili. I've heard lots about this market, and of course I'm [8] .... on seeing locally made goods.

Thanks again and see you soon,

Dieter Hentschel

1D *while*, *whereas* and *whilst*

REFERENCE

page 17

We can use *while*, *whereas* and *whilst* to link two ideas in the same sentence that contrast with each other.

I love listening to jazz, **whilst** my partner can't stand it.

While I used to be quite optimistic when I was younger, nowadays I think I'm more of a realist.

My wife comes from a big family, **whereas** mine is quite small.

We can use *while/whilst* or *whereas* at the beginning of the sentence or in the middle.

If we use *while/whilst/whereas* at the beginning of the sentence, we put a comma at the end of the first statement, before the contrasting statement.

When we use *while/whilst* and *whereas* in the middle of the sentence, we put it directly after the comma.

Whilst Emil enjoys a good steak, I'm a vegetarian.

Emil enjoys a good steak, **whereas** I'm a vegetarian.

Notice that *while* and *whilst* can also be used to introduce a time clause, to describe when two things happen at the same time.

Tim made supper **whilst** I went upstairs for a shower.

While I was stuck in bed, everyone else was enjoying the holiday.

PRACTICE

1 **Match the sentence beginnings (1–6) with the endings (a–f).**

1 Whilst I like Carl as a person,
2 While Marta is very sociable and outgoing,
3 Whereas the unemployment rate in Spain was fourteen percent,
4 Whilst she generally enjoyed his company,
5 Hiro usually enjoys going out in the evening,
6 While I generally remember where I put things,

a there were times when he made her angry.
b her sister is quiet and shy.
c I completely forgot where my keys were.
d whereas I prefer staying in.
e I wouldn't like to work for him.
f it was much higher in other parts of Europe.

2 A **Use the prompts to write sentences using *while*, *whereas* or *whilst*.**

1 an active imagination ✓
often daydream ✗

Whilst I have an active imagination, I don't often daydream.

2 always well prepared for things ✓
good at organising other people ✗
3 enjoy going to parties ✓
talking to new people ✗
4 like to follow a schedule ✓
also happy to make changes at the last minute ✗
5 generally feel comfortable around people ✓
being the centre of attention ✗
6 interested in people ✓
good at listening to other people's problems ✗
7 usually in a good mood ✓
sometimes get stressed easily ✓

B **Write sentences comparing your own personality to that of people you know. Use *while*, *whilst* or *whereas*.**

Whilst I've always been very arty, my brother Felipe isn't creative at all.

2A future probability

REFERENCE

page 22

We use *will/won't* + infinitive without *to* to make predictions about the future, based on our opinions.

I'm pretty sure Italy **will win** tomorrow.

VR **won't replace** real holidays anytime soon.

We can use adverbs like *definitely/certainly/ possibly/probably* with *will/won't*, to say how certain we feel about a prediction.

I'**ll definitely be** there tomorrow.

We **probably won't** come to the party.

Notice that the adverb usually comes after *will* but before *won't*.

We **will probably** come …

We **probably won't** come … ~~We won't probably come …~~

We can also use *will/won't* for things that are sure to happen.

I'**ll be** twenty-two next year.

Use *be going to* for predictions when there is evidence in the present.

It'**s going to rain**! Look at those black clouds!

Use *be certain to* when we are sure that something will happen.

Prices **are certain to rise**.

Use *be likely to* when we think that something will probably happen. We use *unlikely to* or *not likely to* when we think that something probably won't happen.

My team **is likely to reach** the next round.

We **are unlikely to go** on holiday this year.

She **isn't likely to win** that competition.

We use *might*, *may* and *could* + infinitive without *to* when we think that something is possible, but not certain.

Notice that we can use the negative forms *might not* and *may not* to talk about the future, but we can't use ~~*could not*~~ in the same way.

We **might go** to Japan next year.

They **could make** a lot of money with that.

She **may not be able** to see us today.

We use *be due to* when something is scheduled to happen.

He **is due to retire** next year.

The train **is due to depart** at 6 p.m.

PRACTICE

1 Choose the correct words to complete the sentences.

1 Researchers are due **announce** / **to announce** the findings tomorrow.

2 Virtual reality is unlikely **for** / **to** affect my industry.

3 This ambitious study is **certain to** / **certain** have a big impact.

4 My sister is seventeen now, so she **could** / **will** be eighteen on her next birthday.

5 That tech company **may not** / **could not** invest in VR in the future.

6 Machines **won't probably** / **probably won't** replace human workers for many years.

7 Unfortunately, the lab where I work **likely** / **is likely** to close.

8 We **will definitely be** / **will be definitely** at the conference tomorrow, so see you there.

2 Choose the correct options (A–C) to complete the text.

[1].......... robots likely to replace teachers?

The best teachers have personal qualities and communicative skills that robots [2].......... acquire any time soon. For this reason, robots [3].......... replace teachers completely. But according to futurist Dr Bill Sethers, humans and robots [4].......... work well side by side in the classroom of the future. Sethers believes robots [5].......... be used more and more as teaching assistants. 'They [6].......... be ready to comfort a crying child or laugh at students' jokes, but they are good for boring tasks like cleaning the board and checking homework. Also, they're reliable: they never get sick and they're [7].......... ask for a pay rise!' The other surprising advantage of robots [8].......... be motivation. Robots that sing and play games are incredibly popular with young children. Several Japanese companies and one Korean company [9].......... bring out a new generation of robot language teachers in the near future. Judging by the success of the earlier models, these [10].......... be a big hit in schools.

1	**A** Might	**B** Are	**C** Will
2	**A** aren't going to	**B** will	**C** are due to
3	**A** won't probably	**B** could	**C** definitely won't
4	**A** might not	**B** are unlikely to	**C** could
5	**A** are unlikely to	**B** certain to	**C** will
6	**A** may not	**B** might	**C** are going to
7	**A** certain to	**B** unlikely to	**C** due to
8	**A** might	**B** won't	**C** is due to
9	**A** might not	**B** probably won't	**C** are due to
10	**A** definitely won't	**B** will probably	**C** are unlikely to

3 Complete the second sentence using the words in brackets.

1 Some employees will probably work beyond retirement age.
Some employees .... beyond retirement age. (likely)

2 The rainstorm is predicted to arrive at any moment.
The rainstorm .... at any moment. (due)

3 I don't think we'll get there tonight because of airport delays.
We .... tonight because of airport delays. (unlikely)

4 It's possible Jan won't meet us tonight because she isn't feeling well.
Jan .... us tonight because she isn't feeling well. (might)

5 I'm sure the report will back up the findings of our research.
The report .... the findings of our research. (certain)

6 Be careful! Don't spill that coffee!
Be careful! You .... that coffee! (going)

2B quantifiers

REFERENCE

page 23

We use quantifiers with singular, plural and uncountable nouns to specify an amount or number.

	100%	A large amount	A small amount	0%
Uncountable or plural nouns	all any	the majority of in a majority plenty of	hardly any a lack of	no not any
Uncountable nouns		a good deal of	little/a little	
Plural nouns		a large number of	few/a few several a minority of in a minority a handful of	
Singular nouns	every each			no not any

We use *a few* and *a little* to talk about a small amount or number.

There are **a few** tickets left.

I try to spend **a little** bit of time in nature every day.

We use *few* and *little* when there are not as much or as many as we would like.

I have **few** opportunities to get away from the city.

There is **little** chance of me leaving before 6 p.m.

We use *the majority of* to talk about more than 50 percent, and *the minority of* to talk about less than 50 percent. We can also talk about people or things being *in a majority* or *in a minority*.

The majority of people feel more relaxed when they are in the countryside.

I spend **the majority of** my working day sitting at a desk.

Those against the decision were **in a minority**.

We can use *a lack of* to talk about something which there is not enough of, or is missing completely.

There is **a lack of** affordable housing in the city.

We can use *a good deal of* or *plenty of* to talk about when there is a large amount or number of something.

We had **a good deal of** help from the government.

There are **plenty of** opportunities for improvement.

We use *several* or *a handful of* to talk about a small number.

A handful of us went to the concert.

Several of them talked about the importance of downtime.

PRACTICE

1 Choose the correct words to complete the sentences.

1 It was cold, but there was very **little** / **a little** snow.
2 Spending **the little** / **a little** time in a green space can improve your mood.
3 I recently bought **few** / **a few** plants for the office.
4 There are **few** / **a few** things I enjoy more than going for an early morning walk.
5 I spend **a good deal of** / **a handful of** time outdoors.
6 There are **several** / **a good deal of** ways you can improve your mental health.
7 **A few** / **A little** of us are going for a walk later if you want to join us.
8 I would say there has been **a lack of** / **a minority of** focus on the issue.
9 **The majority of** / **Several** people in major cities use public transport.
10 We are so busy that we have **no** / **every** time to just sit and relax.

2 Complete the text with the quantifiers in the box.

a few (x2) a little each handful in a minority lack of no plenty the majority of

Ways to feel closer to nature even if you live in the city

There are [1] .... of ways to feel closer to nature, even if you live in a busy city and spend [2] .... your time working or commuting to work. It only takes [3] .... minutes [4] .... day to do something that will help you to feel refreshed. Adapt your routine so that even when you think you have [5] .... time to spare, you can still enjoy nature. There are a [6] .... of different ways to do this. Get up [7] .... earlier and spend [8] .... minutes outside enjoying the fresh air before you have breakfast or start work. Watch the stars before you go to bed, or go for a walk in your lunch break. Admittedly, people who can spend hours relaxing in nature will be [9] .... For most people working long hours, there will be a [10] .... opportunities. Maybe you'll just have to watch a virtual fish tank on your phone instead and see if that makes a difference.

2C How to ... speculate

REFERENCE

page 27

We use the following phrases when we are speculating, or making guesses about a situation based on the information or evidence we have.

How to speculate

I'd guess .../I'd have thought .../I'd imagine ...
I suppose .../I reckon .../I doubt ...
There's no way ...
She's clearly/obviously ...
He/She's bound to ...
I'm fairly certain/sure that ...
I'm not 100 percent sure, but I'd say ...
I know for a fact that ...
I bet ...
I get the impression that ...

When we are very sure about something, we use:

I'm fairly certain that ...
I'm fairly sure that ...
I know for a fact that ... (this is 100 percent)
I'm not 100 percent sure, but I'd say ...

I'm fairly certain that living in the Antarctic is tough.
I know for a fact that being at sea on your own is not easy.

We use *There's no way that ...* if we're talking about something we think is impossible.

There's no way that they can actually enjoy living there!

If we want to talk about what we think, we can say:

I suppose ... , I reckon ... , I'd have thought ... , I'd imagine that ...

I reckon life on the Space Station must be a bit boring.

When we talk about what we think based on the evidence we have, we can say:

I get the impression that ...
She/He's clearly .../obviously ...
She/He's bound to ...
I bet ...

I bet the sea's pretty cold at that time of year!

PRACTICE

1 Complete the conversations with the words in the box.

clearly	impression	reckon	sure	thought	way

1 A: We're thinking of cycling across France.
B: Really? There's no .... I would even consider doing that!
2 A: When Joe gets back from Chile, he's planning to travel across India on a motorbike.
B: Wow! He's .... very adventurous, isn't he?
3 A: Did you get that job you applied for?
B: Well, I'm not 100 percent .... , but I'm feeling pretty confident about it.
4 A: Have you met Tommy's girlfriend yet?
B: No, but I'm under the .... that she's great company.
5 A: I suggest we call in a consultant to help us deal with the issue.
B: Really? I'd have .... that we could come up with a solution ourselves.
6 A: Do you know when the meeting is due to end?
B: I .... we'll be finished by six.

2 Complete the sentences using the prompts in brackets.

1 .... she might be leaving the company next year. (not 100 percent sure / think)
2 .... the temperature in the Antarctic can go as low as -50 degrees Celsius. (know / fact)
3 .... she could have run all the way around the world. (no / way)
4 .... he enjoys being alone. (get / impression)
5 .... life on the International Space Station isn't always as much fun as it looks. (fairly / certain)
6 With all that running, she's .... get through lots of pairs of shoes! (bound)
7 .... wanted to be an explorer since he was a child. (clearly)
8 I'd .... sailing around the Mediterranean would be quite idyllic. (thought)

3A relative clauses

REFERENCE

page 33

Defining relative clauses

We use defining relative clauses to give essential information about a noun in a sentence. Defining relative clauses tell us which person or thing we are talking about.

I think that's the festival **where Alt-J played years ago**.

We don't use commas before or after defining relative clauses. We can use *that* instead of *who* or *which*.

Fuji Rock uses chopsticks **which/that** are made from local wood.

We can omit the relative pronoun when it is the object of the relative clause.

The organiser (who) we usually talk to is not available.

Relative pronouns

We use relative pronouns in relative clauses. We use: *who/that* for people, *which/that* for things, *whose* for possession, *when* for time and *where* for place.

I met some people **whose** tent collapsed in the night!

We can also use *whose* to refer to cities, countries and other nouns which suggest a group of people.

It's a city **whose** ambition is to be more sustainable.

We omit nouns or pronouns which have been replaced by the relative pronoun.

She's someone who I know well. NOT ~~She's someone who I know her well.~~

Non-defining relative clauses

We use non-defining relative clauses to give extra or non-essential information.

The festival, **which was started by a small group of volunteers**, has run for more than twenty years.

We use commas to separate this clause from the rest of the sentence. We cannot use *that* instead of *who* or *which* in non-defining relative clauses.

The concert, **which attracted thousands of people**, was a huge success,
NOT ~~The concert, that attracted thousands of people, was a huge success.~~

We cannot omit the relative pronoun.

Splendour in the Grass, **which I attended last year**, will be held in July.
NOT ~~Splendour in the Grass, I attended last year, will be held in July.~~

We can use *which* to refer to the whole of a previous clause.

I got sick, **which** meant I could no longer do the job.

Prepositions in relative clauses

In informal English, prepositions usually come at the end of a relative clause.

This is the song **which** she's most famous **for**.

In formal written English, prepositions often come before the relative pronoun. For people, we use *whom*, NOT *who* after the preposition.

He's the person **to whom** I have spoken. (formal)

He's the person **who** I have spoken **to**. (informal)

Where can be replaced by *which … in* in informal English. In more formal English, we use *in which*.

The tent **which we slept in** is broken. (informal)

The tent **in which we slept** is broken. (formal)

PRACTICE

1 Combine the sentences using a relative clause. Add commas where the relative clause is non-defining.

1 WOMAD is an international arts festival. It was founded in 1982 by rock musician Peter Gabriel.
WOMAD .... is an international arts festival.

2 Caterers are invited to the festival. They must use solar power.
Only .... to the festival.

3 Some plastic is used on site. All of it is recyclable.
All .... recyclable.

4 We went to a festival last summer. It was the best festival I've ever been to.
The festival .... I've ever been to.

5 I discussed the problem with someone. She was very understanding.
The person .... was very understanding.

6 The exhibition features paintings by local artists. The exhibition opened last week.
The exhibition .... local artists.

7 The hotel overlooks the beach. The hotel was opened in 1886.
The hotel .... the beach.

8 You should play us a song on your guitar. This is that sort of occasion.
This is the .... a song on your guitar.

2 Look at the relative clauses in Ex 1. In which can you omit the relative pronoun?

3 Join the sentences with a relative clause. Use the relative pronoun in brackets.

1 You're the person. We always rely on you to sort things out. (who)
2 London is the city. I grew up there. (which)
3 They are colleagues. I spend a lot of time with them. (whom)
4 These are places in Laos. You can ride elephants there. (where)
5 This is the album. The band are most famous for this album. (which)
6 We stayed in a hotel. They recycled a lot there. (where)
7 We stopped at a museum. We had never visited the museum before. (which)
8 This is the lady. I was talking to you about this lady. (who)

3B cleft sentences

REFERENCE

page 36

We can use a cleft sentence to emphasise information. *Cleft* means 'divided'. In cleft sentences, one sentence is divided into two parts, each with its own verb.

Juanita **works** with Magdaleno.

(one verb)

It's Magdaleno that Juanita **works** with.

(two verbs, emphasises Magdaleno)

The following structures are used in cleft sentences.

Cleft sentences with *It*	Cleft sentences with *What*
It is/was … who …	*What* + subject + present tense + *is* …
It is/was … that …	*What* + subject + past tense + *was* …

We can use *It* + *be* + *that/who* to emphasise a part of a sentence. In this structure, we emphasise the part of the sentence after the verb *be*.

It was **Jim** who lost his wallet.

(not Paul)

It was **his wallet** that he lost.

(not his bag)

It was **yesterday** that he lost his wallet.

(not two days ago)

We can also use *What* + subject + verb + *be*. In this structure, we emphasise the part of the sentence after *what*, before the verb *be*.

What **I'd like to know** is where it came from!

What **you need to do** is talk to your manager.

Notice that we use the singular form of *be* after *It* and *What* in cleft sentences.

It was my parents I had to thank.

NOT ~~It were my parents …~~

What is most impressive are the songs he recorded at home.

NOT ~~What are most impressive …~~

PRACTICE

1 **Match the sentence beginnings (1–8) with the endings (a–h) to make cleft sentences.**

1 It was Nikolai
2 What worries me
3 It's singing in public
4 What's interesting is
5 It was in Belgium
6 What you need to do is
7 It was last week that
8 What I like about

a that really scares me.
b she went for her interview, not yesterday.
c London is the music scene.
d that they got married, not France.
e speak to your manager.
f the local culture.
g who wrote the book, not Fyodor.
h is the lack of planning for this project.

2 **Complete the conversation with one word in each gap.**

Luisa: Did you watch *The Loved Ones* last night?
Rejane: Of course! It's my favourite soap opera!
Luisa: Wasn't it brilliant? [1] .... I want to know is who stole the laptop!
Rejane: Really? But it's obvious! [2] .... was Julio who stole it!
Luisa: No way! It [3] .... Lena who stole it, not Julio! Why do you think it was Julio?
Rejane: Whenever there's a mystery in *The Loved Ones* [4] .... you need to do is see who looks the most innocent. Then you know they're the guilty one.
Luisa: But what's strange [5] .... that the laptop reappeared at the end.
Rejane: True, but it [6] .... Julio who always does clever things like that. He returned it before he got caught.
Luisa: Hmmm, maybe …

3 **Rewrite the sentences using the words in brackets.**

1 The singer messed up, not the guitarist. (it, who)
It was the singer who messed up, not the guitarist.
2 You need to practise a lot before performing. (what, do)
....
3 Taking deep breaths works for me. (what, is)
....
4 I like acting in public the most. (what, is)
....
5 I'm studying music, not theatre. (it's, that)
....
6 The low salary put me off, not the hours. (it, that)
....

3C H…

REFE…

Vague la…
English. V…
sort of, th…
less factu…

I watch a l… crime drama **and that kind of thing.**

We use vague language when:

- we are not very sure of the precise details of something.
- we can't remember the exact word or information.
- we are having an informal conversation and want to talk generally and sound less direct.

Vague nouns and phrases

We use *thing/things* to refer to something without saying its name.

There are a few **things** I don't like about that film.

We use *bit* to refer to a small piece of something.

I love the **bit** where the animals escape.

We use *stuff* to refer to more than one object, or an uncountable noun.

In the end, they move all their **stuff** into a new flat.

We use *what's her name*? or *what's it called*? when we can't remember the name of someone or something.

The hero is played by that actress – **what's her name**?

Numbers

We use *around* and *about* to give a vague idea of a number.

There are **around** ten episodes in the series.

We use *-odd* after a number, to mean 'about'.

There are 200-**odd** dancers in the final scene.

We use *or so* after a number, to show that the number is not completely accurate.

The storm lasted for two days **or so**.

Adjectives and ages

We use *-ish* to make either an adjective or an age more vague.

She's about twenty-**ish**.

Making a statement less certain

We use *sort of* and *kind of* to make a statement slightly more vague and less certain.

I **sort of** understood what the film was about. (I didn't understand very well.)

It's **kind of** like a modern version of *Groundhog Day*.

Avoiding a long list

We can use phrases such as *and stuff, and everything, and so on, and that kind of thing, or something* instead of finishing a list.

We organised a movie night at home with pizzas, crisps, drinks **and so on**.

He's basically a superhero, so he can fly **and everything**.

PRACTICE

1 Choose the correct options (a–c) to complete the vague statements.

1 I think the films starts at …… .
  a around seven-ish
  b sort of seven o'clock
  c seven o'clock and so on
2 There are …… we should discuss.
  a stuff
  b kind of things
  c a couple of things
3 There are …… people coming to the dinner.
  a kind of twenty
  b twenty-odd
  c twenty and everything
4 There's a lot of action and violence and …… .
  a that kind of thing
  b something like that
  c sort of that
5 Where have you put …… ?
  a my stuff, or something like that
  b my stuff or so
  c all my stuff
6 I think we should wait for …… before speaking to them.
  a a week or so **b** kind of a week **c** a week-ish
7 Her hair has turned a …… colour.
  a grey and so on
  b grey-odd
  c grey-ish
8 I watch all kinds of different things, like drama, mystery, comedy, thrillers …… .
  a and stuff
  b and kind of
  c and something

2 Complete the sentences with the words in the box.

bit	four-ish	name	of
so	something	sort	stuff

1 I never usually eat chocolates, or sweets or …… like that.
2 We expect it to take two years or …… to finish the project.
3 They were …… of planning to leave once he'd found a job.
4 Did you turn the lights out, lock all the doors and that kind …… thing?
5 Do you remember the …… near the beginning of the film, where they first meet?
6 We're meeting Justina at …… .
7 We need to come up with some kind of a plan or …… .
8 You know the film I'm talking about, the one with what's his ……?

3D *do* and *did* for emphasis

REFERENCE

page 41

We can use *do*, *does* or *did* in affirmative sentences to emphasise that what we are saying is true, especially when we are making a contrast with different information or a different opinion.

I **do** really want to go to the concert.
(Perhaps you think I don't want to go.)

I **did** really enjoy their last album.
(I didn't think I would enjoy it.)

He **does** enjoy playing the drums.
(He hates playing the guitar.)

Notice that when we use *do*, *does* or *did* for emphasis, we stress the auxiliary.

I can't stand opera, but I **do** like classical music.

A: He doesn't like jazz music, does he?
B: No, he **does** like jazz, but he doesn't like R&B.

A: You said you would call them.
B: I **did** call them, but they didn't answer.

We can also use *do*, *does* and *did* to emphasise that we feel strongly about something.

I **do** love eating out in expensive restaurants.
He **does** look amazing in that new suit.

We can also use *do*, *does* and *did* to confirm something we think is true, by adding a question tag.

You **do** like spicy food, **don't you?**
He **doesn't** still work there, **does he?**
You **did** remember the passports, **didn't you?**

PRACTICE

1 **Choose the correct options to complete the conversations.**

1 A: You **do** / **don't** really like jazz music, do you?
B: I **do** / **don't** like it. I'm just not very keen on this album.
2 A: We're going to see The Underwater Crew this weekend. Do you want to come?
B: I **do** / **don't** want to come, but I'm not sure I can afford it.
3 A: I hear Francesco is enjoying his new job.
B: He **doesn't** / **does** enjoy it, but he'd like to be paid a bit more.
4 A: You got here on time! I thought you were going to be late.
B: Yes, I **do** / **did** have to run a bit though!
5 A: I don't have any plans for the weekend, but I **do** / **don't** think we should go somewhere. You don't want to watch the football match, do you?
B: No, I **do** / **don't**.
6 A: Hey, are you still coming for dinner?
B: Er, yes. But I **do** / **don't** have to finish this report first.
7 A: Did you check that the music room is free?
B: I **did** / **didn't** send a message, but I haven't heard back yet.
8 A: Have you decided whether to sell your car or not?
B: We **did** / **didn't** discuss it, but we're going to keep it for now.

2 **Complete the sentences with *do*, *don't*, *does*, *doesn't* or *did*.**

1 Nearly everyone had gone by the time I got there, but I .... manage to see Jasmin.
2 I .... play the guitar much now, but I .... play in a few different bands when I was younger.
3 He .... enjoy living in Spain – it's so sunny all the time and the people are so friendly.
4 .... tell me you forgot to bring the passports! We'll have to go home and get them.
5 He's a very difficult manager to work for, but they .... all try to keep him happy.
6 I .... see Angela very often anymore, but I .... see her brother quite a lot.
7 Liv .... have a lot of time for playing music at the moment, but she .... still play the occasional gig at the weekend.
8 Are you still OK to drive us to the festival? You .... offer to the other day.

4A future continuous and future perfect

REFERENCE

page 46

Future continuous

We form the future continuous with *will* + *be* + *ing*. We use it for an action or event that will be in progress at a specific time in the future.

I can't meet at 1.00 because **I'll be taking** Tom to the airport.

This time next week you**'ll be swimming** in the Caribbean Sea.

Don't call me at 8.00 because the band **will be playing**.

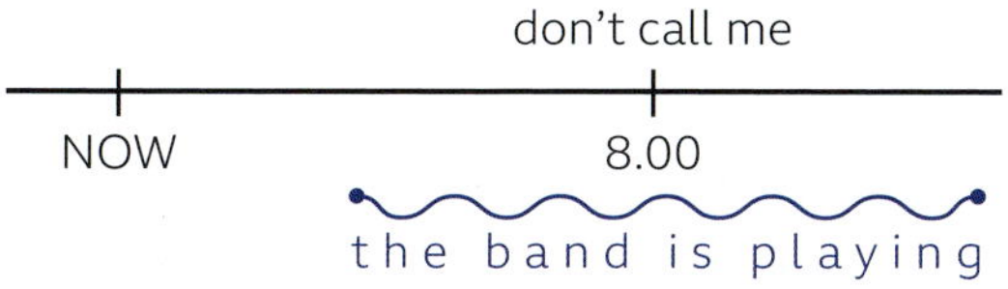

Future perfect

We form the future perfect with *will* + *have* + past participle. We use it for an action or event that will be finished before a specific time in the future.

We often use the future perfect with *by* + a time, meaning *at some time before*.

You can borrow the book next week. **I'll have finished** it by then.

You can't come at 2.00 because we**'ll have left** by then.

We**'ll have eaten** by 3.00, so we can meet you after that.

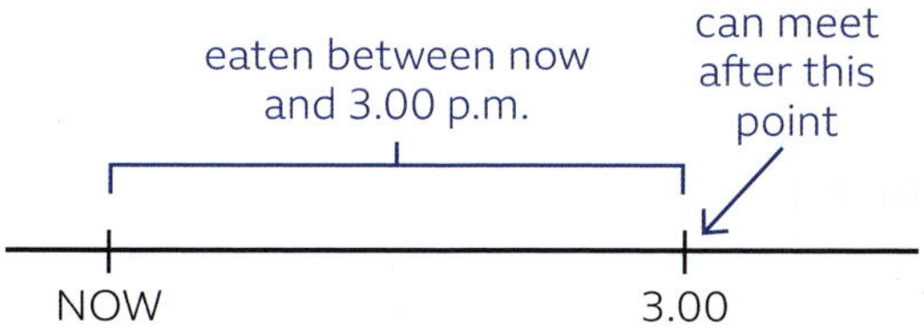

It is possible to use other modal verbs instead of *will* with the future continuous and future perfect.

She **might be travelling** at that time.

This time next week I **could be relaxing** on a beach in Thailand!

I'll call again tomorrow. He **may have forgotten** we'd arranged to meet now.

We **should have completed** the project by the end of next week.

PRACTICE

1 Choose the correct verb forms to complete the sentences.

1 Don't call me at 5 a.m. I'll **be sleeping / have slept**!
2 No, I can't do 2 p.m. I won't **be finishing / have finished** by then.
3 The driver will **be waiting / have waited** for you at the airport.
4 Good luck tomorrow. I'll **be thinking / have thought** of you.
5 Call me on Friday. I'll **be speaking / have spoken** to Amy by then, so I'll know her plans.
6 He can't meet at 7 p.m. because he'll still **be travelling / have travelled**.

2 Complete the second sentence so it has the same meaning as the first. Use the future perfect or continuous form of the verb in brackets.

1 The meeting ends at 3.30.
The meeting .... by 3.45. (end)
2 This time next year we'll be in Germany permanently.
This time next year we .... in Germany. (live)
3 Come over on Saturday, as I'll be free.
Come over on Saturday as I .... anything. (do)
4 Do you need the car later or can I borrow it?
.... the car later, or can I borrow it? (use)
5 We can't go to the gym at 5 a.m. It will still be shut.
The gym .... by 5 a.m. (open)
6 Their football match starts at 2 and finishes at around 4.
The girls .... football at 3.30. (play)

3 Look at the information and complete the sentences (1–6) with the future perfect or future continuous form of the verb in brackets.

4 p.m. – Jack's train arrives. Get there a few minutes before to meet him on the platform. Drive back.

4.10 p.m. – Home!

1 At 3.55, we .... on the platform. (wait)
2 By 4.30, we .... back at the house. (arrive)

10 p.m. bed time!

(the next day) 6 a.m. early start! 6.45 leave for airport.

3 At 11 p.m., I .... (sleep)
4 By 6.45 a.m. the next day, I .... breakfast. (had)

This afternoon – meet Jack and his new girlfriend!

Tomorrow morning – go to British Museum.

5 By tonight, I .... Jack's new girlfriend for the first time. (meet)
6 Tomorrow at 10, I .... the British Museum. (visit)

4B passives

REFERENCE

page 48

Passives

In general, we use the passive to focus on the person or thing affected by an action rather than the person or thing doing the action.

We use the passive when the person or thing that does the action:

- isn't obvious.
- is unknown.
- isn't important.

The theory **has** since **been disproven**.
(We don't know who disproved it and it isn't important.)

General beliefs and opinions

We can also use the passive to talk about general beliefs and opinions. This use is more common in formal writing.

To talk about present beliefs, we use *It is* + *thought/expected/believed/reported* + *that* + clause. We can omit *that* in less formal English.

It is thought (that) a lack of sleep can lead to health problems.

It is believed (that) many children do not get enough sleep nowadays.

To talk about beliefs in the past, we can use the same structure with the past simple or present perfect form of *be.*

In the 4th century BCE, **it was thought** that the Earth was at the centre of the solar system.

It was expected that she would be made CEO within the next year.

It has been suggested that people who have a varied diet have a lower risk of getting cancer.

It has been reported that a huge number of people regularly sleep fewer than six hours a night.

PRACTICE

1 **Put the words into the correct order to complete the sentences.**

1 the / has / population / It / that / reported / thirty percent / been / of
.... suffers from poor sleep.

2 need / thought / most / is / that / It / people
.... about eight hours' sleep a night.

3 get / if / is / you / It / expected / too little / that / sleep
.... , you will not be able to work effectively.

4 1800s / is / the / that / It / believed / in
.... people used to sleep in two blocks of four hours.

5 company / suggested / has / the / that / It / been
.... should allow people to start work later in the morning.

6 reported / it / Last / that / children / week / was
.... had started the fire.

7 In / that / it / Ancient Egypt / believed / was
.... wearing a necklace protected you from bad health.

8 is / It / proportion / that / a / reported / large
.... of people are now out of work.

2 **Complete the article with *it* and the correct passive form of the verbs in brackets.**

Sleep habits from around the world

Siestas

[1] .... (think) that the Spanish tradition of having a sleep in the afternoon dates back thousands of years. In the past, [2] .... (believe) that a siesta was necessary to give farmers time to rest and restore their energy in the hot climate. Nowadays, [3] .... still .... (expect) that many people will go home and enjoy a long lunch and rest with their family.

Late bedtimes for kids

[4] .... (report) recently that parents in countries like New Zealand and Australia put their young children to bed by about 7 p.m., whereas in countries like Spain and Argentina it's common to see young children staying up until late in the evening, after 11 p.m. [5] .... (think) that children in Asian countries sleep less on average that children who live in the USA, Canada and New Zealand.

Alfresco naps

In a recent study, [6] .... (report) that in Scandinavian countries including Norway and Sweden, parents often leave their babies outside to sleep, even in the middle of winter. In these countries, [7] .... (believe) that the fresh air is good for children's health and being outside helps to prevent them from getting sick.

Napping in public

The Japanese practice of *inemuri*, or 'sleeping while present', allows people to multitask. In many Japanese companies, [8] .... (expect) that people will work long hours and might be tired. As a result, [9] .... (considered) quite normal that workers might fall asleep on a park bench or a commuter train, at a dinner party or even during a work meeting.

4C How to ... express agreement and disagreement

REFERENCE

page 51

Giving opinions

We can use a range of phrases for expressing personal opinions, and for expressing agreement and disagreement.

Expressing personal opinions
Personally, I think/feel/believe that ...
In my opinion/view, ...
From my perspective/my point of view, ...
As far as I'm concerned/aware, ...
If you ask me, ...

Expressing agreement and disagreement.

We use these phrases for expressing agreement and disagreement.

Agreeing
I couldn't agree more.
That's a good/fair point.
I take/see your point.
That makes sense.

Disagreeing
I'm not sure.
But on the other hand, ...
I completely disagree with you.

Concession

Sometimes you may agree with part of what someone says, but not all of it.

A: People should be responsible for their own health. It's not up to the government to tell them what to do.

B: **I agree with you up to a point, but** the government also has a duty to look after its people – and health is part of that.

You might also want to show that you acknowledge or understand someone's argument, even if you don't agree with it. This is called concession.

A: Yoga is fun, but it doesn't help you with cardio.

B: **I understand what you're saying, but** it does help you with strength and flexibility.

We use these phrases to express concession, or to partially agree with someone.

Partially agreeing
I agree (with you) up to a point, but ...
I agree to some extent, but ...
I suppose so, but ...
I understand what you're saying, but ...
That's a fair point, although it could also be argued that ...

PRACTICE

1 Match the sentence beginnings (1–8) with the endings (a–h) to make phrases for agreeing, disagreeing or partially agreeing.

1 I couldn't agree
2 In my
3 I agree with you up
4 That's a fair point, although
5 I see your
6 As far as I'm
7 I completely
8 True, but on the other

a disagree with you.
b concerned, you're right.
c opinion, he's correct.
d to a point, but ...
e it could be argued that the opposite is true.
f hand, they could be right.
g point.
h more.

2 Complete each conversation with the words in the box. There are two extra words in each box.

disagree	opinion	perspective	point	sense	suppose

Conversation 1

A: In my [1] .... , to coach a team you need to know everything about the sport.

B: I completely [2] .... with you. Your relationship with the players is more important.

A: I take your [3] .... , but you need to know the game.

B: I [4] .... so, but it's not the most important thing.

agree	ask	fair	hand	perspective	point

Conversation 2

A: If you [5] .... me, it's important to have a new challenge in your life.

B: That's a [6] .... , point, although it's good to take it easy, too!

A: True, but on the other [7] .... , life is about expanding your horizons.

B: I couldn't [8] .... more, as long as it's not too much effort!

3 Complete the second sentence so it has the same meaning as the first. Use the word in brackets.

1 I think it's good to be active.
In .... , it's good to be active. (opinion)

2 The opposite view is that running is bad for your knees.
.... , running is bad for your knees. (hand)

3 I agree with that.
That .... (sense)

4 You're 100 percent correct!
.... more! (couldn't)

5 My point of view is that sport should be free to watch.
.... , sport should be free to watch. (perspective)

6 You might be right.
Yes, I .... (suppose)

7 I partly agree with you.
I agree with you up .... (point)

8 In my view, , it's easy to get motivated to exercise.
As .... , it's easy to get motivated to exercise. (concerned)

1A suffixes

page 8

1 A Look at how we can form adjectives from verbs and nouns by using different suffixes, e.g. *-ed*, *-ous*, *-ful*. What is the root word for each of the adjectives in the table? How has the spelling changed?

experience – experienc**ed**

-ed	-ic
experienc**ed** relax**ed** 1 	optimist**ic**/pessimist**ic** realist**ic** 2 ....
-ous	**-able**
gener**ous** 3 .... 4	reli**able** 5 ....
-ful	**-al**
thought**ful** cheer**ful** 6 .... 7	practic**al** music**al** 8 ....

B Complete the table in Ex 1A with adjectives formed from the verbs and nouns in the box.

adventure ambition artist emotion help hope like talent

2 A Complete the sentences with the correct adjective form of the words in brackets.

1 We can depend on Sam to be here on time. He's very .... (rely).
2 Melissa became quite .... as she was watching the film. (emotion).
3 Al will need some help setting up the new printer. He's not very .... (practice)
4 I love the fact that Leo is always so .... about life! (optimist)
5 Sasha is a really .... musician. (talent)
6 Thanks for moving those boxes – it was really .... (help)
7 It was very .... of you to send those flowers to cheer me up! (thought)
8 I don't think I'll go to the party – I'm not feeling very .... today. (social)
9 I'm not .... enough to go paragliding! (adventure).
10 I'm sure she'll be prime minister one day. She's incredibly .... (ambition)

B VB1.01 | Listen and check your answers.

C Work in pairs. Take turns describing adjectives for your partner to guess.

Student A: This describes someone who plays the guitar and sings, and loves going to watch bands.
Student B: Musical?
Student A: That's right.

1B idioms: memory

page 12

1 A Complete the idioms in bold with the words in the box.

bell ~~ear~~ memory mind tongue tricks

1 He never remembers anything I tell him. Things go **in one** ear **and out the other**!
2 Oh no! I forgot to buy vegetables for the curry. Sorry, it totally **slipped my** ....
3 Hmm ... I'm not sure. I'll need to look at my notes again to **refresh my** ....
4 I'll remember it in a minute. The answer **is on the tip of my** .... !
5 I'm sure I've heard that name before. It definitely **rings a** ....
6 Oh, yes. You were there too, weren't you? My **memory is playing** .... **on me**.

B VB1.02 | Listen and check. Do you have similar idioms in your language?

C Work in pairs. Think of an idiom to use in each situation. More than one may be possible.

1 You went shopping and forgot to buy milk.
2 You're doing a quiz. You know the answer but can't quite remember it.
3 You're discussing a friend's son. The boy is a bad listener and forgets everything.
4 You recognise someone at a party but can't remember their name. You ask your friend.
5 A friend is telling you about a new book. You think you've heard about it before.
6 You and a friend are trying to find a restaurant. You went there years ago. You thought you knew the address, but you were wrong.

D Now roleplay a short conversation with your partner about each situation, using the idioms.

A: So, you went shopping and forgot to buy milk?
B: Yes, sorry. It slipped my mind.
A: Well, how am I supposed to make tea now?

2A word families

page 20

1 A Work in pairs. Complete the table with the correct form of each word.

verb	noun/person	adjective	adverb
research	research/ 1		
predict	prediction	2	predictably
		virtual	virtually
		3	remotely
analyse	4 ..../ analyst	analytical	analytically
	science/ scientist	scientific	5 ....

B Complete the news headlines with the correct forms of words from Ex 1A.

1 **Scientist makes alarming new predictions about global warming**

2 GAMING CEO OFFERS $1,000,000 FOR GAMERS TO DESIGN 2 .... WORLDS

3 **Astronaut says moon rocks were never .... in space lab**

4 **Most workers prefer .... working to being in the office**

5 **BIOLOGIST .... LOSS OF OVER 100,000 ANIMAL SPECIES IN NEXT 10 YEARS**

6 **NEW THEORY ABOUT GRAVITY CANNOT YET BE PROVED 6 ....**

7 Documentary shows what we learnt from 50 years of 7 .... into octopuses

8 **New car can be controlled 8 .... , from over a mile away**

3A the environment

page 32

1 A Match the words in the box with the meanings (1–8).

carbon emissions carbon footprint clean-up (natural) resources recycling renewable solar power sustainable

1 Electricity produced using energy from the sun. ....
2 Things that a country, person or organisation has that they can use. ....
3 An event which is organised in order to make a place clean. ....
4 When gases responsible for global warming are released into the air. ....
5 Used to describe an activity that you can continue without causing damage to the environment. ....
6 Used to describe something which can replace itself naturally, or be easily replaced. ....
7 The process of treating paper, glass, plastic, etc. so it can be used again. ....
8 A measurement of the amount of carbon dioxide that an individual, company or organisation produces. ....

B VB3.01 | Listen and check.

C Complete the sentences with the words and phrases from Ex 1A.

1 We only use wood from forests that are managed in a .... way.
2 We've taken all the paper and glass to the .... centre.
3 We're organising a beach .... to try and get rid of all the plastic.
4 The problem with fossil fuels like coal and gas is that they are not .... , like other energy sources (solar, water and wind).
5 The country is rich in .... , such as wood and minerals.
6 We need to reduce .... by more than 20 percent.
7 It's important for people individually to make changes to reduce their ....
8 .... is very suitable for domestic water heating.

D Work in groups and discuss the questions.

1 What could you do to reduce your carbon footprint?
2 Which sources of renewable energy would work well in your country (e.g., solar power, wind power, etc.)?
3 Is it important to you that the products you buy are made from sustainable materials? Why/Why not?

3B phrasal verbs: communication

page 35

1A Read each conversation and study the phrasal verbs in bold. Then choose the correct words to complete the sentences (1–8).

Ana: Can you hear me or do I need to **speak up**?
Leo: Your microphone's off!
Ana: Thanks for **pointing** that **out**!

1 Ana thinks she needs to speak **louder** / **more quietly**.
2 Ana thanks Leo for **giving her useful information** / **fixing her microphone**.

Sam: Do I need to **spell out** the message again?
Jo: No, it's clear. You can **move on** to a new topic.

3 Sam offers to **keep quiet** / **explain something**.
4 Jo suggests he can **say more about the topic** / **talk about a new topic**.

Maria: Can I **bring up** a new topic: our finances?
Stefan: Our finance director isn't here yet, so we'll **come back** to that later.

5 Maria wants to **start** / **stop** talking about a new topic.
6 Stefan suggests that they **forget about that topic** / **return to that topic later**.

Juan: That speaker **comes across** well. She communicates her ideas clearly.
Mia: Yes, she **got her message across** very well.

7 Juan thinks the speaker speaker created a **positive** / **negative** image of themselves.
8 Mia thinks that the speaker **explained her ideas clearly** / **gave too much information**.

B Choose the correct phrasal verbs to complete the advice for giving a presentation.

1 Always start with a joke, so you **come across** / **come back** as friendly.
2 Make sure you **point out** / **speak up** so everyone can hear you.
3 When you **bring up** / **spell out** a new topic, speak more slowly to emphasise it.
4 To **get your message across** / **speak up** clearly, use visuals like photos or pictures.
5 Only **point out** / **move on to** a new topic when you know the audience has understood the previous point.
6 If someone asks a difficult question, say you'll **come back** / **come across** to it later.

C Work in pairs. Which advice in Ex 1B do you agree with? Why?

4A illness and treatment

page 44

1 A Work in groups. Complete the sentences (1–8) with the words in the boxes.

illness

allergies	~~asthma~~	food poisoning	run-down

1 If you have asthma ...., you find it difficult to breathe in some conditions.
2 You can get .... by eating something that has gone bad.
3 If you're ...., you feel tired and ill.
4 If you have ...., certain things make you sneeze or make your eyes water.

treatment

~~antibiotics~~	first aid	medication	vaccine

5 You take antibiotics if you have an infection that is caused by bacteria.
6 You can get a .... to protect you from the flu.
7 You need .... to treat things like small cuts and bruises.
8 You might take regular .... if you have a long-term health problem.

B Work in groups and discuss the questions.

1 Have you ever had food poisoning?
2 Have you ever taken antibiotics? What for?
3 Do you own a first aid kit? Have you ever used it?
4 Do you suffer from asthma or allergies? Do you take medication for them?
5 What do you do to build up your health when you feel run-down?
6 Have you ever had to have a vaccine to travel to another country?

4C sport: motivation and benefits

page 50

1 A Read the article. Then match the words in bold with the meanings (1–9).

1 the feeling that you are able to do something
2 something which is difficult to achieve
3 working together with other people
4 an advantage of doing something
5 something that you do regularly
6 the feeling of wanting to do something
7 gently persuading someone to do something
8 something which makes you want to do or achieve something
9 the ability to continue doing something, even when you don't really want to do it

B Choose the correct words to complete the sentences.

1 I took up diving because I wanted a new **challenge** / **encouragement** in my life.
2 It takes a lot of **habit** / **discipline** to get up early every morning to train.
3 The thought of getting a medal was a great **challenge** / **incentive** to keep training hard.
4 I don't have the **motivation** / **challenge** to do exercise every day.
5 You can't win a football match without good **incentive** / **teamwork**!
6 My parents always gave me a lot of support and **encouragement** / **incentive** when I was younger.
7 Winning the competition really helped my **discipline** / **confidence**.
8 The main **benefit** / **motivation** of joining a gym is being able to use the equipment.
9 I think it's important for children to develop healthy **habits** / **benefits** at a young age.

C Work in groups and discuss the questions.

1 What activities do you do that involve teamwork?
2 Who gives you encouragement when you find something difficult?
3 What activities do you do that give you confidence?
4 What do you think are the main benefits of joining a gym?
5 What is your motivation for studying English?
6 What do you think is the best way to develop good exercise habits?

Six reasons to do sport

We can't all be sporty, but even if you aren't, there are good reasons to get into the **habit** of doing sport.

Learn **teamwork**

Team sports require cooperation, a skill that may be useful at work and in other situations.

Maintain fitness

Fitness is the most obvious **benefit** of exercise. If you need more of an **incentive** to get you started, remember that people who exercise tend to live healthier lives. Many sports, like running and cycling, help us to build stamina.

Give yourself a **challenge**

Can you run around the track in two minutes or swim the length of a pool underwater? It isn't always about beating your opponent; sometimes, it's about pushing yourself.

Develop **discipline**

Athletes who never give up or who still go to practice when it's wet, cold and dark develop discipline, the ability to keep going when things get tough.

Boost your **confidence**

Many shy kids discover themselves on the sports field: they realise they can run fast or score goals. This gives them a chance to excel, and is a good reason why all children should be given **encouragement** to take part in sports.

Play competitively

For some people, the **motivation** to do sport is to win trophies. This competitive spirit can also be useful in other areas of life.

Lead-in Ex 1A

It is William Shakespeare.

3A Ex 3A Student B

B

Fuji Rock

Where: Japan   When: July/August

Fuji Rock is the biggest music festival in Japan, with between 100,000 and 150,000 people attending every year. The festival is held in a stunning ski resort which is about a 90-minute train ride from Tokyo. It has been running since 1997 and the international crowd has been steadily increasing over the years. Because the festival is held mostly outdoors (with only one indoor stage), attendees must be well prepared for rain and shine. Reflecting its Japanese roots, the festival venue has hot springs where you can relax and also plenty of nature walks.

Fuji Rock is also one of the world's most eco-friendly festivals. The festival organisers put effort into conservation and try to achieve a good balance of music and nature. For example, all the plastic bottles which are collected after the event are recycled to make rubbish bags for the following year's festival. Plastic bottle tops are used to make benches for people to sit on. Paper cups are recycled to make toilet paper and the wooden chopsticks, which are made from wood in the local forest, are recycled to make wooden furniture. Through the Fuji Rock Forest Project, the festival runs a number of schemes that focus on the maintenance and protection of the area around the festival site. One such project is Fuji Rock Paper, which uses the wood cut during forest maintenance that would otherwise go to waste. They use this wood together with the recycled cups and plates from the festival to make branded flyers and pamphlets for the festival. Additionally, every year more than 300 volunteers build and maintain a natural path through the forest, made with wooden boards, to help people with wheelchairs who are attending the festival.

4 Review Ex 2B

1 Myth – Drinking coffee does not stop you from growing.
2 True – There is evidence that vegetarian diets are becoming more popular.
3 Myth – 10,000 steps a day is not necessarily enough to maintain your fitness. We probably need around 15,000.
4 Myth – Sugar is sugar and all sugar can cause health problems.

4B Ex 5 Student A

1 Read the following (true) beliefs about sleep. Add a third belief, which is false.

a It's thought that alternating work and rest (working intensely and then resting) helps us to be more productive.
b It has been suggested that people who don't check their phone or their emails before they go to sleep tend to fall asleep more quickly.
c ....

2 Read your statements to your partner (in a different order). Can they guess which is the false belief?

4B Ex 6B

1 Myth – Sleeping fewer than seven hours a night can lead to health conditions such as Alzheimer's and cardiovascular disease. It has been suggested that former British Prime Minister Margaret Thatcher only needed four hours' sleep, but it was a myth invented to intimidate her political opponents.
2 Myth – It's been shown by research that people who work at night and sleep during the day often feel less rested and have poorer health than those who sleep at night.
3 True – Sleepwalking may include simply sitting up and appearing awake, or it may involve complex activities, such as moving furniture, going to the bathroom, cooking or sometimes even driving.
4 Myth – If you are already tired, then being bored will help you to notice it.
5 Myth – Poor sleep is not a normal part of aging. As we get older, we often get less sleep because our ability to sleep for long periods of time and get into the deep restful stages of sleep can decrease. Older people are lighter sleepers and their sleep is more easily interrupted by light, noise and pain or illness.
6 True – Sleeping more at the weekend is a good way to ensure rest.
7 Myth – Many studies have been conducted which show that people who watch TV in bed tend to sleep less.
8 Myth – Exercising at any time during the day will probably help you to sleep better.
9 True – The blue light emitted by your phone screen (or other devices) reduces the production of melatonin (the hormone that controls your sleep cycle) and this makes it more difficult for you to get to sleep or wake up the next day.

6A Ex 6C

1 Read the article and the notes. Cross out the bullet point that repeats the same idea as the previous note.
2 Edit the other notes to make them more concise. The first has been done for you. Use the ideas you discussed on page 70.
3 Compare your notes with other students.

Deadlines and limitations

To focus on a task, some people need deadlines. Given too much time, many of us produce nothing of value. This is because without any pressure we can't get motivated or focused enough to do the work. One reason for this is procrastination – the habit of delaying a task until the last moment. Another reason is that pressure means we simply have to focus. When something needs doing by a certain time, we take responsibility; we cannot delay or get distracted because then we risk failure.

Similarly, creative activities are sometimes easier when there are limitations placed on us. Complete freedom allows us to dream big, but it doesn't always help us to focus. Sculptor Juan Ignacio Hernandez says, 'I work with stone. The limitations of this material mean I'm always thinking practically: what type and size of stone can I buy locally? What kind of figure does the natural shape of the stone suggest? How much can I cut out of the stone before it breaks? These limitations are part of the creative process.'

< Notes ...

- Deadlines can be really useful for some people when they are doing tasks. Deadlines – useful for doing tasks
- The author says that without deadlines, some people don't do the work.
- Procrastination, which is delaying a task until the final moment before it's due, is a problem for some people.
- Pressure often means we have to focus.
- When we do creative activities, if we're given limitations, it can sometimes be useful because limitations help people to focus.

7A Ex 8

The story of Shariah Harris

Her mother took a wrong turn driving home and they came across some stables that provided riding lessons to inner-city kids. Shariah started taking lessons and soon became passionate about riding horses and playing polo.

The accidental artist

In 1989, Jon developed tinnitus (a condition which causes ringing in the ear), which led to brain surgery. Complications from surgery led to a stroke, which left him with long-lasting physical and mental changes. During his therapy, he was given some colours and he started to draw. What started as a way to relax turned into a new way for Jon to communicate and he started to draw and paint obsessively in abstract ways, often using words as well as images. When he was on holiday, his sister suggested that he send one of his drawings to the *New Yorker*. It was published and Jon started to receive worldwide recognition as an artist.

7 Review Ex 1B

1 The concert was being recorded by a record company, so they had asked the audience not to clap at the end.
2 She fell off the bottom step.
3 They were playing different opponents.

7A Ex 7C Student A

1 Read the sentences in black to your partner so they can rephrase them using a compound adjective. The answers are in blue.

1 The journey is 30 kilometres. It's a thirty-kilometre journey.
2 The doctor has a lot of qualifications. He/She is a well-qualified/highly qualified doctor.
3 It's an opportunity that will change your life. It's a life-changing opportunity.
4 He is famous all around the world for his art. He's world-famous for his art./He's a world-famous artist.
5 The effects of the medicine last a long time. The medicine has long-lasting effects.

2 Listen to your partner's sentences and rephrase them using a compound adjective.

3A Ex 3A Student C

C

Splendour in the Grass

Where: Australia When: July

One of the largest family-friendly music festivals in Australia, Splendour in the Grass is held in Yelgun, New South Wales, and always features an exciting line-up of performers from a range of different genres. As well as great music from all around the world, Splendour in the Grass has a huge array of entertainment to keep everyone happy, from science tents where you can learn from some of Australia's top scientists to dance lessons and an eye-catching arts festival. Splendour in the Grass has something for everyone.

This festival has a great attitude when it comes to the environment and is one of the most sustainable festivals around. It does its best to protect the local area and encourages festival-goers to do the same. The festival appointed Damon Gameau, who is a world-renowned filmmaker and environmental activist, as their Eco Ambassador. One initiative tried to reduce carbon emissions by encouraging people who are attending the festival to catch the bus or share a ride with others. The organisers promote ideas for reducing waste like using your own water bottles and reusable cups, instead of buying disposable plastic. When you buy your festival ticket, you can also choose to offset your carbon footprint by donating extra money, which is used to promote solar energy. Finally, the festival organises a tree-planting session on the Saturday.

6C Ex 5 Student B

Read the information below and take turns to ask for and give advice.

1 Start a conversation. You always get overlooked for promotion even though you are a good worker. Ask your partner for advice about this.

2 Listen to your partner's problem. You know that your partner leaves bags of rubbish in the hall for days. They eventually take them out but there's always a bad smell in the hall. The neighbours are angry about it. Give tactful advice.

3 Start a conversation. Your classmates used to study with you after class. Now they don't want to work with you. Ask your partner for advice about this.

4 Listen to your partner's problem. Student A used to give rides on their motorbike to another friend. But you know that Student A drives too fast and dangerously. The other friend is too scared to do this anymore.

7A Ex 7C Student B

1 Listen to your partner's sentences and rephrase them using a compound adjective.

2 Say the sentences in black to your partner so they can rephrase them using a compound adjective. The answers are in blue.

1 The training course lasts for five years. It's a five-year training course.

2 The shop is full of books which have been owned by other people. It's a second-hand bookshop.

3 The job takes up a lot of time. It's a time-consuming job.

4 The building is twenty metres high. It's a twenty-metre-high building.

5 She is a politician who is respected by a lot of people. She's a well-respected/widely respected politician.

4B Ex 5 Student B

1 Read the following (true) beliefs about sleep. Add a third belief, which is false.

a It's believed that having an afternoon sleep can help you to be more creative.

b It's known that missing even an hour of sleep every night can have serious health consequences.

c ....

2 Read your statements to your partner (in a different order). Can they guess which is the false belief?

7B Ex 7B

1 Read the essay. Why do you think the author called it 'A blessing in disguise'?

A blessing in disguise

Ayodele Aiyegbusi | 24 August

[1]Often in life we find ourselves going through tough times. We struggle and struggle and see only the negative side. But when we look back, maybe years later, we realise things weren't so bad after all. Maybe our difficulties turned out to be a blessing in disguise.

[2]I remember it as if it were yesterday. The rain was falling like needles and a cold wind lifted the dead leaves from the earth. I was eleven years old, waiting for the school bell to ring so I could cycle home. When it finally did, I climbed onto my bike and barely noticed that the road was wet from the rain. I hadn't been cycling more than two minutes when I skidded, fell off and broke my leg.

[3]It was quite a bad break and I had to spend a month lying down. I'd been quite an active child and the worst thing wasn't the pain; it was having to stay in that same position the whole time. I was miserable. I wished I'd paid more attention to the road conditions. I kept thinking, if only I hadn't used my bike that day.

[4]One morning, seeing that I was bored, my mother brought me a drawing pad and some coloured pencils. I started drawing everything around me. One of my earliest pictures was a pair of pigeons on the windowsill. They were walking in circles in a little dance. Another was the rubber plant in the corner of the room. Once, I drew the moon peeking behind the curtains. I had seven brothers and sisters and I drew portraits of them, one every day from Monday to Sunday. And that's how I learnt to draw.

[5]Now, years later, I'm an artist. I work from life, sketching the things around me. I carry pencil and paper everywhere: in cafés, on trains, in hotel rooms. I draw everything, including pigeons dancing on windowsills.

[6]I'll always remember with mixed feelings that time I broke my leg. It was a miserable month, but it showed me that disasters can be opportunities if you look closely enough.

2 Read the essay again. Complete the description of each paragraph (1–6) with the words in the box.

consequence	details	event	good	summary	theme

1 a general introduction and the main .... of the essay
2 a description of the main .... that led to a change
3 more .... about the event and its immediate consequences
4 a description of something .... that happened during a bad time
5 a present .... of the event
6 a .... of the story, and a general message about life

3 Work in pairs. Answer the questions.

1 In paragraph 2, the author describes the weather. What details does he use?
2 In paragraph 3, he says 'I was miserable'. What wishes and regrets did he have?
3 In paragraph 4, he says he 'started drawing everything around [him].' What examples does he give?
4 In paragraph 5, he says he carries 'pencil and paper everywhere.' What examples does he give of 'everywhere'?
5 What lesson did the writer learn from this experience?

1C Top five

SPEAKING OUTPUT | an informal discussion
GOAL | create tourist recommendations for your town/area
MEDIATION SKILL | organising a group task

WARM-UP

1 **Work in pairs. Discuss the questions.**

1. Is your town or area popular with tourists?
2. Do you think your town or area is a good place for a holiday? Why/ Why not?
3. What do you like most about your town or area?

PREPARE

2 **Read the Scenario. What decisions do you need to make?**

SCENARIO

The editor of a local magazine that you contribute to has got touch in with you and some of the other writers.

To	Hyde, Billie; Blyth, Pete; Wood, Campbell
From	Andersson, Leif
Subject	Next feature

Hi everyone,

Local Culture Week is coming up and we'd like to do a little feature on the top five places to visit in our town/area, both for visitors from abroad and from our country.

I'd like you to list your top five in order and give brief reasons why each is good to visit.

Can you guys get something back to me in the next week or so?

Thanks,

Leif

3A MB1.01 | **Listen to the conversation. How does the group decide to organise the task?**

B MB1.01 | **Read the Mediation Skill box. Listen to the conversation in Ex 3A again and tick the phrases you hear.**

MEDIATION SKILL
organising a group task

When deciding how to do something as a group, it's important to clarify the objective and involve everyone in the process.

Make sure the goal is clear
So, they want us to …
OK, so what we have to do is …

Involve people in the process
OK. So how do you want to do this?
Shall we each come up with [a list/some ideas] and then compare?
How about going through [them/everything] one by one?

Give opinions about the best way of doing things
It would be easier if we …
It's going to take too long if we ...
It's better to … first, then later we can ...
Let's take about five minutes each to …
Let's just … first.

4 **Number sentences a–e in the correct order to make a short conversation.**

a Right. So, how shall we start? Shall we pick a couple of ideas and focus on the costs? ……
b Hmm, let's just get a big list of ideas together first and worry about the costs later. ……
c Fine, we can always add more ideas later I guess. ……
d OK, so Maria wants us to come up with some ideas for the party and give her an idea of how much everything would cost. ……
e Making a big list will take too long. Let's just focus on a couple of ideas first. ……

MEDIATE

5A **Work in groups. Read the Scenario again and decide how to organise your group. Then create your top five list, explaining your choices.**

B **Read your lists to the other groups. How similar are they?**

2C Micro gigs

WRITING OUTPUT | an informal summary
GOAL | summarise an informal interview
MEDIATION SKILL | note taking and summarising

WARM-UP

1 Work in pairs. Discuss the questions.

1 How often do you go to gigs or concerts?
2 Do you prefer big or small venues? Why?
3 What are the possible advantages of a very small venue?

PREPARE

2A Read the Scenario. What do you think a 'micro gig' is?

SCENARIO

Your friend Jez sends you this message.

> Hey! I've got to work tonight, so I won't be able to listen to that interview before class. Could you take some notes for me? I'm actually really interested in this whole micro gig idea. I might even set one up myself! 🙂
> 3.52 p.m.

B MB2.01 | Listen to the first part of the interview and check.

3 MB2.01 | Listen again. Use the prompts to make sentences about Sam's micro gigs.

1 micro gig / small concert / people's homes
A micro gig is a small concert which happens in people's homes.
2 Sam / living room / concerts / three years
3 artists / stay / bed and breakfast / part of fee
4 solo artists / fifteen people / big instruments and groups / fewer

4 Read the Mediation Skill box. What type of words are usually 'key' words?

MEDIATION SKILL
note taking and summarising

When taking notes, you don't need to write down every word you hear. Instead, note down the key words (i.e., the ones that give you the most important information). For example, if you heard:

A micro gig is a very small concert, but perhaps the biggest difference is that they happen in people's homes rather than big concert venues.

Your notes might look something like this:

micro gig/small concert/biggest difference/people's homes/not concert venues

Sometimes it's easier to paraphrase certain words rather than writing down exactly what somebody says. Notice the word 'not' is included in the notes above instead of 'rather than', which appears in the interview.

You can then use the notes to summarise the information for someone else. These sentences can be shorter and simpler than what was originally said: A micro gig is a small concert, but the biggest difference is it happens in people's homes, not in concert venues.

Also, you don't need to write down notes for every sentence you hear. Listen for sections that give you the most important information.

5A Look at the transcript of the next section of the interview. Underline the key words in Sam's answers.

Interviewer: How did you get started with all of this?

Sam: I guess it was a bit of an accident really. I had a friend who was a musician, and she wanted to play a gig in the area, but she wasn't really interested in the local venues, as, well, I guess she thought they were a little bit old fashioned, you know? All the bands just sounded the same – there was nothing new or inspiring about any of it.

Interviewer: So, you offered her your place?

Sam: Basically, yes. I said she could use my living room, and I put a couple of posts on social media to promote the event. I came up with the name 'micro gig' to make it sound a bit different, something special, unique.

Interviewer: And was that first gig a success?

Sam: It was a disaster! Very few people came, and it turned out that my living room wasn't great for live sound, but I could still see the potential for it to be a success. I decided I needed to buy better equipment to make the sound better, and that for the next gig I needed to be less lazy about promoting the event. The second gig was a lot better, and I got great feedback. From then on, I was hooked.

B Work in pairs. Compare the key words you underlined.

6 MB2.02 | Listen to the final part of the interview and make notes. Remember to only include the key words.

MEDIATE

7A Read the Scenario again. Write a short summary of the last part of the interview for Jez. Use your notes from Ex 6 to help you.

B Work in pairs. Compare your summaries. Is there anything they mentioned that you didn't?

3C Film challenge

WRITING OUTPUT | a blog post
GOAL | describe a film
MEDIATION SKILL | giving general and personal views

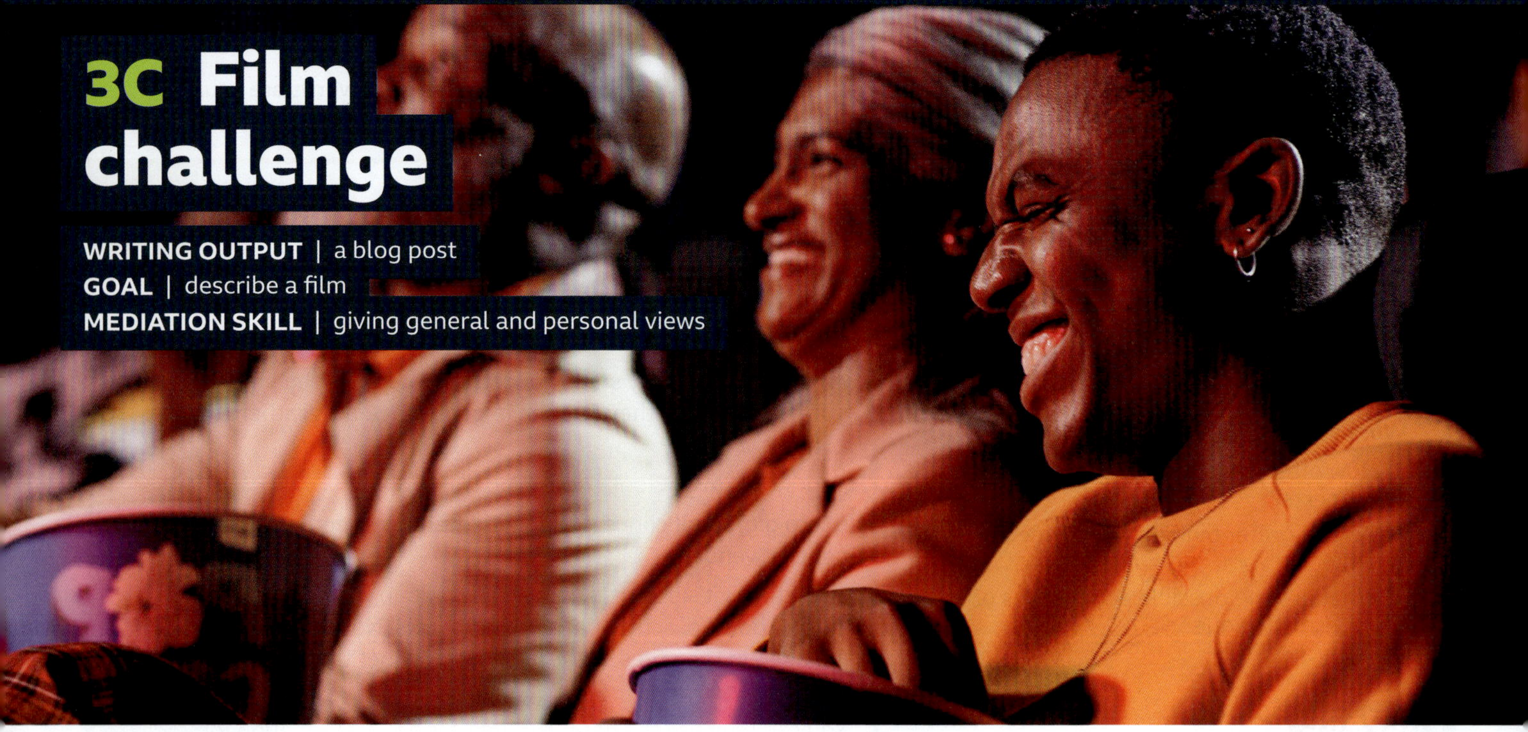

WARM-UP

1 **Work in pairs. Which of the following sentences are true for you and why? Give examples.**

1 I usually like the most popular films.
2 I often like films other people don't like.
3 I have very specific tastes in films.

PREPARE

2 **Read the Scenario. What do you think an 'underrated' film is?**

3 **Read the Mediation Skill box. Underline the phrases in the Scenario that the writer uses to give personal opinions and general opinions.**

MEDIATION SKILL
giving general and personal views

When giving your own interpretation of a story, novel, film or play – especially when you think it is under- or overrated – you might want to contrast your own opinions with what other people think.

Giving personal opinions

For me, it's …
Personally, I …
As far as I'm concerned, it's …

Contrasting general opinions with your own

A lot of people say … , but I …
I've heard people say … , but I think …
It's regarded as … , but I think …

SCENARIO

You are tagged in a social media post.

Maya Lewin
Yesterday at 13.36

Thanks for nominating me for the underrated film challenge, @Nickky Blu! Here are three films that are much better than you think …

My first pick is *Jaws*. Yes, it's regarded as one of the best horror films of all time, but I also think there's another level to it; it's about the value of human life – the choice between making money and looking after people – and that's still an important theme today.

My second choice is a film called *Waterworld*. It got mixed reviews when it was released, but personally I think it's great! The basic plot is that the polar ice caps have melted, which has caused sea levels to rise, so most of the world is underwater. Everyone thought it was ridiculous at the time but given everything that's happening with the environment at the moment, maybe it's not so crazy after all! For me, it's well worth a watch!

My last pick is one of Scarlett Johansson's early films – *Ghost World*. On the surface it's another typical American teen film, but what makes it great for me are the two main characters. They were best friends in high school, but now they've graduated, they start to realise that they're very different people. It's a very real relationship and one I think we can all relate to. I've heard people say it's nothing special, but what do people know?

Anyway, that's my list. Now I nominate @you!

20 Likes | 5 Comments

4 **Complete the posts with the sentences (a–f).**

a For me, it's more than just a comedy.
b some people would say it's not an underrated film
c It's regarded as a complicated film
d I've heard people say it's badly acted
e A lot of people say *Star Wars* is the best sci-fi film ever.
f as far as I'm concerned, it's one of his best performances

Wilco4
20 February at 13:03

Some people say that *Police Academy* is just a funny film. [1] .... It shows how important friendship is at work, and how true friends will stand by each other in difficult times, even when the situation is completely desperate. [2] .... , but for me it's probably the highlight of Steve Guttenberg's career as an actor.

27 11

Neko_Desu
28 February at 14:14

[3] .... I agree that it's a good film, but personally I think that title should go to *Moon*. While *Star Wars* tells a very simple story, basically a good vs. evil children's story, *Moon* has a complex plot that keeps you guessing till the end and asks serious questions about scientific development. [4] .... , but you just need to be a little patient and all of the answers appear by the end.

30 9

You_Can_Call_Me_Mal
4 March at 09:31

If you ask people to name the best Tom Cruise films, not many people would say *Vanilla Sky*, but [5] .... He's really believable as David Aames, a man who has it all and loses it all. While [6] .... , I find that it rarely gets mentioned when people talk about Cruise's greatest films.

16 4

5 **Number sentences a–e in the correct order to make a blog post.**

a … but for me, *Hot Fuzz* is one of the best comedy films made in the last thirty years, if not more. ....

b A lot of people say it's not even as good as other films by Simon Pegg and Edgar Wright, like *Shaun of the Dead*. ....

c Personally, I find it far funnier than any of his other films, as the chemistry between him and his co-star Nick Frost is just magical in this film. ....

d I hear a lot of opinions about the best comedy films, some say *The Wedding Singer*, others talk about *The Hangover* … ....

e As far as I'm concerned, they're the best double act appearing on the screen today. ....

6 **Work in pairs. Take turns completing the sentences with your own ideas.**

1 … is regarded as a very funny film. For me, it's …
2 A lot of people say … is a talented actor. Personally, I think …
3 Everyone thought … was a terrible film. In my case, I …
4 Some people think … films are great, but I think …

7 **Make a list of films that you think are underrated. Think about what other people say about these films, and what you think about them. Make notes about:**

- the characters.
- the plot.
- the themes.

MEDIATE

8A **Write your blog post about three underrated films. Try to contrast what most people think about each film with your own opinion where relevant.**

B **Work in pairs. Show your post to another student. Ask and answer questions about the films you've chosen.**

A: Do you really think *Die Hard* is underrated?
B: Yes, lots of people think it's just an action movie, but for me …

4C Active week

SPEAKING OUTPUT | a group discussion
GOAL | decide how to contribute to an event
MEDIATION SKILL | making group decisions

WARM-UP

1 **Work in groups. Discuss the questions.**

1. Does everyone have a responsibility to have a healthy and active lifestyle? Why/Why not?
2. Is it the government's responsibility to encourage people to be more active? Why/Why not?
3. How much do you enjoy exercise? How do you make it enjoyable?

PREPARE

2 **Read the Scenario. Why can you only choose one activity for Active Week?**

SCENARIO

To Community Group
From Garcia, Abe
Subject Re: Active Week

Hey guys,

It's national Active Week again soon, so we need to come up with an event to encourage people in our community to exercise and be active. I've had a quick brainstorm and this is what I've got so far:

- organising a marathon and inviting people from all over the country to take part.
- organising a football tournament featuring local celebrities.
- organising a walk for the whole town to do together.
- organising a talk from a famous sports star to encourage people to get involved in sport.
- organising a day where people can talk to experts to find the best sport/activity for them.

Can you add this to next week's agenda? We'd probably only be able to do one event as we don't have much time or budget.

Anyway, let me know what you decide.

Abe

3 **MB4.01 | Listen to a meeting about Active Week. Do the group manage to choose one activity?**

4 **MB4.01 | Read the Mediation Skill box. Then listen to the conversation again. Tick the phrases you hear.**

MEDIATION SKILL
making group decisions

Making decisions as a group can be difficult because we often disagree. There are three things we can do to help move the conversation forward.

Ask questions

Find out what everyone thinks and get everyone involved.

So, how does everyone feel about … ?

[Tom] – what do you think about [Sarah's] idea to …

Identify areas of agreement

Highlight areas of agreement. This encourages the people to see what they have in common.

[I think] we all agree that …

None of us want to …

Invite solutions and compromises

We also need to help people resolve things that they don't agree about, either by asking them to come up with a solution, persuading them to change their minds or by offering a compromise.

So, what's the solution?

Is there a way we can do both?

Would that work, [Bruna]?

5 **A** **Work in groups. Read the Scenario again and choose one of Abe's suggestions or think of your own idea. Make sure you each choose something different.**

B **Make notes about the advantages of your suggestion.**

MEDIATE

6 **Get back into your groups. Try to agree on one event for your area. Use the Mediation Skill box to help you to reach compromises where necessary.**

7 **Tell other groups which event you chose. Did you choose the same event, and for the same reasons?**

UNIT 1

Audio 1.01

J = Jamie G = Gini M = Matteo H = Hana

J: Hello and welcome to *Who Am I?* I'm your host Jamie Walker ...

G: ... and I'm Gini Cox.

J: This week we're focusing on identity – all the different elements that make us who we are.

G: That's right. So, we've been interviewing people out on the street, asking them how they would describe their identity. And we've had some really interesting replies.

J: Tell us a bit about yourself.

M: Hi, my name is Matteo and I'm a journalist. I'm thirty-four years old and I'm Brazilian. My mother tongue is Portuguese, but like many Brazilians, I have mixed roots. I'd say that my identity is made up of lots of different things.

J: What do you mean?

M: So, my mother is half Brazilian, half Italian, and my grandmother was Italian, so, I actually have an Italian passport and I spent some time living in Italy when I was younger.

J: Oh, right. So, do you feel that there is an Italian influence on your identity and your personality?

M: Hmm, I don't know about my personality so much. Is my personality connected to my Italian background? I don't know. But I think there is an influence on who I am as a person, you know, the things I do in my everyday life. Like, Italian families love getting together in big groups. That's not something I really enjoy. I do enjoy cooking Italian food though. And I love going to Italy on holiday and speaking the language. So, yeah, I guess the fact I've got Italian heritage is part of my identity, definitely.

J: And how about the UK? How long have you been living here? And do you think it's influenced your sense of identity at all?

M: So, I've been living in the UK for over twenty years now. But I wouldn't say I feel particularly British. I mean, my wife is British, my kids grew up here and I speak the language pretty fluently, but I guess my identity comes more from the place where I grew up, which is Brazil. I definitely feel more at home with my Brazilian and Portuguese friends. And when I listen to Brazilian music, it goes straight to my heart, you know? Like, it makes me think of everything I grew up with – the food, the language, the people – all of that forms a big part of who I am.

G: So, tell us a bit about yourself. What do you think makes you who you are?

H: So, I'm Hana and I'm originally from Korea, but I've lived in lots of different places around the world – mainly the USA but also Hong Kong, Australia, Germany. Now I'm based in Amsterdam, in the Netherlands, which I love. I've been learning Dutch, but it's really hard! So, I've always worked and travelled a lot around other countries and I would say that, um, all of these different places play a part in who I am, far beyond the idea of nationality or belonging to one single place. All of these places and the languages have contributed to the person that I am now.

G: What do you mean?

H: You know, in terms of how I eat and how I choose to live my life, I think there's a lot of Asian influence there. A lot of my favourite dishes to cook are Korean, for example. But I think my identity comes more from my own experiences – the different jobs I've done, the people I've met. I guess my family probably influenced my personality a lot, too.

G: Can you give me some examples?

H: Yeah, so my father is pretty stubborn and I've definitely inherited that from him. I don't think I've inherited anything from my mum – she's very organised, and a great planner, but I'm really not. They've both had a big influence on my attitude to work and studying, though. When I was at school, they encouraged me to work hard and I suppose, because of that, I've always been really focused on my education and my career, even though none of my siblings are. I guess I've always been pretty ambitious.

G: And how about your career? Would you say that's influenced your identity at all?

H: Yeah, definitely. I'm a journalist and that's a big part of my self-identity. I guess, at the end of the day, we are all different and there are lots of influences. Everyone is an individual with different life experiences and a different stories to tell.

Audio 1.02

1 How long have you been living here?

2 Have you ever lived in another country?

3 What have you been doing recently?

4 How long have you been studying English?

Audio 1.05

N = Naomi A = Ayo

N: You know Lagos already, right?

A: A little bit. I came here on another business trip a few years ago. The thing I like about it is the street life. There are some really good markets where you can find handcrafted goods.

N: Oh, that sounds interesting.

A: Yeah, in the centre. And fairly close by, there's Victoria Island, which is sort of your more upscale area. It has designer stores and boutiques and fancy restaurants, that kind of thing. It's kind of the posh area. Do you want to check it out?

N: Um, I'd be happy to go there for a bit, but maybe not more than a couple of hours. It's not really my cup of tea.

A: OK, that's fine.

N: Yeah, I'm not a big fan of shopping generally. I'd rather go to a park and just wander about for a bit.

A: Actually, there *is* a park which you might like. It's called Freedom Park. It has life-size sculptures and an art gallery. And the last time I was there, there was live music.

N: Oh wow, I'm really into live music.

A: Yeah, there was a stage with a band and a dance group. It was awesome.

N: That sounds great. You know, I've heard there are some beaches outside the centre that are worth visiting.

A: Yeah, definitely.

N: It might be nice just to hang out on a beach for a few hours. I think I'd prefer to do that than to go wandering around the shops.

A: We can do that. There are a *few* beaches, if I remember rightly. One's called Tarkwa Bay Beach. It's about twenty minutes out of town and you take a boat to get there. It's idyllic, just beautiful.

N: Oh wow. You know, what I really like doing is surfing. I don't suppose they rent out surfboards, do they?

A: I'm pretty sure they do, actually. I didn't know you were into surfing.

N: I love it.

A: Me too.

N: Shall we just spend the afternoon surfing then, I mean after the markets and the park?

A: Fine with me.

N: Are you sure?

A: Totally! We can go to a street market and Freedom Park in the morning and spend the afternoon on the beach. Excellent! And then we'll find a local restaurant where we can eat some local food in the evening.

N: Sounds good.

A: Have you ever tried jollof rice?

N: Nope. Not yet.

A: You're going to love it!

UNIT 1 REVIEW

Audio R1.01

Stormy weather

Since I was very young, I have always loved the outdoors. As a ten-year-old, I read lots of books about explorers and I was extremely adventurous. I was happy wandering into the woods on my own, or exploring abandoned houses. While most children are curious about the natural world, I was obsessed. I have one particular childhood memory of a day with my grandfather. He was really into hiking and one day, when I was ten, he took me with him. The idea was to go up a hill called Gomez Peak, and we needed to go at a good pace so as to be back by dinnertime. Unfortunately, we got caught in a storm. There was no escape. We tried standing under a pine tree to stay dry, but it didn't work; we got soaked. As we stood there, he kept trying to comfort me, saying, 'It's going to be OK.' He thought I'd be terrified of all the noise and wind. But I wasn't scared – I loved it. I'll never forget listening to the rain falling like drumbeats. To this day, I have never had so much fun in my life!

UNIT 1 VOCABULARY BANK

Audio VB1.01

1 We can depend on Sam to be here on time. He's very reliable.
2 Melissa became quite emotional as she was watching the film.
3 Al will need some help setting up the new printer. He's not very practical.
4 I love the fact that Leo is always so optimistic about life!
5 Sasha is a really talented musician.
6 Thanks for moving those boxes – it was really helpful.
7 It was very thoughtful of you to send those flowers to cheer me up!
8 I don't think I'll go to the party – I'm not feeling very sociable today.
9 I'm not adventurous enough to go paragliding!
10 I'm sure she'll be prime minister one day. She's incredibly ambitious.

Audio VB1.02

1 He never remembers anything I tell him! Things go in one ear and out the other.
2 Oh no! I forgot to buy vegetables for the curry. Sorry, it totally slipped my mind.
3 Hmm … I'm not sure. I'll need to look at my notes again to refresh my memory.
4 I'll remember it in a minute. The answer is on the tip of my tongue!
5 I'm sure I've heard that name before. It definitely rings a bell.
6 Oh, yes. You were there too, weren't you? My memory is playing tricks on me.

UNIT 1 MEDIATION BANK

Audio MB1.01

B = Billie P = Pete C = Campbell

B: Hey! Have you read Leif's email yet?
P: Yeah, so they want us to come up with a top five list of places to visit, right?
C: Yep, our top five, in order.
B: OK. So how do you want to do this? Shall we each come up with a list and then compare?
C: It's going to take too long if we do it like that. How about going through our favourites one by one?
P: Yeah OK. Then we can list the reasons later. Who wants to go first? Billie?
B: OK, well the Museum of Modern Art's got to be on there, obviously.
C: Obviously.
P: And is that number one?
B: Hmm … let's worry about the order later. Let's just get a big list of places together first.
P: OK, so the museum, and what next, the nature park?

UNIT 2

Audio 2.01

1 VR is certain to be used more in the future.
2 The new headsets are due to go on sale next week.
3 This game is going to be a big hit!
4 VR is unlikely to replace our summer holidays.

Audio 2.02

I want you to imagine yourself in paradise. Think about what you can see. What sounds can you hear? What do you feel? If you imagined a white sand beach with gently lapping waves, or a woodland alive with birdsong, I'm guessing you also imagined a feeling of serenity and relaxation. The idea that spending time in nature can be good for our well-being isn't new. It's actually an idea that goes back for thousands of years. The word 'paradise' comes from the Ancient Persian term for park or orchard, which is '*pardaiza*' and I think if you ask most people to imagine paradise, people would think about a white sand beach with waves lapping or with a woodland maybe that's alive with birdsong. They're probably likely to imagine a feeling of serenity and relaxation. And that's the kind of feeling that medics began to try and promote in the UK as early as … sort of … the 1750s. We had doctors travelling around the country, trying to work out what it was like spending time near the sea and whether that's something that could almost be prescribed. And we had sea-bathing hospitals, the idea being that spending time there could help you overcome some of the sort of minor ailments that were common in the 1700s.

In the last 200 years, we've started to sort of lose our connection with some of the preventative effects that spending time in nature can have for us. We've had these incredible advances in technology, in pharmaceuticals, antibiotics, which have meant that we've saved, you know, millions of lives and improved the quality of life in so many countries across the world, but that shift in focus has meant that we've sort of moved away from our ancient nature-based perspectives, and in many cases sort of forgotten that connection that we have with nature.

So the problem now is that for the first time in history, most of the world's population live in big, busy and noisy cities, and they're so different to the kind of environments that we evolved to live in. And whether we're aware of it or not, cities place, you know, a huge amount of stress on our bodies. We're almost in a constant state of alert because we have to navigate things like crossing the road, busy, crowded spaces, threats from passing bicycles. And also the kind of complicated social interactions that we actually start to take for granted now, but that our bodies are constantly trying to deal with and respond to.

So when we live in demanding environments like cities, our body has this desperate need to be able to switch off for downtime. And the natural environment actually provides the perfect kind of setting to allow that kind of restoration to occur.

What's really interesting is that actually just having a view of nature can be enough to see some of these restorative effects. So there's a famous study from the 1980s where hospital patients were shown to recover faster from surgery if they had a view of trees rather than just a window that looked out at the rest of the hospital.

It also looks like the level of biodiversity could be quite important for well-being. It could be that simply seeing or hearing more plants and animals in an environment makes it more fascinating. Which brings us on to the sounds of nature, and several studies have shown that people prefer listening to natural sounds like birdsong or water flowing, compared to the other kinds of sounds they'd hear in a city, for example. But we don't really have a huge amount of data on what kinds of sounds might work best and whether just listening to them is enough. If you just put on a set of headphones on your commute, would that help calm you down enough, or do you need to see, touch, smell, be in nature for it to have the ultimate effect?

Audio 2.05

A: Hey, so, I've been watching this amazing TV series about women with extreme lifestyles. Have you seen it?
B: Yeah, I've been watching that, too. Last week there was one about a woman who's a sea nomad and has spent her whole life at sea.
A: That's right. Amazing. Did you see the one about the astronaut? What was her name … ?
B: Karen Nyberg? Yeah, I saw that one, too.
A: It was incredible, wasn't it?
B: I know. I mean I'd guess it must be so inspiring to see the world like that, from space. Can you imagine?
A: Yeah, it would be incredible, wouldn't it?
B: Absolutely! Although there's no way I would ever consider doing that. I know for a fact that I couldn't go into space. I don't even like getting on a plane! It must be an amazing experience though.
A: Yeah, it was interesting to find out how they actually live up there, you know, the ordinary things that they have to do every day. A lot of it looked pretty tedious, like checking all of the systems and whatever. And that bit about how they keep fit – it was really fascinating!
B: Yeah and how she washes her hair! Did you see that bit?
A: Yeah, it was really interesting to see how she does, you know, normal, everyday things up there. Must be difficult sometimes though – especially being away from people. I mean, she left her three-year-old son at home, and was away for, like, six months. I mean I'd imagine that was really hard.

B: I suppose they had video chats, but it's not really the same, is it?

A: Not at all. And what about that woman who runs around the world? Did you see that one?

B: Yeah, Rosie Swale-Pope I think her name was. I can't believe she's in her 70s and she runs all around the world by herself, pulling that little trailer behind her.

A: I know, and she sleeps in it at night, and then just carries on running in the morning. It's pretty impressive!

B: Yeah, I reckon it must be pretty lonely at times, though.

A: Well, you would think so, but she obviously finds it really rewarding, seeing all those amazing places and meeting interesting people along the way. She's written a book about some of the things that have happened to her. And she raises money for charity.

B: She's clearly the kind of person who just has to keep moving, sort of nomadic.

A: Yes, that's right. I get the impression she's so used to this lifestyle that she wouldn't be happy living anywhere for long. Even when she's back home in the UK, she sometimes prefers to sleep outside in her little trailer than stay inside her house.

B: Oh, really? I'd have thought it'd be exhausting to live like that all the time. And pretty frightening, too. She's bound to feel scared sometimes.

A: I bet she does. Anyway, it's not for me. I can't even bear going camping for the weekend, let alone …

Audio 2.07

If I could travel back in time to any place in the world, I'd go back to Paris in the 1920s. To start with, I'm a huge fan of all the artists and writers from that period, like Ernest Hemingway, F. Scott Fitzgerald, Salvador Dalí, Pablo Picasso, and Gertrude Stein. And they all lived in Paris, so it was a really exciting city at that time. I'd love to meet all of them, but especially Hemingway because I really like his books.

So, what would I do? Well, at that time, there were all these nightclubs and cafés springing up all over Paris, with loads of incredible shows. With that in mind, I'd want to go dancing with F. Scott Fitzgerald and his wife Zelda. I can imagine that being a whole lot of fun. What else? I'd have a long chat with Hemingway and Picasso about their creativity and what they were planning to do next. And last but not least, I'd take Gertrude Stein out to dinner and ask her what she really thought of all these artists with their amazing talent, but also their big egos!

UNIT 2 REVIEW

Audio R2.01

Anyone looking for solitude is unlikely to find it in a 21st-century city, but there are still plenty of places one can be alone. In the 19th century, the American writer Henry Thoreau did an experiment in solitary living. He went to live on a patch of woodland owned by his friend Ralph Waldo Emerson. Thoreau built a hut on the banks of Walden Pond. He spent over two years there and wrote a book, *Walden*, about his experiences.

More recently, the Italian writer Paolo Cognetti left Milan and rented a shepherd's hut near the mountains of Valle d'Aosta. There he lived for several months, surrounded by incredible scenery and very little noise besides the wind. While there, he took time to analyse his life and think about what he might do next. Like Thoreau, he wrote a book: *The Wild Boy*.

Few people are able to escape like Thoreau and Cognetti. The majority of us are lucky if we get a few days on a deserted beach. But there will always be quiet places for those with the desire and resources to find them.

UNIT 2 MEDIATION BANK

Audio MB2.01

I = Interviewer S = Sam

I: Now, anyone that's been listening to the podcast for any length of time will know that I love live music. But it can be difficult to feel any real connection with the artists when you're one of thousands of people in the audience.
So, what's the solution? My next guest may well have the answer. Sam Harrington is one of a small, but growing number of music-lovers hosting 'micro gigs' – an alternative to big concerts.
Sam – welcome to the show.

S: Thanks for having me.

I: So, first things first – what is a 'micro-gig'? Is it just a small concert?

S: Well, yeah, it's a really small concert, but perhaps the biggest difference is that they happen in people's homes rather than big concert venues.

I: Right. And you actually put on micro gigs at your house, is that right?

S: Yeah, I've been using my living room to host concerts for the last three years now. We've probably had about 200 artists play here.

I: Wow, that's a lot!

S: Yeah, and most of them have stayed with us, too. We provide bed and breakfast for all the artists who come and play for us as part of their fee.

I: Nice. And what about the audience? How many people can you actually fit in your living room?

S: Hmmm … It, kind of, depends who's performing. If it's a solo artist with a small instrument, we can probably squeeze around fifteen people in. But with big instruments and groups it's much fewer. We once had someone come with their harp and we only had space for five!

Audio MB2.02

I = Interviewer S = Sam

I: So, why do you do it? What's the attraction of putting on micro gigs?

S: Well, when you go to a big concert the artist or band is usually so far away. You're often in a crowd, which can be uncomfortable, and of course it's often expensive, too. I think music is great when it's a really personal experience, and I love being able to chat with the musicians about the music they make. It's a much more satisfying experience.

I: Sure, but you're never going to have, say, Elton John in your house, are you? I'm guessing the artists don't get paid that much for doing such a small show, so what's in it for them?

S: Haha! Well, Elton is very welcome! But, yeah, you're right, they don't get paid a lot, but I think most artists we have here find it a very positive experience. It's a great place to interact with your audience and to make a very direct connection with people. Music, and art, doesn't always have to be about numbers. Indeed, some famous artists actually use small venues like ours to try out new songs and get feedback from a small audience.

I: Right. So, do people actually know who's playing in advance or is it a surprise?

S: No, we don't have gig listings or anything, we like to keep it a surprise! People just turn up and hope they can get in.

I: And do they always like the artists you invite?

S: Not always! I remember a very angry, shouty, singer songwriter we had here a couple of years ago. He was pretty rude and some of the people who came along really didn't like him.

I: Oh, really? So, was it a bit of a disaster then?

S: No, not at all. Music isn't always about everyone having fun. Sometimes it's good to listen to something that's not your usual thing, and even if you don't like it, it's an experience, something to talk about with your friends, or something that makes you think. And sometimes you change your mind about things you think you don't like. A lot of our regular customers had never seen live hip hop before, for example, but they loved some of the artists who've come to play here. I mean, yeah, it's great to see your favourite artist, but it's good to be a musical explorer, too.

I: Absolutely. Sam – thanks for coming on the show.

UNIT 3

Audio 3.01

1 Burning Man festival, which takes place at the end of August, attracts huge crowds.

4 The festival appointed Damon Gameau, who is a world-renowned filmmaker, as their Eco Ambassador.

Audio 3.03

P = Pauline K = Katherine R = Rufus M = Mahmoud

P: We've all been there. You've practised a thousand times. You know your lines and you know how to say them. Yet when the time comes to perform, your legs turn to jelly and you just want to hide in the corner. Stage fright affects even the most experienced performers, and can make or break anyone just starting out. So, how do we cope with it? I'm Pauline Hazany and this week I interviewed a few well-known performers to find out. First up is professional musician, Katherine Sherrell, who I caught up with backstage on the first night of her UK tour.

P: Katherine, you used to get pretty bad stage fright, didn't you?

K: Yeah, I did, for years. Every time I had to go on stage, I could hardly stand up, I was shaking so much. I just got so nervous. It was awful. And my time on stage seemed to go on forever!

P: So, what happened? Did things just improve the more you performed?

K: Well, sort of. It was a couple of things, really. Firstly, I told a friend, a fellow musician, about my nerves, and he said something surprising. He said, it's not about you; it's about the music. He also told me to stop worrying about the audience. You know, they want a great night out; they've paid for their tickets, and they're on my side. From that moment, I had a different approach; I was calmer and more relaxed. And it's served me well ever since.

P: Sounds like good advice. Have you picked up any more tips that could help our listeners?

K: Something else I do is focus on my posture, how I stand, and even how I walk on stage before the gig starts. I remember I've been doing this for years and I imagine I'm ten feet tall and that nothing can stop me!

P: The second person I spoke to was Rufus Gerrard, a stage actor who's played all kinds of roles from Hamlet to Frodo in the theatre version of *The Lord of the Rings*. I caught up with Rufus during a rehearsal for his new play, Arthur Miller's *The Crucible*.

P: Rufus, hi.

R: Hi, Pauline.

P: Tell us about stage fright.

R: It's a real problem, even for experienced actors. You feel as if you're going to die of fright. It can hit you at any time and you have to find a way to overcome it.

P: So how do you cope with it?

R: In my case, I learnt quite early on in my career that what I needed to do was prepare both physically and mentally. So, physically I started doing stretching exercises for about fifteen minutes before every performance. And mentally I started using visualisation. Basically, I'd imagine myself not in front of a big, scary audience, but in front of my friends and family, people who'd supported me all my life, and I'd see them smiling and clapping. I also tried to erase myself and my ego, so I was no longer Rufus Gerrard acting in front of an audience, but I was the character in the play. It's the character that's important, not me.

P: And it worked?

R: Yeah, it made all the difference.

P: My last interview was with motivational speaker, Mahmoud Jalil. Mahmoud regularly gives presentations to hundreds of people around the world, so he knows a thing or two about how to stay cool under pressure. I met up with him in a café a couple of hours before he was due on stage.
So, you're on pretty soon, aren't you, Mahmoud?

M: Er, yeah. I've got about an hour or so before I need to get ready.

P: So, how are you feeling? Getting nervous yet?

M: Haha! Not really. I used to get incredibly nervous before giving my talks though. I mean like a total disaster.

P: So what changed?

M: Well, it was the build-up beforehand that scared me. I used to spend hours going over the performance in my head. Was everyone going to like it? Would I forget what to say? Every time I had to go on stage, it was like the worst day of my life! And then one day I made a decision to just stop caring so much. I said to myself – what's the worst thing that can happen? That I forget what I'm trying to say? Or the technology breaks down? But if that happens, how much does it matter? Will it be the end of the world if I get lost and have to read my notes? The answer was no. And that was how it all changed for me. I mean, it was so liberating.

P: So you just needed a change of mindset?

M: Basically, yeah. What worked for me was approaching the presentation differently. I still get nervous, but I don't spend hours and hours preparing and imagining all the worst things that can happen. Now it's under control.

Audio 3.05

A = Alice S = Sam R = Ravi

A: Hey, have any of you guys seen *The Queen's Gambit* yet?

S: Yeah, I have. It's amazing, isn't it? I binge-watched the entire thing in a couple of days!

R: Really? Wow. It must be good, then. What's it about?

A: So, it's about a woman, Beth Harmon, who is a chess prodigy.

R: Chess?

A: Yeah, but trust me, it's good. Anyway, it's set in the USA around the 1950s and it shows her rise to becoming, like, a world-class chess player, you know, beating all the grand masters and that kind of thing.

R: Is it a true story?

S: Hmm ... I don't think so. It's based on a book by Walter Tevis. I'm pretty sure the main character is fictional.

A: Well, yes but she's kind of based on a real person, Vera Menchik, who was a chess star, or something like that. So, the story is sort of real. It's beautifully written though, isn't it? And she's such an intriguing character.

S: Yeah, definitely. It really takes us into her world. The acting is fantastic.

A: Yes, I loved that bit at the end when ... well, I won't spoil it for you, but it's really good. And it's beautiful to watch, too. You know, the costumes and stuff. It's done really well.

R: Ah, OK. Well, it sounds good. I'll add it to my watch-list.

A: Yeah, do – it's well worth a watch. What about you then? Have you binged-watched anything recently?

R: Me? Yeah, I'm watching a programme called *Big Little Lies* at the moment. It's amazing!

A: Oh, really? I remember hearing about it, but I don't think I ever watched it. Wasn't it the one about the women, set in California? It's like a murder mystery or something.

S: That's right. Oh, it's brilliant. It's based on a book by ... um ... what's her name, you know that Australian author ... Liane Moriarty. It tells the story of five young-ish women in California who become involved in this murder investigation. And the acting is brilliant, you know, really powerful. So, every episode is sort of incredibly tense and gripping to watch.

A: Sounds good.

S: It's got a fantastic cast, as well – Nicole Kidman, Reese Witherspoon and they give these really powerful, realistic performances.

A: Sounds great. Just my kind of thing.

S: Yeah, I think you'd love it. You get really caught up in the drama and that kind of thing, all the plot twists. But it's also visually stunning to watch. Every scene is beautifully shot. It's perfect for a late-night binge-watching session.

A: Brilliant! The show I'm watching at the moment has got about ten seasons, or something like that. But I'm getting through them really quickly, so now I'll have something to watch when I'm finished.

R: Yeah, good to know ...

S: I definitely ...

Audio 3.06

A = Alice S = Sam

A: So, it's about a woman, Beth Harmon, who is a chess prodigy. It's set in the USA around the 1950s and it shows her rise to becoming, like, a world-class chess player, you know, beating all the grand masters and that kind of thing.

A: Yes, I loved that bit at the end when … well, I won't spoil it for you, but it's really good. And it's beautiful to watch, too, you know, the costumes and stuff. It's done really well.

A: It's like a murder mystery or something.

S: That's right. Oh, it's brilliant. It's based on a book by um, what's her name? You know, that Australian author … Liane Moriarty. It tells the story of five young-ish women …

S: Every episode is sort of incredibly tense and gripping to watch. You get really caught up in the drama and that kind of thing, all the plot twists …

A: The show I'm watching at the moment has got about ten seasons, or something like that.

UNIT 3 REVIEW

Audio R3.01

The show goes on

I once took on the challenge of trying to put on a show with people who had never performed on stage before. At first it seemed impossible. People kept messing up their lines. After a few weeks, I really didn't want to continue, but everyone was so enthusiastic that in the end, I did agree to carry on. But then I realised that we were trying to rehearse in the evenings, when everyone was tired. So I came up with the idea of rehearsing early in the mornings instead, which was much more successful because everyone was fresh. What I liked about working with people new to acting was that they were completely free – they had no expectations to live up to.

As the day of the performance approached, I must admit I became more nervous. We had put up posters to attract an audience, but I wasn't sure how many would attend. Thankfully, the theatre was full. My amateur cast ended up giving an incredible performance, and the audience loved it!

UNIT 3 VOCABULARY BANK

Audio VB3.01

1 solar power
2 natural resources
3 clean-up
4 carbon emissions
5 sustainable
6 renewable
7 recycling
8 carbon footprint

UNIT 4

Audio 4.01

1 This time next year, I'll have graduated from university.
2 I hope we'll have cut down on junk food by then.
3 When you next see me, I'll have started working out.
4 I hope you'll have found a new job by the summer.

Audio 4.02

P = Presenter M = Matthew
TV P = TV Presenter

P: Matthew Walker researches how you spend around a third of your life.

M: I'm a sleep scientist.

P: Actually, one of the world's leading sleep scientists. At the root of sleep science lies a puzzle. All these hours lying down, eyes shut. Why? Why do we sleep? It's not just that it seems a monumental waste of time.

M: Sleep actually seems to be the most idiotic of all things that human beings could do because when you're asleep, you're not finding a mate, you're not reproducing, you're not caring for your young, you're not finding food, and in fact, it's been suggested that if sleep doesn't serve an absolutely vital function, then it's the biggest mistake the evolutionary process has ever made.

P: Managing eight hours' shut-eye is for me just a dream. And it turns out I'm not alone. There's evidence that in many parts of the developed world, we're sleeping less and less. A poll in 1942 found Americans were sleeping eight hours a night.

M: Now, on a recent National Sleep Foundation survey, what they found was that the average adult in America was down to sleeping six hours and thirty-one minutes a night. In the United Kingdom it was six hours and forty-nine minutes. Japan perhaps the worst down to six hours and twenty-two minutes.

P: Only ten percent of Japanese adults, according to this survey, were getting eight hours or more.

TV P: Good morning, this is Diana Speed welcoming you to the network and reminding you that if you've forgotten that the clocks went forward last night so the time is now twenty past five on Sunday the twenty-ninth of March …

P: Researchers have studied what happens in countries after clocks are adjusted in spring and autumn.

M: What they found was that in the spring, when we lose one hour of sleep, there was a twenty-four percent relative increase in heart attacks the following day, whilst in the autumn, in the fall, when we gain an hour of sleep, there was actually a twenty-one percent reduction in relative heart attack rates.

P: When the clocks go forward and we lose an hour's sleep, there are also more hospital admissions and more car accidents.
It also turns out that during sleep, we're able to reorganise information in the brain rather as though we were putting together the components of an IKEA furniture pack. And when we wake up, 'Eureka!' Every language has a variation of the English phrase 'sleep on it', 'sleep on the problem'. 'Dormici su, … la nuit porte conseil,' …

M: Yeah, I think there's probably a reason that no one has ever told you to stay awake on a problem.

Audio 4.03

It's been suggested that if sleep doesn't serve an absolutely vital function, then it's the biggest mistake the evolutionary process has ever made.

Audio 4.06

M = Martin L = Leah

M: I read this article the other day about how much exercise we should do. It recommended 150 minutes of moderate exercise a week, which sounds about right to me. What do you think?

L: Hmmm, I'm not sure. I agree with you up to a point, but it depends, doesn't it? I mean, it depends on your age, your general health, and whether or not you're sporty. For most people, I'd say about an hour a day is enough to keep you fit and healthy. That's what I do, and I enjoy it.

M: An hour a day?! That's a lot, if you ask me!

L: Do you think so? It depends what kind of exercise, I guess. In my opinion, there's a big difference between, say, walking for an hour and playing football for an hour. So if you're doing a contact sport like football or basketball, you might only want to do that, say, two or three days a week. But you can easily do moderate exercise every day, like walking or jogging or swimming.

M: Yeah, that's a good point. Not all exercise is equal. But I completely disagree with you that everyone needs to do an hour a day. That's way too much for most people!

L: I know what you mean. Most people would find it hard to fit in exercise every day, but I'm talking about an ideal number. So, how much exercise do you do?

M: What, you mean vigorous exercise – sweating and getting out of breath?

L: Yeah.

M: None.

L: Really?

M: Yeah. But remember, I'm on my feet all day at work, aren't I? So I don't have the stamina to spend my evenings running around as well.

L: Oh, I see your point.

M: I know in theory I should go to the gym and all that stuff, but on the other hand, I think doing too much exercise is just as bad as doing too little.
L: True.
M: I do a physical job, and I'm exhausted by the evening. As far as I'm concerned, if you do physical work during the day, you don't need to go to a gym or do anything else.
L: Hm. That's a fair point, although it could also be argued that you just need a different type of exercise, like stretching or yoga or something to help you relax.
M: No thanks! That's what the TV's for.
L: Well, you could at least kick a ball around every now and then, or walk the dog.
M: I couldn't agree more, but I don't have a dog.
L: Well, walk the cat, then.
M: Ha ha.

Audio 4.08

I would say that my modern lifestyle is quite different from the traditional lifestyle of, say, my grandmother. Especially as a young woman. Nowadays, most young women where I come from get a good education and go out to work, whereas in the past, in my grandmother's generation, that didn't happen so much. My grandmother left school when she was young, and married my grandfather. She never went out to work, although she used to earn money by sewing, and making suits for people. She dedicated her life to looking after everybody, her parents, her aunt, her children, her grandchildren. She cooked and kept the house clean. She would get up early and go down to the market to buy fresh fruit and vegetables from the local farmers, freshly caught fish and seafood from the fishermen. We still have a market that sells local produce. I suppose that tradition is still quite strong. But it's much smaller than it used to be, and people do most of their shopping in the supermarket, so it's much more difficult for the local fishermen and the farmers to make money. Their lifestyle is disappearing, and we only have a small window of opportunity to save it. A lot of farmers are now choosing to run 'Agritourism' businesses instead – essentially providing holidays on the farm – which is something that didn't exist before. Another tradition that is under threat is home cooking. My grandmother made home-made pasta and bread every day. She would spend hours preparing meals for the family. She lived a simple life. Nowadays, I think the expectations of young people are very different. We don't have so much time to spend at home, so a lot of the traditional skills of cooking and making things at home have been lost. These days, it seems like nobody has time for those lengthy recipes. We use a machine or we buy food that is ready-made and put it in the microwave, so I would say that this is another tradition which is in danger of disappearing. Also, when something breaks, we throw it away and buy a replacement, but I remember my grandfather was always repairing things and making them work again. Our modern-day lifestyle is much more focused on consumerism than in the past. Perhaps it's time to make a change.

UNIT 4 REVIEW

Audio R4.01

Health is the new wealth

Tara Williams, Monday 25 February, 13.00 GMT

In recent years, health and fitness has grown into a multi-billion-dollar industry as many of us strive to eat healthily and stay in shape. With modern technology, the average lifestyle has become increasingly sedentary. We are also busier and in general work longer hours than in the past. So, to make up for it, we follow healthy-eating gurus on Instagram, try to vary our diet by drinking fresh vegetable juice and eating superfood salads. We join gyms, buy fitness technology, take online yoga classes and do regular workouts. It is thought that Americans spend more than $40 billion trying to improve their health and fitness every year.

And future trends look even more extreme. Some are predicting that within the next ten years, a lot of fitness training will have moved outside. The benefits of training outdoors include exposure to the sun and fresh air, and running where the ground isn't flat. In addition, it's likely that more of us will be wearing personal tracking devices, which will offer us computer-generated personal training programmes based on our individual health metrics.

UNIT 4 MEDIATION BANK

Audio MB4.01

B = Bruna C = Costas J = Jim P = Penny

B: Right, so next on the agenda is Active Week. Abe's sent through a list of ideas, but I've actually got another option I'd like to discuss. How does everyone feel about putting on some dance classes in the town square? It's active, and it doesn't need to be competitive, so everyone can join in.
C: Yeah, that's a nice idea Bruna, and I think we all agree that we need to find an activity that everyone can do. But I just don't know if dancing is popular enough. We want to get as many people involved as possible. Remember when we did the fun run a couple of years ago? People absolutely loved that.
B: Good point, so what does everyone think of that idea – about doing a fun run again?
J: Sounds good to me.
P: Yeah, the fun run was good, but I think we should try and do something different every year, which is why dance classes are such a great idea. We've never done them before.
J: That's a good point, Penny.
B: OK, thanks for the input, everyone. So, we all agree that we want something everyone can do, and I think we all want the biggest attendance possible, but Penny is worried about doing something we've done before. So, what's the solution?
C: Well, perhaps we could try and do both? Have two events instead of one this year? That way, if you're not interested in dance classes, you can do the fun run.
J: Would that work, Bruna?
B: Hmm … Abe did say we should try and choose one activity, but I can suggest two and see what he says?
P: OK, great. Thanks, Bruna!

UNIT 1

Opener: BBC Vlogs

1 In my family, I probably take after my mother. She really enjoys the cinema, she enjoys reading, she enjoys travelling and that's, kind of, what I've spent a large part of my life trying to do. And I think I probably got that interest in those subjects from her.

2 Oh, I take after my father, Edward. He lives in Indiana. He has a passion for science and he's the person who gave me my love for reading and my love for books. As you can see, I've tonnes of books. And we have the very same eye colour.

3 Hmm … I believe I take after a combination of both my father and my mother. My father was a pragmatic man and the peacemaker of the family and I believe that I demonstrate those skills. My mother is very sociable and also very career focused, er, I believe that I've also got those characteristics as well. I've also been told that I look like my mother, which I consider a compliment because, er, I think my mother looks great.

4 In my family, I take after my father, more than my mother. We both have dark hair, we have dark senses of humour, er, and we both love language.

5 Who do I take after in my family? I don't think there's anyone like me to be quite honest. The rest of my family wishes they were like me, but there can only be one.

1D: BBC Street Interviews
Exs 2A and 2B

Elaine: I would describe myself as, erm, liberal, erm, I'm quite, er, happy-go-lucky, erm, I try to make the best that I can out of life, so quite positive I think?

Anna: I would say I'm bubbly, a passionate and committed person. Erm, I, I'm a people person, so I like to interact with different types of people and, like, er, get to know all different walks of life.

Valeria: So, my personality is quite curious and enthusiastic.

Elijah: Optimistic, loving and, er, creative. But sometimes I'm a bit grumpy.

Gwen: Er, I think I'm quite outgoing, erm, quite sociable, erm, I like to chat to people, meet new people, go to parties, and stuff like that – so I think I'm quite an outgoing person.

Roisin: Erm, I would say I'm friendly, welcoming … maybe a bit funny sometimes.

Collin: I'm optimistic, er, I like people, erm, I never give up.

1D: BBC Street Interviews
Exs 2A and 2C

Elaine: Generally speaking, I'm reasonably confident, erm, in social situations, erm, due to the nature of the work that I do – I recruit people worldwide. Erm, so my personality will change depending on the people that I am talking with because, erm, I will need to be a little bit more professional in how I come across, erm, in that situation.

Anna: Er, so at work, maybe I'm more serious, whereas when I go to, like, a café with my friends, er, I'm a lot more relaxed.

Valeria: I can be quite direct at work, erm, and, I think with my friends, I can be quite compassionate.

Elijah: So, if I'm hanging out with friends, I might be more talkative. If I'm with my mother, er, maybe I'll listen a little more.

Gwen: Yeah, I'm … I'd say I'm confident in most situations, but then sometimes like everybody, you know, maybe your mood's not that great and, you know, you can maybe feel, I don't know, sometimes walk into a party and just think, 'Oh, I don't want to be here!'. So, yeah, I think it varies, but not necessarily the situation, more just how I'm feeling inside myself.

Roisin: Erm, I'm probably less confident when I meet new people, whilst when I'm with my friends, I'm a bit more confident, a bit more chatty, a bit more comfortable.

Collin: Erm, doesn't change.

UNIT 2

Opener: BBC Vlogs

1 Erm, social media has a lot of impact on my life. It is a great way to keep in touch with people in different countries that I know. Erm, it's also a little bit distracting sometimes and I sometimes spend more time on it than I would like to.

2 Erm, social media has, er, quite a big impact on my professional life – I'm a furniture painter so I have a Facebook page where I have a community of followers that either buy my furniture or I create tutorials for them, so they can learn about what it is I do.

3 Social media has a big impact on my life. I don't post a lot of photos, but I spend way too much time looking at other photos.

4 I completely love social media. I don't know what I would do without it. I don't know how I did without it before it was, er, invented. Um, I just like to be able to text my friends, message my friends, erm, swap photos, arrange things, buy things. Erm, I think it's just the best thing ever.

5 Social media doesn't have a very large impact on my life. Personally, I think social media is quite harmful and I also think it's something that you grow out of as you get a little bit older. So, maybe I'm now at an age where I don't really spend much time either investing content into it or investing time into it, learning about other people. So, I would say its impact gets smaller and smaller every day that I get older.

2D: BBC Entertainment
Exs 2A and 2B

Dr Black: So, this is one of the last paintings van Gogh ever painted. Those final months of his life were probably the most astonishing artistic outpouring in history. And especially astonishing because van Gogh did it with no hope of praise or reward. Each of these pictures now is worth tens of millions of pounds, yet in his lifetime, he was a commercial disaster. Sold only one painting, and that to the sister of a friend. We have here possibly the greatest artist of all time, but when he died, you could have sold his entire body of work and got about enough money to buy a sofa and a couple of chairs. If you follow me now. …

The Doctor: Now, he'll probably be in the local café - sort of orangey light, chairs and tables outside.

Amy: Like this?

The Doctor: That's the one.

Amy: Or indeed like that.

The Doctor: Yeah, exactly like that.

The Doctor: Hello, I'm the Doctor.

Vincent: I knew it!

The Doctor: Sorry?

Vincent: My brother's always sending doctors, but you won't be able to help.

The Doctor: No, not that kind of doctor. That's incredible, don't you think, Amy?

Amy: Absolutely. One of my favourites.

Vincent: One of my favourite whats? You've never seen my work before.

Amy: Ah, yes. One of my favourite paintings that I've ever seen, genuinely!

Vincent: Then you can't have seen many paintings, then. I know it's terrible. It's the best I could do.

Vincent: It's not much. I live on my own. But you should be OK for one night. ONE night. Sorry about all the clutter.

The Doctor: Some clutter.

Vincent: I've come to accept the only person who's going to love my paintings is me.

Amy: Wow. I mean, really. Wow.

Vincent: Yeah, I know it's a mess. I'll have a proper clear-out. I must, I really must. Coffee, anyone?

The Doctor: Not for me, actually. You know, you should be careful with these. They're, they're ... precious.

Vincent: Precious to me, not precious to anyone else.
Amy: They're precious to me.
Vincent: You're very kind. And kindness is most welcome.
The Doctor: OK, so let's talk about you, then. What are you interested in?
Vincent: Well, look around. Art. It seems to me there's so much more to the world than the average eye is allowed to see. I believe, if you look hard, there are more wonders in this universe than you could ever have dreamed of.
The Doctor: You don't have to tell me.
Vincent: I only wish I had something of real value to give you.
The Doctor: Oh, no, no. I could never accept such an extraordinary gift.
The Doctor: Are you thinking what I'm thinking?
Amy: I was thinking I may need some food or something before we leave.
The Doctor: Well, no, you're not thinking exactly what I'm thinking. Vincent! Got something I'd like to show you. Maybe just tidy yourself up a bit first.
The Doctor: Now, you know we've had quite a few chats about the possibility there might be more to life than normal people imagine?
Vincent: Yes.
The Doctor: Well, brace yourself, Vinny.
Vincent: Where are we?
The Doctor: Paris. 2010. And this is the mighty Musée D'Orsay, home to many of the greatest paintings in history.
Vincent: Oh, that's wonderful.
The Doctor: Er, ignore that. I've got something more important.
The Doctor: Dr Black – I just wondered, between you and me, in 100 words, where do you think van Gogh rates in the history of art?
Dr Black: Well, er, big question. But, to me, van Gogh is the finest painter of them all. Certainly, the most popular, great painter of all time, the most beloved. His command of colour, the most magnificent. To my mind, that strange, wild man who roamed the fields of Provence was not only the world's greatest artist, but also one of the greatest men who ever lived.
The Doctor: Vincent. Sorry. I'm sorry. Is it too much?
Vincent: No. They are tears of joy. Thank you, sir. Thank you.
Dr Black: You're welcome. You're welcome.
Vincent: Sorry about the beard.

UNIT 3

Opener: BBC Vlogs

1 I really love, er, theatre. You can't beat the atmosphere before the curtain goes up. And every night is different … special. Theatre is special.
2 I like going to musical performances, like classical concerts, er, and jazz performances. Jazz is especially exciting. Er, it's usually at a small club. The musicians play in their own style, in their own way, and I like how they interact with each other, er, and the other musicians, to bring the music to life.
3 I love going to live comedy performances because they really improve my mood and, er, they make you see the funny side of otherwise particularly volatile situations.
4 I love going to music festivals. I love seeing my favourite artists play live, I love exploring new bands that I've never heard of before and I always find that the food at music festivals is amazing – the different food stalls with lots of different cuisines from around the world, I absolutely love. And it is fun to camp with your friends.
5 One of my favourite things to watch live is sports, especially football. And if it's my team Tottenham, even better. I find being in the stadium so exhilarating and it's so full of energy just the atmosphere that's created by the crowd. Um, whether they're singing and cheering because they're excited about what's happening on the pitch or even when they're angry at something that's going on, there's just so much energy there that you can't recreate that when you're watching football on TV in your living room, for example.

3D: BBC Street Interviews
Exs 2A and 2B

Kaelan: I like jazz music – I'm a jazz musician myself. I like jazz because it allows me to express myself freely and improvise.
Roisin: Erm, I listen to mostly hip hop and rap. Erm, but I also enjoy more singing songs, stuff that's a little bit more relaxed. I'd say, I'm pretty general.
Ryan: Oh, I like all sorts of music, but I'd say probably rock music is my favourite. Er, just because I play guitar, so I … I like, yeah. I like stuff with guitars and drums, things like that.
Aslan: Er, I like all music. I like film scores, I like hip hop, I like rock. Pretty much anything really.
Oby: Erm, I enjoy listening to rap music because of all the different aspects of it, like the lyrics and the beat behind it.
Leanne: Erm, I prefer, er, kind of, a soft rock. Erm, I quite like … I like singing along. Erm, so, something that's, er, yeah got a good tune to it as well.
Sophia: I listen to a … a wide range of music, but my main would be R&B, contemporary R&B, erm, just because it's very chilled and relaxing. Erm, and I also listen to rap when I'm working out at the gym, yeah.
Lucy: I quite enjoy hip hop music, 'cause I like the rhythms and I think it's quite good to dance to.

3D: BBC Street Interviews
Exs 2A and 2C

Kaelan: Very important because it's my career! So, yeah. It's, yeah, very important to me.
Roisin: Erm, I'd say very important. I don't listen to music every day, but I love going to concerts … I do listen to music on Spotify, like public platforms, but I don't play any instruments.
Ryan: Very important, I'd say. Erm, it's the … you know … always listening to music when I walk around – it's the soundtrack to my life, I suppose.
Aslan: Erm, I would say music is very important. Erm, there's certain bits of work where I do listen to music while I'm working and there's certain bits of work where I don't, where I can't, if it's very technical or if it's … if I'm trying to be very creative, then I can and do listen to music while I work.
Oby: Erm, music is very important to me. I don't play the piano anymore, but I used to.
Leanne: Erm, yeah, quite important. Erm, I … I have to say I don't like, erm, sort of, er, orchestra music so much, erm, but I do like, erm, sort of, background music, listening to, erm, relaxing things.
Sophia: Very important, I'd say. When I wake up, the first thing I do is put on my music, when I'm brushing my teeth, listening to music, on the tube listening to music. Even at … when I'm at work I listen to music to be honest, so yeah, it's very important.
Lucy: Music is really important to me because although I don't go to festivals, I do listen to it a lot at home and I play the piano as an instrument.

UNIT 4

Opener: BBC Vlogs

1 Um, the one thing I'd like to do to change, erm, or to improve my health, is to go out more often. Erm, to erm, do much more fitness outside – outdoors – because due to the nature of my job, I, erm, I mostly sit down. Erm, I'm in a sitting position, like, more than six or seven hours a day. So, I think I should go out more with my bike and, you know, go on a long-distance bicycle ride.
2 One thing I could do to improve my health would be to get more sleep each night. To do that, I would switch my phone off before I go to bed and stop scrolling through social media.
3 Definitely my eating. Erm, I ordered three pizzas for myself a couple of days ago. So, yeah. Changes and improvements can be made. And will be made.
4 If there's one thing I would do to change my life, it would be to take more exercise and perhaps go to the gym, because I have a sailing boat, which I sail on my own, and I would be happier if it was easier to get in and out of the boat and to be able to control the sails for the wind and not capsize.

5 I try to be a healthy person, but one thing that I could change to improve my health is trying to do more exercise every day.
6 I try hard to be healthy – to eat the right things, to eat plenty of fruit and vegetables – and I try to exercise at least three times a week. But the one thing that I really need to do to improve my health is to drink more water.

4D: BBC Documentary
Exs 2A and 2B

Narrator: From the blackness of space our home is a blue planet. But now, satellite cameras capture a kaleidoscope of extraordinary colour.
Mr Dai and his son are nomads. They've travelled across China just in time for the bloom. These flowers will eventually produce almost 20 percent of all the world's rapeseed oil. But they're not here for the oil. They've come to make honey.

CAPTION: Beekeeping is the most important part of our income. Our livelihood depends on it.

Narrator: But the weather is not on their side. The view from space is almost completely white. Thick cloud is blocking the sun. It's just too cold for the bees to fly.

CAPTION: It's still too cold. They don't want to come out.

CAPTION: If it stays like this for a few more days, there is no way we will make any honey.

Narrator: With a chill in the air, these bees aren't going anywhere. And time is running out.
In two weeks, the rapeseed farmers will spray pesticides over the fields, making it a dangerous place for the bees. They must move on before the spraying starts. All they can do is sit and wait for the sun.
After three grey days, the clouds finally part and one and a half million bees head out to work. They must visit two million flowers to make just one jar of honey. The bees drink the sugary nectar from the flowers they visit and transfer it to the hive where it becomes honey. Food for the long winter months.
But the bees are more than just honey makers. They are one of the world's most important crop pollinators, helping plants produce fruits, seeds and vegetables. But now pesticides are contributing to a worldwide decline in the number of honeybees, and their future is under threat.
Mr Dai's window of opportunity is short, but the bees have been hard at work. He has plenty of honey. And not a moment too soon. The fields will be sprayed in two days. It's time to move on.

IRREGULAR VERB TABLE

Verb	Past simple	Past participle
admit	admitted	admitted
be	was	been
become	became	become
begin	began	begun
bite	bit	bitten
blow	blew	blown
break	broke	broken
bring	brought	brought
build	built	built
burn	burnt/burned	burnt/burned
buy	bought	bought
catch	caught	caught
choose	chose	chosen
come	came	come
cost	cost	cost
cut	cut	cut
deny	denied	denied
do	did	done
draw	drew	drawn
drink	drank	drunk
drive	drove	driven
earn	earned/earnt	earned/earnt
eat	ate	eaten
fall	fell	fallen
feed	fed	fed
feel	felt	felt
find	found	found
forget	forgot	forgotten
freeze	froze	frozen
get	got	got
give	gave	given
go	went	gone
grow	grew	grown
have	had	had
hear	heard	heard
hit	hit	hit
hold	held	held
hurt	hurt	hurt
keep	kept	kept

Verb	Past simple	Past participle
know	knew	known
lead	led	led
learn	learned/learnt	learned/learnt
leave	left	left
let	let	let
lie	lay	lain
lose	lost	lost
make	made	made
mean	meant	meant
meet	met	met
pay	paid	paid
put	put	put
read	read	read
ride	rode	ridden
run	ran	run
say	said	said
see	saw	seen
sell	sold	sold
send	sent	sent
show	showed	shown
shut	shut	shut
sing	sang	sung
sit	sat	sat
sleep	slept	slept
speak	spoke	spoken
spend	spent	spent
spill	spilled/spilt	spilled/spilt
stand	stood	stood
swim	swam	swum
take	took	taken
teach	taught	taught
tell	told	told
think	thought	thought
throw	threw	thrown
understand	understood	understood
wake	woke	woken
wear	wore	worn
win	won	won
write	wrote	written

Pearson Education Limited
KAO Two
KAO Park
Hockham Way
Harlow, Essex
CM17 9SR
England
and Associated Companies throughout the world.

pearson.com/languages

First published 2023

ISBN: 978-1-292-44067-5

Set in BBC Reith Sans

Printed and bound by Neografia, Slovakia

Acknowledgements
Written by Antonia Clare and JJ Wilson
The publishers and authors would like to thank the following people for their feedback and comments during the development of the material: Charlotte Buckmaster, Charlotte Rowe, Billie Jago, Dorota Walesiak.

Text Credits:
Articles on page 26 adapted from The last of the sea nomads, Johnny Langenheim, 18 Sep 2010, Guardian News and Media Limited and The British grandmother running to Kathmandu, Financial Times, 6 April 2020 (Usborne, S), copyright The Financial Times Limited 2020; Article on page 57 adapted from First day horror stories: 'I crashed into a colleague's parked car', BBC, Alex Taylor, 10 November 2020; Article on page 69 adapted from How did our ancestors avoid distractions?, BBC, research by Miriam Quick

Image Credits:
Alamy Stock Photo: BLM Photo 33; **BBC Studios:** 7, 16, 17, 19, 28, 31, 40, 41, 43, 52, 55, 60, 65, 67, 76, 79, 88, 89, 91, 100, 101; **Brit Worgan:** 81; **Eldon Lindsay / Cornell Athletics:** 82; **Future Publishing:** Susannah Ireland 100, **Getty Images:** 27, 10'000 Hours 55, 10, 68, 74, 92, 146, Adam Hester 7, akinbostanci 6, Alejandra de la Fuente 60, AleksandarNakic 62, 63, Alexander Spatari 84, Anders Andersson 14, Anna Efetova 23, Apisak Kanjanapusit 52, 53, Carol Yepes 143, CasarsaGuru 83, Claudia Burlotti 152, CliqueImages 139, cunfek 21, d3sign 25, 95, Daniel Tsai 149, Daria Botieva / Eyeem 111, Dougal Waters 24, Drakula Images 11, electravk 68, FG Trade 152, FilippoBacci 152, Fine Art / Contributor 28, 29, Flashpop 11, fotog 125, Francesco Carta fotografo 71, Frans Lemmens 32, freedom_naruk 23, Geber86 18, Georgy Dorofeev / EyeEm 11, gremlin 59, Hinterhaus Productions 11, 45, 118, hobo_018 93, Ian Ross Pettigrew 11, Jamie Garbutt 47, Jessica Peterson 12, 13, JGalione 68, JohnnyGreig 150, Jonathan Knowles 67, Jose Luis Pelaez Inc 138, Julia Gunther 38, Jun Sato / Contributor 142, Justin Lambert 11, 84, Klaus Vedfelt 97, 148, KOLOstock 114, Kyle Monk 80, Laura Olivas 45, lechatnoir 35, Leland Bobbe 21, Lidia Utkin 84, Lilly Roadstones 152, Luis Alvarez 133, LumiNola 57, mapodile 155, Mark Metcalfe / Stringer 144, Marko Geber 11, martin-dm 22, 156, Maskot 11, Michal Kostka / EyeEm 103, Mireya Acierto 152, MoMo Productions 60, Morsa Images 84, 86, 136, MStudioImages 68, Nick David 153, OsakaWayne Studios 60, Prasit photo 98, Rafa Cortés Pascual / EyeEm 149, recep-bg 72, Reza Estakhrian 31, RichLegg 120, Rifka Hayati 46, RyanJLane 35, sarayut Thaneerat 10, skynesher 152, SolStock 34, 60, South_agency 79, SrdjanPav 135, Tara Moore 72, 152, Thomas Barwick 91, 23, 73, 84, Tim Robberts 152, Tom Werner 58, 72, 152, TommL 51, Vasily Pindyurin 21, View Pictures / Contributor 141, VioletaStoimenova 50, vorDa 56, Wachirawit Iemlerkchai 116, We Are 48, Westend61 19, 43, 8, 20, 23, 35, 45, 49, 60, 72, 84, 84, 149, 154, Yerbol Mukhanbetzhanov / EyeEm 44; **NASA:** 27; **Panos Pictures:** James Morgan 26; **Shutterstock:** ANTSTUDIO 70, Kurt Strumpf/AP 76, 77, Supamotion 35

Cover Images: *Front:* **Alamy Stock Photo:** Westend61 GmbH; **Getty Images:** adamkaz, Hinterhaus Productions, We Are

Illustrated by
Stephen Collins (Central Illustration Agency) 111, 129; Ben Hasler (NB Illustration) 96; Sam Kalda (Folio) 87; Rupert Van Wyk (Beehive Illustration) 69; Mark Willey (Designers Educational) 85

MIX
Paper from responsible sources
FSC™ C128612
www.fsc.org

BBC

Speak out

3RD EDITION

B2

Split 1

Units 1–4

Workbook

Pearson Education Limited
KAO Two
KAO Park
Hockham Way
Harlow, Essex
CM17 9SR
England
and Associated Companies throughout the world.

pearson.com/languages

First published 2023

ISBN: 978-1-292-44067-5

Set in BBC Reith Sans

Printed and bound by Neografia, Slovakia

Acknowledgements
Written by Helen Chilton

Image Credit(s):
Getty Images: 10'000 Hours/DigitalVision 32, BeyondImages/E+ 14, CSA Images/Vetta 27, Drazen/E+ 37, Eduardo Fonseca Arraes/Moment 12, FatCamera/E+ 49, fotografixx/iStock 13, Jim Craigmyle/Stone 54-55, Jonathan Knowles/Stone 9, Karen Schuld/Tetra images 25, katleho Seisa/E+ 11, Klaus Vedfelt/DigitalVision 18, MoMo Productions/DigitalVision 51, Monty Rakusen/Image Source 47, Peter Muller/Image Source 35, Richard Bailey/Corbis 33, skynesher/E+ 41, suteishi/E+ 23, Tara Moore/DigitalVision 33, Tim Robberts/DigitalVision 33, timandtim/Digital Vision 7, Westend61 33

Cover Images: Front: **Alamy Stock Photo:** Westend61 GmbH; **Getty Images:** adamkaz, Hinterhaus Productions, We Are

Illustrated by: Rupert Van Wyk (Beehive Illustration): 21

FSC
www.fsc.org
MIX
Paper from responsible sources
FSC™ C128612

CONTENTS

Lesson 1A

GRAMMAR | present perfect simple and continuous
VOCABULARY | personality adjectives; suffixes
PRONUNCIATION | weak forms of *have* and *been*

VOCABULARY

personality adjectives

1 A Choose the correct word to complete the sentences.

1 He's so ....! He's planning to open two new restaurants by the end of the year.
 a adventurous b ambitious c hopeful

2 Hilda is the most .... person I know. She seems to disagree with everything I say.
 a argumentative b rebellious c stubborn

3 People often go through a .... stage of life, where they want to break rules.
 a rebellious b curious c stubborn

4 I think I'm pretty .... I've climbed a mountain, trekked through the Amazon – that kind of thing.
 a outgoing b stubborn c adventurous

5 My sister's very .... Once she's made her mind up, she won't change it.
 a outgoing b stubborn c argumentative

6 My twin brother and I are completely different. I'm quite shy, whereas he's very ....
 a rebellious b ambitious c outgoing

B Complete the conversation with the adjectives in the box.

adventurous ambitious argumentative cheerful curious outgoing rebellious stubborn

A: Do you get on well with your brother and sister?

B: Usually, but my brother can be a bit [1] .... Whatever my opinion is, he'll almost always tell me I'm wrong. He's quite [2] ...., too. He never follows rules and sometimes gets in trouble at school.

A: Oh, dear! Your sister's always very [3] .... She seems to enjoy life.

B: Yeah, she does. She's quite [4] .... and has got loads of friends. I'm quieter than her. Anyway, what about you and your brother?

A: We get on fine. He's a lot older than me, so he's working now. He's quite [5] .... Like, he's already going for a promotion.

B: He sounds quite [6] ...., as well. Doesn't he go mountain climbing?

A: Yeah, he's very [7] .... about the world – wants to know everything and try everything.

B: I wish my brother was more like yours!

A: Oh, he isn't perfect. He can be very [8] .... and won't change his mind for anything!

suffixes

2 Complete the sentences with the adjective form of the words in brackets.

1 Our new teacher's really .... (help) – she sent a list of useful websites to the group.

2 I'm not .... (art) at all. I can't even draw simple objects.

3 Wow! That musician was so .... (talent)! Imagine being able to play the piano like that.

4 I'm quite an .... (emotion) person – I always cry at the end of films.

5 I think you need to be more .... (realist). Can you really be a professional footballer?

6 Jade isn't very .... (like). She says unpleasant things about people behind their backs.

7 Rupert is an .... (experience) lawyer with over 30 years in the industry.

GRAMMAR

present perfect simple and continuous

3 A Choose the correct word or phrase to complete the sentences.

1 I**'ve called** / **been calling** / **'m calling** the doctor's all morning, but no one's answering.

2 Have you **had** / **having** / **been having** your hair cut? It's looks great!

3 Felix has **been** / **had** / **been having** lessons recently and is making great progress so far.

4 How many times have you **visited** / **been visiting** / **been** Canada?

5 I've **studied** / **study** / **been studying** Japanese for just over a year now.

6 She's **raised** / **been raising** / **raising** €1,000 for charity.

B Complete the blog post using the correct form of the verbs in brackets.

Something I'm working on

Ellie Behr | Fri 23 Oct | 10.27 GMT

Regular followers of my blog will know that, I [1] .... always .... (be) a shy, quiet person who hates conflict and walks away from any kind of argument. Recently, though, I [2] .... (work) on being more assertive, by which I mean being stronger and more confident. I [3] .... (have) three sessions with a life coach, who [4] .... (help) me to finally understand that being assertive is not the same as being aggressive, and that people have more respect for you when you stand up for yourself. Recently, I [5] .... (practise) the things we've talked about and it [6] .... (be) a real eye-opener!

C **Use the prompts to write present perfect simple or present perfect continuous sentences.**

1 I / see / that new Wes Anderson film / five times now.
2 You / work / on that report / all morning!
3 Have / you go / anywhere interesting recently?
4 Ben / never try / horse-riding / because he / scared of horses!
5 He / take / a year off / go travelling.
6 I / look / for you / the last half an hour!

PRONUNCIATION

4A **1.01 | weak forms of *have* and *been* | Listen and choose the correct words to complete the sentences.**

1 **He's never been** / **She's never been** to Poland.
2 How long **have you been** / **have they been** studying in Manchester?
3 What's **he been** / **she been** up to this week?
4 **They've been** / **I've been** trying to book flights to Mexico all morning.
5 **She's been** / **He's been** waiting here for the last four hours.

B **1.01 | Listen again and repeat.**

LISTENING

5A **1.02 | Listen to an interview about identity. Put the topics in the order they are discussed.**

a Other factors that influence our identity
b How to find yourself
c The elements that form our identity
d How we develop our sense of self
e The importance of self-identity

B **1.02 | Listen to the interview again. Complete the sentences with no more than three words from the recording.**

1 Identity is a combination of your ……, your likes and dislikes, your moral code and what motivates you.
2 Without a clear sense of self, it can be difficult to …… .
3 Parents provide …… for how their children should behave.
4 Your identity isn't …… – it develops over the course of your life.
5 Our relationships and experiences …… our sense of self.

C **1.03 | Listen to the speaker's final advice again and write what you hear. You will hear the sentence only once.**

……

……

WRITING

a blog post

6A **Read the blog post. How has the writer changed? Complete the summary with words from the text.**

I'm not the person I once was

When I was a young kid, I was pretty adventurous. I was always out in the woods near home, climbing trees and swimming in the river. As a teenager, I was a bit of a risk-taker and didn't think twice about the stuff I did: snowboarding, sky-diving, you name it! I think I've changed considerably since then. These days I much prefer indoor activities and I've been a music teacher for the last four years. I've become a lot calmer as a result! I'm still curious about the world, but I haven't done anything 'extreme' for a long time!

I'm definitely less [1] …… and no longer a [2] …… . Nowadays, [3] …… are more my thing, and my role as a [4] …… has calmed me down. That doesn't mean I'm not [5] …… about what's going on around me. I just choose not to take part in [6] …… sports like snowboarding and sky-diving anymore!

B **Read the comments. Underline examples of the present perfect simple and continuous.**

Astrid94
14.07 | 2 Nov

I would say that I've actually changed very little. I've always been very close to my family and we agree on most things. You'll often find us all on the golf course, too – recently I've taken up the sport so I can join my parents and brothers for a game!

JosephER
14.22 | 2 Nov

I've changed loads! As a young child I was quiet like my mum, who brought me up on her own, but in my teenage years I was rebellious and hated school with a passion. I think I've outgrown that, and I've been channelling my energy into being ambitious instead.

I_Kara
14:39 | 2 Nov

I've always had two sides to my personality. In my work as a gym instructor, I'm patient and cheerful, but in my personal life, I'm a total stress-head, though I've been working on that! I still love nothing more than getting together with friends and debating all the issues important to us.

C **Make notes about how these things have changed as you have got older. Then write a blog post. Write 100–140 words.**

- your personality
- your interests
- your values

Lesson 1B

GRAMMAR | infinitive and *-ing* forms
VOCABULARY | collocations about memory; idioms: memory
PRONUNCIATION | chunking: two-part collocations

VOCABULARY

collocations about memory

1 **Choose the correct word or phrase to complete the sentences.**

1 I **remember every detail** / **learn things by heart** / **brought back memories** of that day – the sunlight on my pillow, the smell of my mother's cooking downstairs …
2 My **short-term** / **long-term** / **perfect recall** memory is terrible. I can't even remember what I had for breakfast!
3 You need to learn your lines by **recall** / **memory** / **heart** when you're acting on stage.
4 Oh, that programme **remembered every detail** / **brought back memories** / **had a good memory** for me. I used to work in the building that was featured in it.
5 What are your earliest **long-term** / **short-term** / **childhood** memories?
6 I haven't **brought** / **got** / **learned** a good memory – I never remember anything!

idioms: memory

2A **Match the idioms (1–6) with the sentences which have a similar meaning (a–f).**

1 Things go in one ear and out the other.
2 It slipped my mind.
3 Can you refresh my memory?
4 It's on the tip of my tongue.
5 That rings a bell.
6 My memory's playing tricks on me.

a It sounds familiar.
b I forgot.
c I quickly forget.
d I've remembered that incorrectly.
e I can't quite remember it!
f Please remind me.

B **Complete the sentences with the correct form of the idioms in the box.**

in one ear and out the other memory is playing tricks on me on the tip of my tongue refresh my memory rings a bell slip my mind

1 Now, what was it? No, don't tell me – it's ……………… .
2 That name definitely ……………… . Did she used to work here?
3 I thought I'd sent that already. I guess my ……………… .
4 Now, ……………… – what time are we starting tomorrow again?
5 You never listen! Honestly, it all goes ……………… .
6 I forgot the milk! Sorry, it totally ……………… .

PRONUNCIATION

3A **1.04 | chunking: two-part collocations | Listen and complete the sentences.**

1 My ……………… is better than my ……………… .
2 I've got ……………… when it comes to phone numbers!
3 This song brings back a lot of ……………… .

B **1.04 | Listen again and repeat.**

GRAMMAR

infinitive and *-ing* forms

4A **Choose the correct words to complete the sentences.**

1 I think the plan is **to meet** / **meeting** Max outside the venue.
2 Annoyingly, he forgot **to set** / **setting** a timer and burnt the dinner.
3 I remember **to get up** / **getting up** early and watching TV.
4 No, he stopped **to go** / **going** to Spanish classes last month.
5 Mum rang – she wants **to have** / **having** dinner with you tonight.
6 Remember **to lock** / **locking** the door when you leave.

B **Complete the anecdote with the correct form of the verbs in brackets.**

As a child, my primary goal was [1] ……………… (climb) the really big mountain I could see from my bedroom window. I did some exercise every day – which involved running up and down the stairs – [2] ……………… (improve) my stamina, so I could make the climb.

Then, one morning, I remember [3] ……………… (set off) with some sandwiches in my schoolbag, announcing to my dad I'd be back in time for dinner after my day's climbing. I walked and walked, and eventually turned back so as [4] ……………… (make sure) I was home before dark. I was tired and looking forward to [5] ……………… (have) a big bowl of soup.

In reality, I'd only been gone an hour, with my dad trailing me from a distance. The whole family still laugh about my adventure – but I'm going to try [6] ……………… (reach) the top of that mountain one day!

READING

5 A Skim the article and tick the topics that are mentioned.

1 What happens in the brain
2 How we adapt stories to our audience
3 How and why we adapt stories
4 Why we forget things
5 What the research tells us
6 How people experience things differently

B Scan the article again and underline the following information.

1 Why our memories are useful to us
2 Why we make minor changes every time we tell a story
3 What we call memories that are entirely invented
4 The name for the process of changing our memory according to who we're talking to
5 What we do when we can't remember something

C Read the article again choose the correct option (a–c).

1 What does the writer say in the second paragraph?
  a We often change stories that we think make us look bad.
  b We may or may not be aware that we are adapting our stories.
  c We usually know how someone will react to a story.
2 What point does the writer make in the fourth paragraph?
  a Despite changes, memories are likely to be relatively accurate.
  b We invent more 'facts' each time we recall a memory.
  c A memory becomes what we last described it to be.
3 What would make the best alternative title for the article?
  a How our memories change as we get older
  b Your memory may not be as good as you think it is
  c Why it is sometimes difficult to remember things

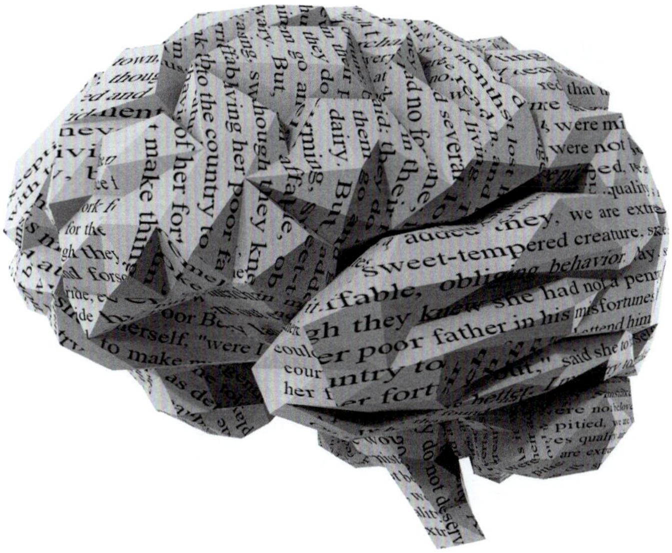

Why you can't trust your own memory

Ayodele Odetoyinbo | Mon 27 Jun

Have you got a good memory? If you answered 'yes', then you might want to think again. Research has shown that our memories may not be as reliable as we think. Since our memories help us recall past events, learn from our mistakes and play a part in creating our identities, this may not be the best news!

When we describe something that has happened to us, we often make tiny adjustments each time we tell it, without even realising we're doing it. The reason for this could be because we wish that what we are saying is true, or we want our listener to think in a particular way about what we're telling them. For example, we might want to make them laugh or feel sorry for us – in which case, we may make changes consciously. When we recall the story again in the future, it is likely to be rather different to what we really experienced.

And think about those times when you were with friends and you experienced something amazing, exciting or terrible together. You can be almost certain that their memory of the occasion isn't quite the same as yours, even though you experienced exactly the same thing. Sometimes we even create 'false memories' based on stories we know about ourselves that we don't remember. But because we have heard them so many times, as we imagine them, we turn them into memories.

Also, when we talk about what we remember to different people, the way we tell the story may change – and when we do that, the memory changes, too. This is known as the 'audience-tuning' effect. The way you tell a story to someone becomes your memory of what happened, whether or not it is accurate. Our memories change over time depending on our reasons for re-telling them and how we re-tell them. Even as we go over a memory in our heads, we are likely to make small changes to it. And if we can't bring to mind some of the smaller details, we will fill in the gaps over time. What's more, we tend not to question our memories once they are made. So, whatever was our most recent version of the memory becomes the memory itself.

So, next time someone asks whether you're telling the truth and you think you are – you actually may not be!

Lesson 1C

HOW TO ... | express personal preferences
VOCABULARY | emotions and feelings
PRONUNCIATION | word stress: dependent prepositions

VOCABULARY

emotions and feelings

1 A Complete the sentences with *about*, *by*, *into*, *of* or *on*.

1 I'm really passionate .... travel – I love visiting new cities!
2 Melania sounds fed up .... everything today – let's go and cheer her up.
3 I'm terrified .... flying even though I know it's the safest form of transport.
4 Katya was thrilled .... the present you gave her for her birthday.
5 I'm not keen .... going to museums. I just find them really boring.
6 She's really .... Japanese culture. We're hoping to go to Tokyo next year.
7 I'm quite fond .... my auntie – she's such a great listener.
8 I think she's feeling a bit nervous .... the journey.

B Choose the correct phrases to complete the diary.

Day 1

I'm absolutely [1]**passionate about / fond of / fed up of** Spanish food, so I've booked myself onto a cooking course here in Madrid. I felt a little bit [2]**not keen on / thrilled by / nervous about** talking to people in Spanish because I haven't done it for ages, but it went well.

Day 2

We made paella today – a famous Spanish rice dish. I'm not that [3]**terrified of / nervous about / keen on** rice, but this dish is delicious! Tomorrow we're learning some knife skills. To be honest, I'm really [4]**terrified of / thrilled about / passionate about** cutting myself – I tend to have a lot of accidents and I'm getting a bit [5]**keen on / fond of / fed up of** being so clumsy.

Day 3

Phew! Everything went well and we learned about the various ingredients to use in tapas – small snacks. I'm [6]**fed up of / really into / not keen on** them because there's such a lot of variety and they're so tasty. Flying home tomorrow!

How to ...

express personal preferences

2 A 1.05 | Listen to a conversation between three friends. What are the speakers talking about? Do they reach a compromise?

B 1.05 | Listen again and complete the extracts with the missing words.

1 Backpacking's not really ....
2 Sorry, it's just that I'm .... camping.
3 .... go to lots of different places, but stay in some decent hotels?
4 Well, ... go to Thailand.
5 I'd be happy to do a bit of sunbathing, but I .... do it all day.
6 How about travelling around Europe instead? Does that ....?

PRONUNCIATION

3 A | word stress: dependent prepositions | Read the sentences. Underline the stress in the phrases in bold.

1 I'm quite **fond of** boat trips, actually. They're a great way to see the city.
2 The kids aren't **keen on** trying unusual foods.
3 Dan's **terrified of** driving in foreign countries and so am I!
4 I'm not **really into** visiting museums. I find a lot of them really boring.
5 I always feel **nervous about** getting lost when I'm in a new city.
6 Katie's quite **passionate about** culture and the arts.

B 1.06 | Now listen and check.

SPEAKING

4 A 1.07 | Complete the personal introduction with the phrases (a–f). Then listen and check.

Hi, I'm Jack. I'm [1].................... learning languages and [2].................... them for a few years now. [3].................... languages is that they give you lots of insight into new cultures. [4].................... people shouting loudly at waiters in English when they're in another country. [5].................... give it a go and get it wrong than not try at all. I'm [6].................... when it comes to learning languages and I can speak three pretty fluently now!

a quite ambitious
b I'd rather
c I've been studying
d The thing I love about
e passionate about
f I can't stand hearing

B Talk about your own hobbies and interests. Use the model in Ex 4A. Record your answer if you can.

Speak anywhere Go to the interactive speaking practice

Lesson 1D

GRAMMAR | *while, whereas* and *whilst*
LISTENING | personality traits

GRAMMAR

while, *whereas* and *whilst*

1 A Match the sentence beginnings (1–6) with the endings (a–f).

1 I've always been pretty shy,
2 Whilst I love musicals,
3 I cleaned the bathroom,
4 My brother loves going out,
5 I read an entire book
6 Whilst I'm usually pretty organised,

a my partner absolutely hates them!
b while I was waiting for my connecting flight.
c I was a bit of a mess that day.
d whereas my twin sister is very outgoing.
e whereas I'm more of a stay-at-home type.
f whilst my flatmate made dinner.

B Complete each sentence with one phrase from box A and one phrase from box B.

A

confident with friends · meeting new people · mowed the lawn · my parents · self-esteem · to see you

B

cleaned the house · intimidated by people at work · not very sociable · too much work to do · very confident · walking home

1 Whilst I'm ...., I feel ....
2 Whilst I'd love ...., I've got ....
3 I love ...., whereas Tom is ....
4 I called .... whilst I was ....
5 Whilst Tom ...., I ....
6 Dad lacks ...., whilst mum is ....

LISTENING

2 A 1.08 | Listen to the lecture and match the personality traits (1–5) with their definitions (a–e).

1 openness
2 conscientiousness
3 extroversion
4 agreeableness
5 neuroticism

a how helpful and understanding you are towards others
b how energetic, sociable and confident you are
c how responsible and reliable you are
d how likely you are to feel emotions like sadness and anxiety
e how happy you are to try new things and hear new ideas

B 1.08 | Listen again and complete each sentence with one or two words.

1 The lecturer says that a .... of the five main personality traits does not exist.
2 A conscientious person is ...., keeps their promises and admits their mistakes.
3 In an ...., a conscientious person will do all their work and turn up on time.
4 The lecturer says that it's unlikely an extrovert will be described as a .... person.
5 If you can understand the .... of other people, you are an agreeable person.
6 The lecturer says that neurotic people tend to have a higher number of ....

C 1.09 | Listen to the final sentence again and write what you hear. You will hear the sentence only once.

....

....

Lesson 2A

GRAMMAR | future probability
VOCABULARY | science and technology; word families
PRONUNCIATION | connected speech: future probability

VOCABULARY

science and technology

1 Complete the sentences with the words in the box.

analyse	findings	predicted	remotely
researchers	smart	tech industry	virtual reality

1 .... technology didn't exist when my parents were younger – they couldn't even access the internet on their phones!
2 Could you help me .... the results of the experiment? It'll take me ages to review them on my own.
3 In my role, I can work ...., so I don't need to go into the office every day.
4 As ...., the tests were highly successful.
5 Don't forget to include the .... of the study in your report.
6 .... have discovered that VR can provide many of the same benefits as real-world experiences.
7 My mum works in the .... as a software engineer. I hope to follow in her footsteps.
8 I've been practising golf using .... It's almost as good as being on the course.

word families

2 Choose the correct word to complete the sentences.

1 The outcome of the board meeting was entirely .... I knew I'd be forced to resign.
a remote **b** predictable **c** scientific
2 Have you completed the chemical .... yet? We'll need the results of it fairly soon.
a analysis **b** science **c** prediction
3 I'm planning to do some .... into VR in my postgraduate degree.
a analysis **b** predictions **c** research
4 If you want to be a data scientist, you need a highly .... mind.
a analytical **b** virtual **c** predictable
5 There is absolutely no .... evidence to back up your claim.
a remote **b** virtual **c** scientific
6 It's incredible that vehicles on the Moon can be controlled ...., don't you think?
a scientifically **b** remotely **c** virtually

GRAMMAR

future probability

3A Choose the correct word or phrase to complete the sentences.

1 Paulo says he **definitely won't** / **will definitely** / **won't definitely** stop trying to get into his first-choice university.
2 Lisa thinks it's **likely** / **certain** / **unlikely** she'll win the photography competition because there were so many great entries.
3 It's **won't** / **certain to** / **due to** rain the minute I get out of the car because I haven't brought my umbrella!
4 Hurry up! Bryony's train is **won't** / **likely to** / **due to** arrive any minute now.
5 Pasha says he **may not** / **definitely will** / **won't** be able to come tonight, but he'll do his best.
6 They said I **could** / **will** / **might** work remotely, but I didn't want to. I prefer going into the office.

B Complete the second sentence so that it means the same as the first, using the correct form of the words in brackets.

1 I don't think this experiment is going to work.
This experiment .... (likely) work.
2 Paula says she's about to start a new project involving VR.
Paula says she .... (going) start a new a project involving VR.
3 I don't think attending a gig virtually is something I'll ever do – I'd rather be there in person.
I don't think .... (ever) a gig virtually – I'd much rather be there in person.
4 I'm sure VR will be used in school classrooms eventually.
VR .... (certain) be used in school classrooms eventually.
5 You're handing in your report today, aren't you?
You're .... (due) your report today, aren't you?
6 I've thought about finding a job in the tech industry, but I haven't decided yet.
I .... (might) a job in the tech industry, but I haven't decided yet.

PRONUNCIATION

4A 2.01 | connected speech: future probability | Listen and complete the sentences.

1 VR is .... come down in price eventually.
2 Robert's .... start his new job on Monday.
3 Are you .... bring your headset with you?
4 You're .... catch anything out in the open.
5 Joseph .... study law at university.
6 VR is .... be in every household by 2030.

B 2.01 | Listen again and repeat.

READING

5 A Read the article and choose the main topic (a or b) of each paragraph (1–6).

Paragraph 1

a checking how experiments have gone

b making necessary changes to experiments

Paragraph 2

a ensuring things are being done properly

b carrying out daily tasks and duties

Paragraph 3

a discussing work with seniors

b writing up

Paragraph 4

a motivating other people

b teaching in a lab

Paragraph 5

a gaining inspiration for work

b chatting to others in the field

Paragraph 6

a offering students useful advice

b providing assistance to students

B Read the article again. Are the statements True (T) or False (F)?

1 Students are given regular support on the experiments they're doing.

2 Daniela refuses to do certain tasks outside of the lab.

3 Daniela does not especially enjoy one important part of her job.

4 Daniela says she is sometimes jealous of her students' ability to come up with ideas.

5 Daniela usually finds her conference talks go well.

6 Daniela thinks students should not work too hard in the lab.

A day in the life ...

research scientist Dr Daniela Brown

8.45 a.m.

[1]Based at a university, I supervise research students as they carry out experiments in the lab. It's my role to keep them – the students *and* the experiments! – on track, so the first thing I do when I arrive is to take a look at the results of any experiments that were running overnight. If an experiment didn't go as predicted, I might adapt it and get the students to repeat it in a slightly different way.

9.30–10.30 a.m.

[2]After this, I head to my office to go through my emails. That can take some time! I could do it remotely, but when I go home in the evening, I prefer to switch off. My job can be pretty stressful and I think it's important to have some down-time. While I'm in my office, I might also do a bit of reading. I'll maybe look through scientific journals or reference books. I also like to make sure I'm doing all the technical stuff for the experiments right, so I'll double-check on techniques and report back to the students if need be.

10.35 a.m.–1.00 p.m.

[3]Then I'll grab a coffee and settle down to analyse the results of previous days' experiments, and I might spend some time reporting on my findings, too. Getting papers published for others to read is an essential part of any research job, though I prefer practical work, so writing up can seem a bit like hard work! Thankfully, I have my own supervisor who I can approach with any questions or ask for help if I get stuck. It's important for any researcher to be able to discuss ideas with other experts.

13.45–4.30 p.m.

[4]After lunch, I'll spend some time in the lab with the students. They will have questions of their own, though I can't always answer them! In science, there's always trial and error, but I encourage them to find solutions and new ways of doing things. I don't pretend to know it all because I certainly don't. What always amazes me is that someone will always come up with a way of doing something that I've never even thought about.

9.00 a.m.–5.00 p.m. (on occasion)

[5]Occasionally, my day will involve attending a scientific conference instead. I haven't presented at one yet, but it's fascinating to see what else is going on out there in the scientific community, and it often informs what I might decide to work on next.

6.00 p.m.

[6]Before my working day ends, I will go back to the lab after a bit more time in my office to see how the research students have got on during the day and to answer their questions. I'll also help out with setting up any experiments that will run overnight. I'll remind students not to work too late and to get some much-needed rest before I log off and head out of the lab myself.

Lesson 2B

GRAMMAR | quantifiers
VOCABULARY | nature
PRONUNCIATION | connected speech: quantifiers

VOCABULARY

nature

1 A Match the sentence beginnings (1–6) with the endings (a–f) to make sentences.

1 Look at the way the sunlight is
2 I love deserted beaches like this –
3 The coastline stretches for 3,000 km
4 This entire area is
5 You can cycle down this track
6 I just sat on the river bank,

a from one end of the country to another.
b creating a beautiful pattern on the ground.
c known for its amazing scenery.
d watching the boats go by.
e all the way into the city.
f no one around for miles and miles.

B Complete the text with nature words or phrases.

WILLOWS WELL-BEING RETREAT

Location

Surrounded by [1] .... the only thing interrupting the peace at the Willows Well-being Retreat is the sound of birdsong and leaves moving on the trees. Or if you find yourself standing on the [2] ...., the gentle sound of water rushing by.

Facilities

- World-class dining
- Freshwater swimming pool
- Large [3] .... amongst the trees for yoga classes.

Activities

From forest bathing to hiking along ancient [4] .... through the landscape, there is a wide variety of well-being activities to choose from during your stay. For those who prefer being less active, simply sit and enjoy the beautiful [5] .... around you or bathe in the [6] .... shining warmly through the trees.

We look forward to welcoming you at Willows!

GRAMMAR

quantifiers

2 A Choose the correct word or phrase to complete the sentences.

1 I suspect there are **few / a little / a few** rooftop gardens in this area because the houses don't have flat roofs.
2 **No / None / Not any** wildflowers should be taken from these woods as it will have a negative effect on the ecosystem.
3 Only a **little / majority / minority** of residents are in favour of the plans to change the shared lawn into a vegetable plot.
4 There's **a minority / a little / little** countryside left in the region – it's almost all been built on.
5 I found **a handful of / a lack of / plenty of** new cycling routes round here – not many, but it might be interesting to see where they go.
6 I know **a little / a few / few** people who really enjoy gardening, but it's not really my thing.

B Read the sentences and correct the quantifiers in bold.

1 There are only a **little** of vegan restaurants in the city where I live.
2 **Few** of my friends live in the countryside, but most live in urban areas.
3 **No** time I go to the beach I come back feeling refreshed and relaxed. It's awesome.
4 There are **a handful of** parks in my town at all, so we have to play football at the sports centre.
5 There's a definite **little** of green spaces in my local neighbourhood.
6 I see very **a little** wildlife in my garden because I live in the city.
7 I spend a good **majority** of time walking in the forest near my house.
8 There are **no** open spaces in my city, but the ones we do have are pleasant.

PRONUNCIATION

3 A 2.02 | connected speech: quantifiers | Draw a line ‿ between any words that link together in the phrases in bold. Then listen and check.

1 There's **a lack of** attractive green spaces in my town.
2 Only **a handful of** people I know live in the countryside.
3 I spend **a good deal of** time outdoors.
4 **Several of the** beaches nearby are quite good.
5 Young people who like gardening **are in a minority**.

B 2.02 | Listen and repeat.

LISTENING

4 A 2.03 | Listen to the introduction to a radio programme. Choose the correct topic (a–c).

a The benefits of gardening as we get older
b How people of all ages enjoy gardening together
c Young people who enjoy gardening

B 2.04 | Listen to the next part of the radio programme and answer the questions.

Which speaker … ?

a says how pleased they are that they have learned about plants? ....
b became interested in gardening because of a local scheme? ....
c noticed a difference in their mood after doing some gardening? ....
d Is excited about something that is going to happen soon? ....
e became suddenly more aware of their surroundings? ....
f mentions one reason that gardening may have a particular benefit? ....

C 2.04 | Listen again. Are the statements True (T) or False (F)?

1. Speaker 1 started gardening because she wanted to test a theory.
2. Speaker 1 is confident about why she had benefitted from time in the garden.
3. Speaker 2 likes getting away from her living accommodation for a while.
4. Speaker 2 quickly came to realise that gardening could be interesting.
5. Speaker 2 understands that different tasks should be done at different times of year.
6. Speaker 3 did not use to know exactly why seaside landscapes were so beautiful.
7. Speaker 3 has little idea of what she is really doing with the plants on her balcony.

D 2.05 | Listen to the final speaker again and write what you hear. You will hear the sentence only once.

....

WRITING

a for-and-against essay

5 A Read the article and choose the main topic (a–c).

a The benefits of walking in the rain.
b Why people dislike walking in the rain.
c How to enjoy walking in the rain.

B Complete the article with *although*, *despite*, *however* or *while*.

Wet weather walking

Cary Stuart | Thurs 12 Aug | 10.12 GMT

[1] .... the fact that we're repeatedly told to spend more time in nature, few of us actually do. [2] .... it's true that it's often raining and cold in the UK, there are ways to making walking in wet weather more appealing.

You may have heard the expression, 'There's no such thing as bad weather – only bad clothing'. [3] .... it's easy enough to buy wet weather gear, it means making a bit more effort to get out of the house. [4] ...., if you take that extra step, you might just find it was worth it.

To avoid getting really wet on your walk, try taking a route through woodland, where the trees provide cover. [5] ...., remember that rain can still drip through the branches, so don't take off your raincoat just yet!

The best way to enjoy a walk in the rain is to set off with the right attitude. Then, [6] .... the fact you're getting a little wet, you can really start to appreciate nature in all weathers.

C Correct the mistakes in the sentences.

1. Despite I love living in the city, I also like getting out into the countryside from time to time.
2. My apartment has got a fantastic view. Although, I'm starting to find it a little small.
3. Despite many people I know prefer renting, I've decided to save up and buy a house.
4. However there can be a great sense of community in villages, everyone knows your business, too!
5. Although the fact that public transport is so good in the city, many people still insist on driving.
6. I think there are very few downsides to living in the country. Despite, I'll admit it can be boring at times.

D You are going to write a for-and-against essay about whether spending time indoors or outdoors is better for our well-being. Make notes in each column.

for	against

E Write your essay using your notes to help you. Write 100–140 words.

Lesson 2C

HOW TO ... | speculate
VOCABULARY | lifestyle adjectives
PRONUNCIATION | stress to show certainty

VOCABULARY

lifestyle adjectives

1 Choose the correct word to complete the magazine article.

An interview with ...

a storm chaser

In this week's 'Interview with a ...', Zen Magazine talked to Micky Nguyen, who has the fascinating-sounding job of storm chaser.

Zen Magazine (ZM): Being a storm chaser sounds like a pretty [1]**harsh / unique** job! I've never even heard of it.

Micky Nguyen (MN): You're right! The work is far from [2]**ordinary / modest**, and I never expected to do this for a living. More and more people are starting to do it, though.

ZM: So, tell us what it involves. Following storms around ... ?

MN: Yeah, I have to get up close to storms so that I can place sensors to record weather data. The conditions can be [3]**rewarding / harsh**, particularly in winter when most storms occur.

ZM: Why is there a need for what you do?

MN: It helps weather forecasters be able to give better storm warnings. It's [4]**tedious / rewarding** in that way because I know I'm helping people.

ZM: You drive all over the country – isn't that [5]**unique / exhausting**?

MN: I do get tired, yes. And there are risks. I could get struck by lightning! I never have, though. That sense of danger is exciting but I'm very careful.

ZM: Well, it certainly doesn't sound boring!

MN: Never! I used to work in an office and the work was pretty [6]**tedious / rewarding**. The days would stretch on forever. The salary was better – I'm on quite [7]**unique / modest** pay now in comparison, but I wouldn't change a thing!

How to ...

speculate

2A 2.06 | **Listen to three conversations between friends. What do they speculate about?**

B 2.06 | **Match the sentence beginnings (1–8) with the endings (a–h). Then listen again and check.**

1 I suppose it depends
2 I'd have thought it
3 I reckon you could
4 I bet we'll settle in
5 I know for a fact that
6 There's no way I'll
7 I doubt there'll be
8 I'd imagine the

a easily get cut off though.
b forget home so easily!
c on how remote it is.
d farmers will stay ...
e in no time!
f anyone here in 100 years' time!
g we're going to meet ...
h wouldn't feel so small.

PRONUNCIATION

3 2.07 | **stress to show certainty** | **Listen and underline the stressed word in each sentence.**

1 There's no way I'd ever consider travelling solo round the world.
2 I know for a fact that I'd feel like I was in prison on a tiny boat.
3 He's obviously not happy where he is at the moment.
4 You're clearly not someone who wants a conventional lifestyle.
5 Tom's bound to live a life of adventure – he can't keep still!

SPEAKING

4A 2.08 | **Complete the conversation with one word in each gap. Then listen and check.**

Oli: I'd [1]........ Kwame's feeling nervous about the play tomorrow.
Cara: It's the first night, right? I get the [2]........ he's feeling pretty confident, actually.
Oli: Oh, yeah?
Cara: Yes – I know for a [3]........ that he's learned his lines off by heart.
Oli: Well, I'd guess you have to, really. There's no [4]........ I could be an actor.
Cara: Why not? I'm 100% [5]........ that you'd be brilliant at it!
Oli: No, I'd be [6]........ to get stage fright!

B 2.09 | **You are Cara in the conversation in Ex 4A. Listen and speak after the beep. Record the conversation if you can.**

C **Listen to your recording and compare it to Ex 4A.**

Speak anywhere Go to the interactive speaking practice

Lesson 2D

VOCABULARY | extreme adjectives
READING | time travel

VOCABULARY

extreme adjectives

1 **Choose the correct word to complete the sentences.**

1 Paris during the 1920s was home to the **astonishing** / **incredible** / **finest** writers and artists of the age.
2 Have you ever seen a van Gogh painting in real life? They're **magnificent** / **mighty** / **precious**.
3 The **finest** / **mighty** / **precious** Amazon River winds its way through the rainforest.
4 The museum contains valuable pieces of jewellery which contain **precious** / **finest** / **mighty** stones.
5 Only the **magnificent** / **incredible** / **finest** coffee beans are used in this unique blend.
6 I can't believe how fast you can run – it's **astonishing** / **mighty** / **precious**!

READING

2A **Skim the article quickly and answer the questions.**

Do scientists think it is possible to:
1 travel forwards in time?
2 travel backwards in time?

B **Complete the sentences with words from the article. Write between one and three words.**

1 The writer says that we do not find our own kind of time travel ....
2 The writer suggests that un-doing .... would be a good reason to travel back in time.
3 The writer refers to a theory known as ...., which involves complex mathematics.
4 If we lived on the ISS for a long time, we wouldn't need to apply ....
5 Einstein's .... tell us that backwards time travel is theoretically possible.
6 Unfortunately, the .... make travelling back in time impossible in reality.
7 Scientists are aware of ...., although it is impossible to see it.
8 Tunnels, known as ...., could allow us to travel enormous distances.

C **Read the article again. What would make a good concluding sentence?**

a It looks as though time travel to the future is more likely than to the past!
b For the moment, maths can only suggest that time travel is possible – but watch this 'space'!
c You never know, time travel could be a reality in the *very* near future!

Is time travel actually possible?

Sofia Valdez | 20th Oct | 12.02 GMT

You may have seen *Doctor Who, Back to the Future* or read *The Time Traveller's Wife*, but can you imagine yourself jumping into the future or back into the past? Is it even a possibility? Here's what the scientists say.

We all travel through time, second by second, minute by minute, hour by hour. But there doesn't seem to be anything incredible about that (unless you stop and think about it) because it's our norm, and, much as we might like to go backwards in time, perhaps to correct our mistakes or experience something fantastic again, we can only go forwards. Scientists say we can travel faster if we want to. But explaining *that* involves Einstein and theories and physics and maths, and something known as 'space-time'. (It's all a bit complicated.)

Astronauts are the nearest we have to *actual* time travellers. They can be in space for several weeks or months. When they're on the International Space Station (ISS), they're moving faster than the rest of us back on Earth. This actually creates a situation where they're going slower in time than we are on Earth. (It's true, trust us.) If they were there for years, they'd age better than the rest of us. So, perhaps space travel is better than face creams and anti-aging diets!

But can we go *back* in time? Unfortunately, Earth's physics simply don't allow it. But if we return to Einstein for a minute, we know that some of his mathematical calculations do indeed suggest travelling back in time is possible. The problem is that although Einstein might have *theoretically* proven we can go back in time, in fact, all the other laws of physics really do make it impossible.

This doesn't stop scientists from trying, though! We know that dark matter exists (parts of the universe that we can't see because they don't give off energy or light – as far as we know). And in that dark matter, there *might* be 'wormholes' (theoretical tunnels through space and time). If there are, we could travel from one area of space to another – which could be billions of kilometres away *and* in a different place in time.

GRAMMAR

1 Choose the correct words to complete the sentences.

1 How long have you **learned** / **been learning** Japanese?
2 I've **emailed** / **been emailing** her three times today.
3 How many times have you **been** / **been going** to India?
4 Have you **had** / **been having** your hair cut? It's looks great!
5 I'm so tired because I've **worked** / **been working** a lot today, and I still haven't finished.

2 Complete the email with the correct form of the verbs in brackets.

Hey Alex!

How's life? Things are pretty much the same here, although I had a pretty terrible day yesterday! I tried [1] .... (repair) the washing machine myself – bad idea! It flooded the kitchen. I wanted [2] .... (save) money by doing it myself but in the end, it cost me a fortune. Because I was messing about so long with that, I forgot [3] .... (go) to my dentist's appointment for the third time, so they've taken me off their system. Then I stopped [4] .... (get) some shopping on my way back from the gym – I got to the till and realised I didn't have my bank card with me. It was a nightmare!

What else? Oh, I know. Do you remember [5] .... (go) to that festival where we met Andi and Niamh? I bumped into them the other week. I was in the park and they stopped [6] .... (say) hello. They asked how you were.

The only other thing to report is that I'm thinking of looking for a new job. My idea is [7] .... (retrain) as a physiotherapist. I just want [8] .... (do) something more worthwhile with my life.

Anyway, I'm looking forward to [9] .... (see) you in September for our holiday!

Speak again soon,

Chris

3 Use the prompts to write sentences using *while*, *whilst* or *whereas*.

1 enjoy writing stories ✓
a brilliant imagination ✗
2 actually quite shy ✓
love performing on stage ✓
3 can organise other people ✓
organise myself ✗
4 happy to listen to people's problems ✓
like giving advice ✗
5 enjoy playing football ✗ (never)
enjoy watching it ✓ (always)

4 Complete the article with the correct future form of the words in brackets.

What next?

If you're due [1] .... (leave) university soon and feel a little overwhelmed about what's [2] .... (happen), don't worry! With a little planning, it [3] .... (might not be) quite as scary as it sounds.

If you know you definitely [4] .... (not enjoy) a graduate job in a big firm, there are other options. You [5] .... (be able) to apply for a postgraduate course as soon as you graduate, and you [6] .... (also be) in a good place to start your own business. You certainly [7] .... (not need) a ton of money if you're offering a service such as web design or social media influencing. But you may [8] .... (able) to apply for a bank loan if you want to start, say, an online shop.

Another possibility is to take a gap year to consider your future. While you're travelling, you're likely [9] .... (meet) new people and discover more about the world, which [10] .... (give) you new ideas about your future.

5 Choose the correct word or phrase to complete the sentences.

1 Only **a few** / **a little** / **a lack of** cheese on my spaghetti, please!
2 The **minority of** / **lack of** / **majority of** affordable housing in this country is a real issue.
3 There **are some** / **aren't any** / **are little** places left for the Escape Room event, I'm afraid.
4 The **majority** / **minority** / **plenty** of people who live here have family in the area.
5 **Very few** / **Plenty of** / **Quite a few** people know the secret ingredient – just me and my father.

VOCABULARY

6 Match the personality adjectives in the box with the descriptions (1–5).

adventurous	argumentative	
curious	rebellious	stubborn

1 He was an awful teenager. He refused to do what he was told and caused trouble instead.
2 It doesn't matter what we're talking about, my brother always seems to disagree.
3 My daughter just loves finding out new things. She's always asking questions.
4 She's already climbed Mount Everest. Apparently, she's now planning to trek through the Amazon!
5 It doesn't matter what you tell him – he won't change his mind.

7 Complete the sentences with the adjective form of the words in brackets.

1 Sofia's quite an .... (experience) skater now and is entering her first major championship.
2 I'm pretty .... (optimist) about the future of the planet – we're making great progress.
3 Tonya isn't a .... (rely) employee and often turns up late or not at all.
4 I'm feeling quite .... (emotion) after seeing my daughter graduate.
5 I've never been very .... (practice). I can't even change a lightbulb!

8 Complete the text with the words in the box.

brought	by heart	childhood	detail	memory	recall	short-term

We have near-perfect [1] .... when it comes to dangerous or threatening things that have happened to us, but it's impossible for us to remember every [2] .... Over time, we forget things, regardless of the fact we like to think we have a good [3] .... While our [4] .... memory might work pretty well soon after acquiring new information, if we don't make the effort to learn things [5] ...., we won't remember them for long at all, especially if they aren't important for our survival.

9 Choose the correct words to complete the sentences.

1 Oh, that name **slipped my mind / rings a bell**! Is she the one that used to work on reception?
2 I can never remember things like dates. They just **go in one ear and out the other / refresh my memory**.
3 Didn't I leave the keys on the table? My memory is **ringing a bell / playing tricks on me**.
4 No, don't tell me. Hold on, it's **gone in one ear and out the other / on the tip of my tongue**!
5 I know you've told me the story before but go on, **refresh my memory / slip my mind**.

10 Complete the phrasal verbs in the sentences with *about, by, into, of, on* or *up*.

1 I'm really fed .... of living in this town – it's so boring. Nothing ever happens!
2 I'm quite fond .... going to the cinema on Mondays, when it's quiet.
3 My brother's really .... futsal. It's like football, but with a smaller ball.
4 So, what are you passionate ....? Personally, I love music and fashion.
5 Mum's not keen .... soup – let's make pasta for lunch instead.

11 Choose the correct word or phrase to complete the sentences.

1 Further .... seems to confirm that VR can have a positive impact on recall.
a analysis **b** researchers **c** findings
2 According to recent data, only twenty percent of people in the .... industry are women.
a smart **b** remote **c** tech
3 As ...., participants that played video games demonstrated better social skills.
a findings **b** predicted **c** analysis
4 .... working on the project have said they expect to have results by the end of the year.
a Researchers **b** Findings **c** Tech industry
5 The company has said these .... will revolutionise the field of VR.
a analysis **b** tech **c** findings

12 Complete the conversation with the correct form of the words in brackets.

A: How's the [1] .... (research) going?
B: Well, as [2] .... (predict), it's taking a long time. But I've done all the [3] .... (analyse) of the experiments, so I'll meet the deadline.
A: Good for you! Do you think you'll become a full-time [4] .... (research) after this?
B: I'm not sure. I definitely want to do some kind of [5] .... (science) work related to my studies, though. How's your job?
A: OK. I've been offered the opportunity to work [6] .... (remote) and just go into the office once a week, which would really suit me.

13 Complete the sentences with the words in the box.

deserted	riverbank	scenery	sunlight	woodland

1 The .... is so bright, it's hurting my eyes!
2 Fishing is so boring. You just sit on the .... all day, not talking.
3 Urgh! I'm sick of work. I wish I were on a .... beach somewhere, lying in the sun.
4 This area of .... is made up of hundreds of different types of trees.
5 The .... around here is amazing. I could look at it for hours.

14 Choose the correct words to complete the sentences.

1 This TV series is really **tedious / rewarding**. I don't think I'll finish it.
2 I think you're **ordinary / unique** – there's no one else like you!
3 I'm quite **modest / harsh**. I don't like to make my achievements seem better than they are.
4 I'm going to tell you the truth. It might sound **harsh / exhausting**, but at least it will be honest.
5 It's really **rewarding / ordinary** when I put the effort in, and achieve something at the end.

15 Choose the correct meanings for the adjectives.

1 The royal palace is truly **magnificent**.
a very impressive **b** very expensive
2 It's **astonishing** how successful the blog has been.
a very exciting **b** very surprising
3 Mm, this is the **finest** cheese I've ever tasted!
a the best **b** the softest
4 I love your baby! She must be so **precious** to you.
a very important **b** very expensive
5 What an **incredible** view! You're lucky to live here.
a completely impossible **b** extremely great

Lesson 3A

GRAMMAR | relative clauses
VOCABULARY | festivals; the environment
PRONUNCIATION | pitch in non-defining relative clauses

VOCABULARY

festivals

1 **Complete the blog post with the correct form of the words in the box.**

act atmosphere attend attract festival-goer line-up organiser venue

SherryG
Mon 30 Jul | 09.33

Just back from 1 .... WOMAD festival and it was awesome! There was a fantastic 2 .... of artists from all over the world – not just music but dance and other arts, too. I saw as many 3 .... as I could during the four days I was there and none of them disappointed. The 4 .... was amazing – everyone was singing, dancing and having a great time.

The festival grounds are huge, and all of the 5 .... certainly did a good job of making it easy to get around the enormous 6 ...., which stretched over several large fields. It's a beautiful place, too – no wonder the festival 7 .... such a massive number of people. I think there were about 40,000 8 .... in total! You should definitely go!

the environment

2 **Choose the correct word to complete the sentences.**

1 Driving less is the simplest way for individuals to reduce their carbon **footprint** / **power** / **emission**.
2 We need to move away from natural **emissions** / **power** / **resources** such as oil and gas and look for sustainable alternatives.
3 We've introduced a **recycling** / **renewable** / **clean-up** scheme at work for cardboard, glass and metal.
4 Carbon **emissions** / **power** / **footprints** will drop by forty percent if the current targets are met.
5 More and more organisations are turning to **clean-up** / **renewable** / **recycling** energy such as wind and solar power.
6 We can't depend on solar **resources** / **emissions** / **power** in our country because the weather's so bad!

GRAMMAR

relative clauses

3A **The sentences below have a mistake. Choose the best option to correct the mistake.**

1 Everyone <u>in which</u> we've spoken to has really enjoyed the event.
a what **b** which **c** who
2 My mum, <u>that is</u> a singer-songwriter, is appearing at the Edinburgh Festival this year.
a who's **b** which **c** whose
3 That's the album <u>which is</u> they're most famous for.
a when **b** what **c** that
4 Camp Bestival, <u>who</u> attracts thousands of visitors every year, takes place in the UK.
a where **b** which **c** that

B **Read the sentences in Ex 3A again. In which can you omit the relative pronoun?**

PRONUNCIATION

4A **3.01 | pitch in non-defining relative clauses | Listen and underline the clauses with a lower pitch.**

1 Glastonbury Festival, which has been running since 1970, attracts over 200,000 visitors.
2 The band, who had never played to such a large crowd before, felt very nervous.
3 The headline act, which will perform this evening, is expected to draw a huge crowd.
4 Billie Eilish, who has sold over 5 million records worldwide, will be on stage at nine.
5 The orchestra, which is bigger than ever, will play on the Sticks stage this afternoon.
6 Woodstock, which took place over three days in 1969, was a turning point in music.

B **3.01 | Listen again and repeat.**

READING

5A Read the article and tick the topics that are mentioned.

eco-businesses food waste green festivals
product quality renewable energy
sustainable products transport water usage

Be a greener festival-goer!

Here are our top tips to help you cut your festival carbon footprint ...

Tip 1: Go to environmentally-friendly festivals

Start off in the right way by choosing to attend a green festival, whose organisers will make cleaner decisions on your behalf, including powering their grounds with green energy, providing recycling bins, and committing to environmental policies.

Tip 2: Stay local

Instead of travelling long distances to go a festival, choose one that is closer to home. Bands often do the festival circuit around the country, so you'll still get to see your favourite performers. You'll also have the opportunity to see up-and-coming bands in your area and add some new favourites.

Tip 3: Re-think your 'stuff'

It's easy to pack your rucksack full of mini-bottles of shampoo, shower gel and hair products, but too many of these still come in unnecessary plastic packaging. Fortunately, there are alternatives: you can take – or make – shampoo bars, bamboo toothbrushes, and natural deodorants; and some companies have refill stations, where you can take along a reusable container and fill up with your favourite toiletries before the festival.

Tip 4: Buy once, buy well

Many festival-goers actually leave their tents behind after the event, not realising the majority end up in landfill. So, instead of purchasing a single-use festival tent, invest in something high-quality and reusable. It'll be more comfortable, too. And go plastic-free by taking along reusable water bottles and coffee cups.

Tip 5: Be an electricity saver

Festivals usually have charging points for mobile phones but these come at a cost. Why not take your own pocket charger? All you have to do is wind it up and it'll provide charge for your phone. And why not decorate your tent with solar-powered fairy lights to make it stand out from the crowd – and help you find your way home at night!

B Read the text and answer the questions. Use no more than three words for each answer.

1 What are many green festivals committing to?

....

2 To fill up your reusable containers, where should you take them to?

....

3 What can you do if you use reusable water bottles and coffee cups?

....

4 What do you need to do to use a pocket charger?

....

WRITING

a formal email

6A Read the email from a local resident to the organisers of a festival. What is the purpose of the email?

[1] Hi,

I live in the countryside where XFest is held annually. Every year, I [2] get more and more fed up with the mess left behind by festival-goers, who [3] couldn't care less about the damage they are causing to the local environment.

I have been involved in clean-up operations for the last few years and [4] hate the amount of waste that is left in the fields. I know that some of the camping gear is rescued and given to homeless charities, but this doesn't [5] sort out the problem of it being buried or the ground being damaged.

Is there no way you can insist on campers leaving the place as they found it?

[6] Can't wait to hear from you all!

Suki Wolensson, Kent

B Read the email again. Replace the underlined informal phrases (1–6) with their more formal equivalents (a–f).

a become increasingly frustrated by
b strongly disapprove of
c address the issue of
d I look forward to your response.
e appear to have little concern
f To whom it may concern,

C Imagine you are one of the organisers of XFest. Plan a formal response to the email in Ex 6A.

D Write your formal email. Write 100–140 words.

7 Read the question. Then plan, write and review your answer. You must write at least 75 words.

Governments should make people look after their local environment. Do you agree or disagree with this statement? Why/Why not?

Lesson 3B

GRAMMAR | cleft sentences
VOCABULARY | phrasal verbs: performing; phrasal verbs: communication
PRONUNCIATION | emphatic stress

VOCABULARY

phrasal verbs: performing

1 A Choose the correct phrase to complete the sentences.

1 The play certainly didn't .... my expectations. It was all pretty disappointing.
  a come up with **b** live up to **c** end up
2 Stand-up comedians often have to .... heckling from members of the audience.
  a put up with **b** end up **c** carry on
3 I totally .... my lines in our dress rehearsal. Let's hope things go well on opening night.
  a put me off **b** fell back on **c** messed up
4 Who .... the name for this show? *Fairy Lights* sounds like a children's programme!
  a lived up to **b** carried on **c** came up with
5 I slipped on stage and .... falling into the orchestra pit! It was so embarrassing!
  a ended up **b** fell back on **c** carried on

B Complete the forum posts with the phrasal verbs in the box. There are two you don't need.

came up with	carry on	ended up	fall back on
live up to	mess up	put up with	put you off

Calling all street performers!

Felix99 Yesterday at 9.36 p.m.

Hi, all! I'm currently studying music at uni, but I'm struggling to pay the fees this term. I'm a pretty decent musician, so I'm thinking of doing a bit of busking to help me [1].............. with my studies. And maybe if I fail all of my exams it'll give me something to [2].............. ! Ha ha! So, what's the job really like? Thanks!

Comments

Perry Yesterday at 9.48 p.m.

Hey, Felix. I'm a busker and [3].............. the idea in the same way you did – to get a bit of extra cash. Obviously, it means a lot of performing out in the cold and you can be there for hours! Don't let that [4].............., though – it's fun and if you're good enough, you can earn a decent amount. Good luck!

Kittykat02 Yesterday at 10.01 p.m.

I [5].............. busking for a bit last year and it was hard work. You'll have to [6].............. a lot of difficult people and you **WILL** get cold and stiff after a while. It's still great fun though.

phrasal verbs: communication

2 Choose the correct words to complete the text messages.

Hey, Antonio! How did the presentation go?
4.32

Hey! Yeah, not too bad. They kept asking me to [1]**speak up / bring up** though because my mic wasn't working properly.
4.35

Oh, really? But did you still manage to [2]**come across your message / get your message across**?
4.36

More or less. I did have to [3]**spell out / speak up** the need for us to be better at recycling. Every day I find plastic in the normal bin, loads of waste paper by the photocopier ... We've talked about it before so it's a bit frustrating having to keep [4]**coming back to / pointing out** the same point.
4. 37

Yeah, that must be pretty annoying! Did you [5]**move on / bring up** your idea for the renewable energy programme?
4. 38

No, I decided to leave that for now. Anyway, how did your interview go?
4. 39

Well, they said I [6]**spoke up / came across** well, but I didn't get the job. In the feedback, they [7]**pointed out that / came back to** the candidate who got the job had a lot more experience.
4.41

Oh, no! Sorry, mate. Well, never mind. Take what you can from the experience and [8]**come back to / move on from** it.

Thanks, I will!

GRAMMAR

cleft sentences

3 A Match the sentences beginnings (1–6) with the endings (a–f).

1 What theatre performers enjoy
2 It was my school drama teacher, Ms White
3 What I hoped to get across in the screenplay
4 What happened next
5 What Hannah wanted to do as a child
6 What I'd really like to find out
7 It was only when we finished the play
8 What I really love about being in a band

a who suggested I apply to acting school.
b was that Johannes fell off the stage!
c is making music with my friends.
d is getting immediate feedback from the audience.
e that we discovered there was a talent scout in the crowd.
f was become an opera singer.
g is whether I'm playing the lead role.
h was the character's sense of despair.

B The sentences below have a mistake. Choose the best option to correct the mistake.

1 That I want to know is how to get into film acting.
a It's b What c How

2 It was Candice who wants to go into the circus, not Toni.
a who want b which wants c who wanted

3 It were my grandparents who gave me my 'lucky' socks.
a was b is c are

4 It the performers did was pretend to be audience members.
a They're b It's c What

PRONUNCIATION

4 A 3.02 | emphatic stress | Listen and underline the stressed words.

1 What I like watching are the less well-known acts.
2 It was Max who left the car unlocked, not me.
3 What sounds better to me is finishing on a minor chord.
4 It's you who likes Italian opera – that's why I got the tickets!

B 3.02 | Listen again and repeat.

LISTENING

5 A 3.03 | Listen to a conversation between two friends, about a stage performance. Number the pictures in the correct order.

B 3.03 | Listen again. Are the statements True (T) or False (F)?

1 Alex's partner did not think she had got her lines wrong.
2 Katy worried that she would make mistakes on stage.
3 Katy thinks it may have been her fault that there was a problem with Alex's costume.
4 The crew in charge of the scenery were able to resolve an issue straightaway.
5 All the audience members wanted a refund of their tickets.
6 Katy thinks that people who watch a performance want the actors to do well.

C 3.04 | Listen and complete the phrases.

1 It was like, a total ....!
2 I'd practised, like, a .... times!
3 I could hardly stand up, I was .... so much.
4 … it was like the .... day of my life!
5 You feel as if you're going to die of ....
6 I bet your time on stage seemed to go on ....!

D 3.05 | Listen to the recording and write what you hear. You will hear the sentence only once.

....

Lesson 3C

HOW TO ... | use vague language
VOCABULARY | film and TV
PRONUNCIATION | linking and elision

VOCABULARY

film and TV

1 A Complete the review with the words in the box. There is one word which you do not need.

based	cast	costumes	ending	scenes
set	soundtrack	subtitles	twist	

Review of Daniel Craig's last James Bond film, *No Time to Die*

★★★★

Many James Bond films are [1] .... on novels by Ian Fleming, but this one was written specially for the film. The [2] .... includes Daniel Craig as the retired (!) James Bond, along with Ralph Fiennes as M, Ben Wishaw as Q, and Léa Seydoux as Madeleine.

The film is [3] .... in Italy and on a remote island, and the scenery – as always in James Bond films – is stunning. There are the usual action-filled car chase [4] ...., which are always fun, as well as some more emotional ones, for example, when Bond is with his girlfriend – and her young child. The [5] .... is unexpected! I wouldn't call it a [6] .... as such, but there are certainly some surprises!

As for the [7] ...., well, it's the usual James Bond suit and nothing else very exciting. The [8] .... is as great as ever, with dramatic music throughout and the well-known James Bond theme, though unfortunately, we never actually hear the full tune!

B Choose the correct word to complete the sentences.

1 I have to put the **soundtrack** / **costumes** / **subtitles** on when I watch a film because I can't hear very well.
2 My current favourite series is **cast / set / based** in Sweden – it's a 'Scandi noir' murder mystery.
3 I love a good **twist** / **ending** / **set** in a film or novel – it's exciting to find out what happens next.
4 I thought the **cast** / **scene** / **set** was brilliant. The main actor doesn't usually play mean characters!
5 I loved the **ending** / **scene** / **subtitle** where James meets the new 007. It makes you wonder what's going to happen.
6 It annoys me when they make a film **subtitled** / **based** / **set** on a best-selling book and then change the ending!

How to ...

use vague language

2 A 3.06 | Listen and tick the phrases you hear.

and stuff	bits	old-ish	sort of
something like that	that kind of thing		

B 3.07 | Match the questions (1–5) with the vague replies (a–e). Then listen and check.

1 Who's that guy who played the thief in *Lupin*?
2 When was the *Great Gatsby* supposed to be set?
3 How old do you think the actor in *Maid* is?
4 Did you enjoy watching *The Originals*?
5 Is *Money Heist* a dark story?

a I'd say she's young-ish ... maybe late 20s?
b It was OK. It's sort of for a younger audience, really.
c It's what's his name – oh, you know!
d I suppose it is, a bit. But I like that kind of thing.
e Around the 1920s, I think.

PRONUNCIATION

3 3.08 | linking and elision | Listen and complete the sentences. Then listen again and repeat.

1 I love .... in a good mystery series.
2 I like the film. It's .... a combination of action and thriller.
3 I love dramas that are .... real events.
4 *The Crystal Maze*? Oh, that's where they run around and find crystals or ...., isn't it?

SPEAKING

4 A 3.09 | Complete the conversation with one word in each gap. Then listen and check.

Peter: Have you seen that TV programme *The Crown*?
Alex: Yeah. I've watched the first series.
Peter: What's it [1] .... ?
Alex: It's about the British Royal Family. Each series concentrates on a different period of time and the events that took place then. It's a [2] .... slow in places for me, but it's interesting enough.
Peter: Does it show real events [3] .... stuff? Or is it all made up?
Alex: It's based on real things that happened, but I think they sort [4] .... use a bit of artistic licence – you know, they don't really know what people said [5] .... anything so they have to make that up.

B 3.10 | You are Alex in Ex 4A. Listen and speak after the beep. Record the conversation if you can and compare yourself to Ex 4A.

Speak anywhere Go to the interactive speaking practice

Lesson 3D

GRAMMAR | *do* and *did* for emphasis
LISTENING | a music podcast

GRAMMAR

do and *did* for emphasis

1 A **Choose the correct word to complete the sentences.**

1 I really **did** / **didn't** / **don't** delete your Spotify account! You must've done it by mistake.
2 I know you think hiking that mountain is possible in a single day but I just **did** / **don't** / **do**.
3 Oh, I **do** / **did** / **didn't** love this song when I was younger – I would dance to it all the time.
4 I **do** / **don't** / **didn't** listen to electronic music – just not the kind that you like!
5 **Do** / **Does** / **Don't** come over after the concert if you have time.
6 I **do** / **didn't** / **did** use to get up at midday when I was younger, but I don't now!

B **Complete the sentences with *do, don't, does, doesn't* or *did*.**

1 I .... want to go to the gig, but I just can't afford it right now.
2 Saira does have expensive tastes in clothes, ... she?
3 I .... call the venue to check the gig was still on, but no one answered.
4 You .... remember to send that gift to Mario, didn't you?
5 I loved The Sparks' last two albums, but I really .... like this one.
6 You .... like spaghetti with meatballs, don't you?
7 You .... know I'm not into jazz. I've told you before.
8 He .... like your band, but he just doesn't like crowded places.

LISTENING

2 A **3.11 | Listen to the introduction to a music podcast and answer the questions.**

1 Which genre are they talking about?
2 Who is Elijah?
3 Who is Bethany?

B **3.12 | Listen to the next part of the podcast and choose the correct option (a–c).**

1 How does Bethany think some people react when they hear jazz?
 a They feel anxious.
 b They feel annoyed.
 c They feel confused.
2 What does Elijah think puts people off about jazz?
 a the unusual techniques used
 b the sound of certain instruments
 c the lack of real tunes
3 What do Elijah and Bethany agree on?
 a Some kinds of jazz are easier to listen to.
 b People should avoid jazz if they don't like it.
 c Only jazz musicians understand it properly.

C **3.12 | Listen to the main part of the podcast again. Complete the sentences with no more than three words from the recording.**

1 Bethany says it's hard to know what will happen in jazz because some musicians .... while playing.
2 Bethany says we tend not to like music or other things that make us feel ....
3 Elijah describes a .... called 'noodling', in which the musicians move away from the main tune.
4 Elijah says noodling can seem .... but says that it has structure and tune.
5 Elijah thinks jazz has an .... and shows a lot of creativity.
6 Bethany says that basic and structured jazz makes a .... to jazz music for people.

D **3.13 | Listen to the final sentence again and write what you hear. You will hear the sentence only once.**

....

Lesson 4A

GRAMMAR | future continuous and future perfect
VOCABULARY | health and lifestyle; illness and treatment
PRONUNCIATION | connected speech: future perfect

VOCABULARY

health and lifestyle

1 **Complete the sentences with the correct form of the verbs in the box.**

do (x2) cut expand keep (x2) stay transform vary work

1 It's very important, especially as you get older, to .... mentally active. Doing puzzles is great for your brain.
2 I've .... down on the amount of fat and sugar I consume and feel much healthier now.
3 You really need to .... your horizons and get out and about more.
4 It's hard to find time to .... in shape when you've got a full-time job and a family to look after.
5 Research shows that .... regular workouts is good for you both mentally and physically.
6 I .... a sedentary job for years and was very unfit. Then I retrained as a yoga teacher and now I'm healthier than ever!
7 I've always .... long hours and I'm often too tired to make a proper meal when I get home.
8 Last year, my sister totally .... her lifestyle. She became a vegan and started doing more exercise.
9 It's important to .... your diet as much as you can and include all food groups in your meals.
10 I took up running last year and hopefully, if I .... up my progress, I'll do a marathon soon!

illness and treatment

2 A **Complete the table with the words in the box.**

allergies antibiotics asthma first aid food poisoning medication run-down vaccine

illness	treatment

B **Complete the sentences with words to describe illness and treatment.**

1 The whole group got.................... from the restaurant and were very sick.
2 I suffer from .... all year round and often have itchy eyes and sneeze a lot.
3 I did a .... course so that I could help anyone who suddenly became ill or injured.
4 If you want to find out whether your .... can be taken with other medicines, please consult your doctor.
5 Patients are given .... to help fight against diseases.
6 Sophie's feeling a bit ...., so won't be coming to school today.

GRAMMAR

future continuous and future perfect

3 A **The sentences below have a mistake. Choose the best option to correct the mistake.**

1 In two years' time I'll be completing my degree and hopefully found a job.
 a I'll have completed **b** I'm completing
 c I completed
2 This time next week, you'll have swum in the sea and thinking of me back at home!
 a you'll be swimming **b** you'll swim
 c you're swimming
3 If I'm lucky, I'll have got a visa and work in Australia by next summer.
 a I'll work **b** working **c** be working
4 I'll be finishing lunch by 1 p.m., so we could go for a walk then.
 a I've finished **b** I'll have finished **c** I finished

B **Complete the blog post with the future continuous or future perfect form of the verbs in brackets.**

Going Vegan

Going vegan has been a gradual process for me. By this time next month, I'll [1] .... (be) vegan for a whole year.

I became vegetarian first: I'll [2] .... (celebrate) three years without meat or fish next week. It was hard to give up my favourites, but now I barely think about what I no longer eat – only what I'll [3] .... (have) for my next meal! I've become very inventive – you have to be when you're vegan – and I might [4] .... (set up) my own vegan meal business soon.

Personally, I did it because I developed a mild allergy to milk and dairy products, so I had to cut down on them. I'll [5] .... (go) to the doctor's soon and we'll see whether things have improved – I think my allergy will [6] .... (improve) because my symptoms are much better.

There are lots of benefits to going vegan, for both personal benefit and the planet's. If I can convince my parents to go vegan, I'll [7] .... (do) a pretty good job of getting my message across. However, it's important to remember that you may not always get everything you need from a vegan diet – I'll [8] .... (write) a blog soon about the vitamin supplements that can be helpful for staying on top form. Watch this space!

PRONUNCIATION

4 A **4.01 | connected speech: future perfect | Listen and complete the sentences.**

1 By this time next week, ... this project.
2 Hopefully, ... meat entirely by then.
3 With any luck, ... a house by then.
4 Come round at 7 p.m. – .... dinner by then.
5 By this time next week, ... from university!

B **4.01 | Listen again and repeat.**

READING

5 A Skim the article and choose the main topic (a–c).

a The benefits of different kinds of diet
b The reality behind commonly held beliefs
c The reasons we're lied to about what we eat

B Read the article again. Are the statements True (T) or False (F)?

The writer …

1 thinks food producers try to trick customers into paying too much for food.
2 will continue to buy the expensive health foods that she particularly likes.
3 feels that the message about fat has been very clearly stated.
4 does not intend to limit the amount of high-fat food she eats.
5 is confused about whether or not people should take extra vitamins.
6 has believed information provided on food packaging in the past.

C Read the article again and answer the questions. Use no more than three words for each answer.

1 What are superfoods meant to stop?

....

2 What does the writer think food manufacturers want from people?

....

3 What phrase does the writer use to describe the act of labelling food low in fat?

....

4 What is the writer happy to continue eating?

....

Health myths busted!

We all want to be healthier, but with so much (mis)information out there, it can be difficult to know which changes are actually worth making. So, here is the truth about four common food myths, which may help you make up your mind …

Myth 1: Superfoods are a thing

Sorry, but superfoods *aren't* a thing! Yep, you heard right. While we've all been filling our trolleys with blueberries, ginger and coconut, it turns out that, yes, they do us good, but they're no better than other fruit and veg. 'Super' foods are promoted because they supposedly contain huge amounts of antioxidants (substances that prevent cell damage in our bodies), and the message is that we should buy as many as we can. These (often exotic) foods are – surprise, surprise – very expensive, though. I know what I'll be getting from now on: cheap 'ordinary' veg that I love just as much!

Myth 2: All fat is bad fat

We've been told (over and over again) that we should cut down on foods that contain saturated fats, such as butter, cream and cheese, and eat plenty of foods that are great for heart, eye and brain health (think Omega 3 in oily fish). But the jury seems to be out on whether saturated fats *really* cause heart disease, and whether foods that contain cholesterol (a fat which can be found in eggs) *actually* raise cholesterol in our blood. I think I'll be carrying on with less butter and more salmon, just in case …

Myth 3: You don't need supplements

OK, so this one's hotly debated! Many say that if you have a varied diet, you'll get everything your body needs, and that manufacturers only promote vitamins and supplements so they can fill their pockets with our hard-earned cash! But it turns out there *are* arguments *for* supplements in certain circumstances: those with health conditions including diabetes, pregnant women and people over 50 *can* benefit from additional vitamins. Who knew?

Myth 4: low fat = low calorie

Nope! It's just another marketing trick! Look in supermarkets and you'll see 'low-fat', 'fat free', 'diet' and 'light' in lots of labels. I've certainly fallen into that trap! While they might truthfully be low in fat, they may also be highly processed and full of sugar to make them tasty. 'You're better off having a few nuts or full-fat items like cheese and yoghurt than eating so-called "diet" products', says one specialist. I, for one, will be following this advice. So, bring on the ice cream (just not too much of it)!

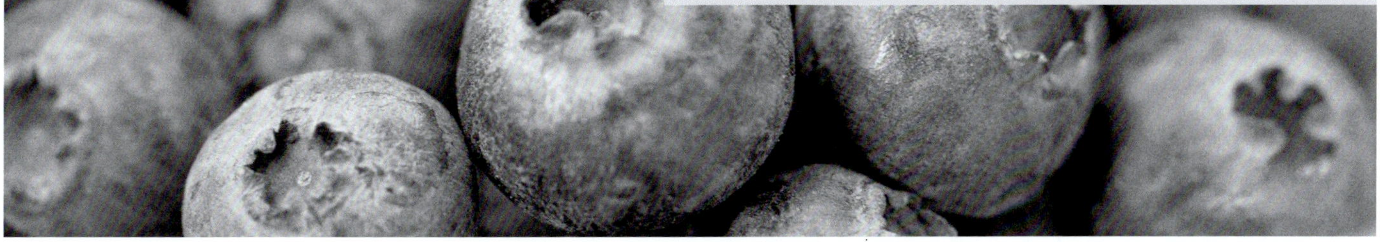

Lesson 4B

GRAMMAR | passives
VOCABULARY | sleep
PRONUNCIATION | sentence stress: content and function words

VOCABULARY

sleep

1 A Complete the conversation with the words in the box.

deep	dropping off	exhausted	keep
nightmare	oversleep	sleeper	snore

Doctor: Thanks for coming to the sleep clinic. I'd like to ask you a few questions before we run some tests.

Fran: Sure. I've just been so [1] .... lately and I don't know why! I go to bed early, but often [2] .... and end up being late for work.

Doctor: What time do you usually go to bed?

Fran: About ten o'clock. I don't have any problems [3] .... and I'm never awake past 11 p.m.

Doctor: Do you wake during the night?

Fran: Only if I'm having a [4] .... But I usually go back to sleep again once I'm calmer.

Doctor: And do you [5] .... ? I mean, has anyone ever told you that you do?

Fran: Sometimes – if I've gone to bed *really* tired. I [6] .... my husband awake then because I'm so loud – so he says! I think I must be quite a heavy [7] ....

Doctor: Why's that?

Fran: Well, I usually wake up with a headache. When my alarm goes off, it's like I must've been in a really [8] .... sleep and I struggle to wake up.

Doctor: Well, that doesn't sound good. What we're going to do at the clinic is …

B Choose the correct word or phrase to complete the sentences.

1 I'm .... – I never wake up, even if there's a thunderclap outside!
  a a heavy sleeper **b** an insomniac **c** exhausted

2 There was a noisy party last night which .... us awake.
  a kept **b** overslept **c** dropped

3 I .... today – I just didn't hear my alarm.
  a kept awake **b** overslept **c** lied in

4 She says she always takes a short .... on the train after work.
  a nap **b** nightmare **c** snore

5 I rarely get a .... – my kids are up at dawn practically every day!
  a drop off **b** lie-in **c** nap

6 My husband says that I .... and keep him awake at night.
  a oversleep **b** drop off **c** snore

GRAMMAR

passives

2 Complete the article about sleep disorders using the correct passive form of the verbs in brackets.

Why do people …

… sleepwalk?

It [1] .... (suggest) that sleepwalking runs in families. If you have a family member who walks in their sleep, it [2] .... generally .... (accept) that you are ten times more likely to do it yourself. It [3] .... also .... (suspect) that stress, illness and medication can make sleepwalking more likely. It [4] .... once .... (assume) to be dangerous to wake a sleepwalker, but this [5] .... now .... (not consider) to be a problem. However, it should be done quietly and carefully to keep distress to a minimum.

… talk in their sleep?

Talking in your sleep [6] .... (define) as a sleep disorder where the sleep-talker doesn't know what they're doing. Speech [7] .... more easily .... (understand) when it occurs during REM sleep (when people are dreaming). Anyone can sleep-talk, but it [8] .... (observe) most often in men and children. Records show that sleep-talking [9] .... (notice) by ancient Greek philosophers about 2,500 years ago, so it [10] .... (not discover) recently. Sleep-talking isn't usually a problem and does not require treatment.

PRONUNCIATION

3 A | sentence stress: content and function words | Read the sentences and predict which words will be stressed the most.

1 It was thought that eating cheese before bedtime gives you nightmares.
2 It's been suggested that using your phone in bed makes it harder to drop off.
3 It's believed that up to fifteen percent of the population are sleepwalkers.
4 It's estimated that most people sleep for fewer than seven hours a night.

B 4.02 | Listen and check.

LISTENING

4 A 4.03 | Listen to the introduction to a radio programme. What kind of programme is it?

B 4.04 | Listen to the next part of the programme and choose the correct option(s) (a–c).

1 What does Rob say about using a sleep tracker?
  a It provided some useful information.
  b It helped him learn to relax.
  c It caused him problems.
2 How did Jenna feel before using her technique?
  a worried about her future
  b scared about being kept awake
  c relieved to get some sleep during the day
3 What does Jenna say helped her sleep better?
  a reading before she went to sleep
  b learning about sleep psychology
  c quitting an old habit
4 What does Álvaro say about nuts?
  a He says they should be avoided at night.
  b He is pleased he can eat more of his favourite kind.
  c He doesn't fully understand how they work.
5 What does Sonya say about the techniques?
  a She finds them quite difficult to do.
  b She thinks they sound rather unusual.
  c She is not very keen to have a go at them.

C 4.05 | Listen to the recording and write what you hear. You will hear the sentence only once.

....

WRITING

an article

5 A Read the article and tick the topics that are mentioned.

dreams lack of sleep napping nightmares
sleep and disability sleep behaviours
sleep cycles sleep positions

B Complete the article (1–5) with the sentences (a–e).

a In addition to this, they can involve anxiety, too.
b as well as sleep paralysis, where you wake up, but are unable to move.
c Moreover, their dreams involve feelings, smells and sounds rather than sight.
d Furthermore, they make friends easily, but don't enjoy being the centre of attention.
e A lack of sleep not only affects your mental health, but also your physical health.

C You are going to write an article about what kind of sleeper you are. Plan your article. Choose three ideas to write about from Ex 5A.

D Write an article about what kind of sleeper you are.

Six Amazing Facts You Didn't Know About Sleep

Sleep has fascinated experts for centuries and new information is being discovered all the time. So, we've put together six of the most amazing facts we could find on the topic.

- Most nightmares are not frightening. They often include feelings of sadness, guilt and confusion. [1] .... They happen most often when someone is feeling worried.
- The position you prefer to sleep in *might* reflect your personality. For example, people who sleep on their backs in the 'starfish' position tend to be good listeners. [2] ....
- [3] .... For example, you won't cope with pain as well when you don't sleep much.
- Contrary to what some people may think, blind people do dream. [4] .... Also, interestingly, deaf people use sign language when they dream.
- Everyone dreams, but they might not remember them. Those that do remember will have forgotten fifty percent of the dream within five minutes of waking. The most common dreams include teeth falling out, forgetting to prepare for an exam, and trying to run but not getting anywhere.
- Some unusual sleep behaviours include parasomnia or making unusual movements in your sleep; 'exploding head syndrome' where someone wakes to a loud noise that is only in their head, [5] .... Don't worry if this happens to you – it just means your brain's woken up before the rest of your body has!

Lesson 4C

HOW TO ... | express agreement and disagreement
VOCABULARY | exercise; sport: motivation and benefits
PRONUNCIATION | stress in phrases for partial agreement

VOCABULARY

exercise

1 **Choose the correct word or phrase to complete the sentences.**

1 You need a lot of **flexibility / stamina / moderate exercise** to be able to finish a marathon. They take a long time to run!
2 It's important to do some **aerobic / low-impact / stamina** exercise because it makes your heart beat faster.
3 **Strength / Flexibility / Low-impact** training doesn't have to mean hours lifting weights – you can build muscle using your own body weight at home.
4 An example of **aerobic / high-impact / low-impact** training is yoga, which is gentle but strengthening.
5 I do **moderate / vigorous / stamina** exercise every day, just a 20-minute walk around the park.
6 **High-impact / Flexibility / Strength** exercise includes things like running and ball sports, such as football or tennis.

sport: motivation and benefits

2 **Complete the fundraising page with the words in the box. There is one word which you do not need.**

benefit challenge confidence discipline encouragement incentive teamwork

Cycling for the kids!

£1,258 raised by **3,480 supporters** DONATE

So, this year I'm planning a huge [1] .... for myself and I need your [2] .... to get me going!

I'm going to cycle the length of the country in as short a time as possible. The [3] .... for me to raise money for a children's charity that is close to my heart, and the [4] .... to them is being able to fund more research to make lives better.

I'm going to need a lot of [5] .... to make sure I get up early to train before work, even when it's dark or cold. Most of my weekends will be spent cycling long-distance routes. I also need to build my [6] .... for cycling bigger roads, though I'll take quieter ones when possible.

Follow the link to find out more about the charity or donate now.

How to ...

express agreement and disagreement

3 A **4.06 | Listen to a conversation between two friends. What are they talking about?**

B **4.06 | Listen again. Do the friends agree (A), disagree (D) or partially agree (PA) with each other about the statements (1–6)?**

1 Micro-HITT training doesn't seem worth the effort.
2 One benefit of micro-HITT is that it's quick.
3 Everesting sounds like a manageable challenge.
4 New cyclists could cope with Everesting.
5 The man needs to find a relaxing form of exercise.
6 Yogalates helps with physical and mental health.

PRONUNCIATION

4 A **4.07 | stress in phrases for partial agreement | Listen and underline the main stressed word in each of the phrases in bold.**

1 **I agree up to a point**, but don't you think the government should play a role, too?
2 **I take your point**, but that's what footballers expect to get paid.
3 **That's a fair point**, but don't you think they get enough exercise at school?

B **4.07 | Listen again and repeat the sentences.**

SPEAKING

5 A **4.08 | Complete the conversation with phrases for agreeing and disagreeing. Then listen and check.**

Marla: Let's do something. It would be a shame to stay in on a day like this.
Dan: I [1] .... more. What shall we do? Want to try bouldering with me? Come on ...
Marla: Climbing over massive rocks all day? No, thanks. It sounds exhausting.
Dan: I know what [2] ...., but you did say you want to improve your strength a bit ...
Marla: That's a fair [3] ...., but I've got work tomorrow and I don't want to be worn out.
Dan: You go to the gym all the time – you'll be fine!
Marla: I completely [4] ....! Last time we went jogging it took me a week to recover!
Dan: All right. I take [5] .... You do need a lot of stamina. But on the [6] ...., if you stay here all day, you'll never get fitter!

B **4.09 | You are Dan in the conversation in Ex 5A. Listen and speak after the beep. Record the conversation if you can.**

C **Listen to your recording and compare it to Ex 5A.**

Speak anywhere Go to the interactive speaking practice

Lesson 4D

VOCABULARY | phrases related to time
READING | disappearing traditional skills and lifestyles

VOCABULARY

phrases related to time

1 **Choose the correct option(s) to complete the sentences.**

1. **Time is running out** / **It's time to move on** for endangered animals and we need to take action.
2. We got to the theatre **just in time** / **not a moment too soon** for the start of the play.
3. We've got a very short **future under threat** / **window of opportunity** to carry out the conservation project.
4. I've got some new boots and **time is running out** / **not a moment too soon** – the old ones were wearing out!
5. The future of our planet **is still under threat** / **has a short window of opportunity** and we must keep making changes to our habits.
6. **It's just in time for** / **It's time to move on from** this job. I've become very bored.
7. The community are increasingly concerned that their traditional way of life is **under threat** / **running out**.
8. Right, I think it's probably **just in time** / **time** to go home or I'll miss the last train!

READING

2 A **Read the article. What is its purpose?**

B **Read the article again. Are the statements True (T) or False (F)?**

1. Kerry does not believe readers are aware of the skill practised by her great-grandfather.
2. Kerry suggests that people who wore clogs could not afford to replace them regularly.
3. Nisse says that Franco-Provençal speakers moved out to the countryside from cities.
4. Nisse speaks a different language to his grandparents because he does not need to use the language they speak.
5. Özkan believes that the way people worked in the past used a lot of time and energy.
6. Özkan ithinks that technology can only solve one kind of problem.
7. Agata is not impressed with her grandparents' lifestyle choice.
8. Agata would be happy to move on from every aspect of traditional life.

Should we care about losing traditional skills and ways of life?

Do you know how to make bread? Or fix a hole in your socks? Or even how to light a fire? For all too many of us, the answer to all of these questions is 'no'. Basic life skills that were once a staple part of everyday life have all but disappeared. But is this a bad thing?

YES!

Kerry, UK: My great-grandad used to make clogs. I bet you don't even know what they are! Well, they're shoes made from leather and wood. They last a long time. This is why they were chosen by low-paid workers who put in long days at cotton mills, in coal mines and on boats that transported goods along canals. A very limited number of clog-makers still exist, but their future is under threat, as so few people wear clogs now. It would be a shame if such a great skill – and fantastic style of footwear – disappeared forever.

Nisse, Switzerland: Time is running out for my grandparents' language, Franco-Provençal. They live in an isolated part of Switzerland, and because my parents (like many) moved away to find work, I never learned it. Now it's dying out, despite attempts to get people learning it. I understand it, but I only speak Swiss-German – the most common language in Switzerland. Lots of books used to be written in Franco-Provençal. The window of opportunity for reviving the language is short. If no one can speak it, how will we learn about the history of our country?

NO!

Özkan, Turkey: People make a lot of fuss about 'lost' skills and ways of life. But if they were so good in the first place, why did they disappear? It's time to move on. My grandparents lived tough lives as farmers, using traditional skills – but only because that's what was available then. It wasn't considered 'traditional' at the time! As far as I can tell, traditional skills and ways of life were very hard. Technology has solved so many problems and many people are a lot better off in all kinds of ways – not just financially, but health- and time-wise, too.

Agata, Poland: When I visit my great-grandparents in their village, I feel like I've gone back in time by a century. I suppose I have in a way because they stick to the 'old ways' and don't live as comfortably and easily as they could do – well, that's only my opinion. They don't enjoy using modern technology, anyway! For me, when a new app or phone model comes out, it's not a moment too soon. I will say this, though: I always seem to arrive just in time when my great-grandma's cooked some traditional dumplings – delicious! That way of life should never disappear!

GRAMMAR

1 Combine the sentences using a relative clause. Omit the pronoun where possible.

1 Nick works at the theatre. The one over there.
That's .... works.
2 We met a girl at your cousin's barbecues. Is that her?
Is that .... your cousin's barbecue?
3 A guy got his car stuck in the mud. I think that's him over there.
I think that's .... got stuck in the mud.
4 The venue has been very successful. It opened last year.
The venue, ..., has been very successful.
5 Remember the hotel we stayed in for our honeymoon? They closed it!
They closed .... in for our honeymoon!

2 Match the sentence beginnings (1–6) with the endings (a–f).

1 It was Felicity
2 What I want to know
3 It's Helena that
4 It was Ankoma who
5 What you need to do
6 What I'd like to

a is wash your hands.
b who told me.
c do is go to sleep!
d is what you were doing!
e told everyone.
f you need to speak to.

3 Complete the conversation with the correct form of *do* to add emphasis.

A: Are you going to the company party on Thursday?
B: I [1] .... want to go but it's on the other side of London from me. It'll be fun, though.
A: Hmm, well, I didn't want to go last year either but I must admit, I [2] .... enjoy it in the end.
B: Yes, and there's a DJ again, isn't there?
A: Well, you [3] .... love a good dance, but I really [4] ....! I hate it.
B: Fair enough. The quiz should be good though. I think Emir's running it this year.
A: Well, he [5] .... like testing us all, doesn't he?
B: That's true. I'm rubbish at quizzes but I [6] .... like the theme last time – 90s pop music.
A: My team won! I think Mike was unhappy – he [7] .... like to show off his knowledge!

4 Complete the text with the future continuous or future perfect forms of the verbs in brackets.

We'll no doubt [1] .... (hear) more and more weather forecasts about violent storms and flooding. The sad thing is that we probably [2] .... (get used to) such reports by then. And that will only be if we still *have* weather reporters: scientists believe that as well as the weather having become more extreme, our society may also [3] .... (fall) apart by 2050!

By 2050, the South Pole [4] .... (shrink) considerably, sea levels [5] .... (rise) by 30 cm, temperatures [6] .... (increase) dramatically, and civilisation as we know it [7] .... (start) to collapse. The worst thing is that we [8] .... (do) it all to ourselves: it will be our own fault.

5 The sentences below have a mistake. Choose the best option to correct the mistake.

1 There is generally accepted that film-making is a serious form of art.
a It's b It was c There are
2 What's Going On by Marvin Gaye is consider to be one of the best albums of all time.
a is considered being b considers being
c is considered to be
3 In the late 1800s, they believe widely that the Earth was flat.
a it's widely believe b it was widely believed
c they widely believe it
4 Despite evidence to the contrary, Vitamin C thought still is to cure the common cold.
a still are thinking b it's still thought
c is still thought

VOCABULARY

6 Choose the correct words to complete the sentences.

1 The **line-up** / **act** for the festival is superb, with over 50 bands performing over the weekend.
2 The **festival-goers** / **atmosphere** at music festivals is always amazing.
3 I think the **organisers** / **festival-goers** have done a great job of the layout.
4 Sanjay's never **attended** / **attracted** a festival before so we should look after him.
5 Donauinselfest is the world's biggest music festival, **attending** / **attracting** three million people!

7 Complete the sentences with the words in the box.

emissions	footprint	power	recycling	resources

1 In an effort to reduce their carbon .... music festivals are going greener.
2 Lollapalooza has it own programme to encourage festival-goers to do more ....
3 Reducing the number of plastic bottles that are made can help lower carbon .... from the factories that produce them.
4 Many people who attend the Paléo Festival in Switzerland use public transport to avoid unnecessary use of natural ....
5 At the We Love Green festival in France, festival-goers can generate .... by cycling at the festival's 'electric pedals' station.

8 Replace the words in bold with the correct form of the phrasal verbs in the box.

come up with	fall back on	live up to	mess up	put someone off

1 I've **thought of** a brilliant idea for a new play.
2 You should stay at uni so you have something else to **use** if the band doesn't work out.
3 Your act was incredible – how can I ever **be as good as** that?

4 I **got** all my lines **wrong** on stage – it was really embarrassing.
5 Stop making silly faces – you're **distracting** me.

9 Complete the phrasal verbs with *across*, *back*, *on to*, *out* or *up*.

1 You come .... as such a friendly person, but you're actually quite mean!
2 OK, let's move .... to the issue of parking for the event.
3 Can you speak .... a bit, please? We can't hear you at the back.
4 I'll come .... to the topic of recycling later, if I may.
5 My teacher spelled .... exactly what we had to do for our homework.

10 Complete the sentences with the words in the box.

based on	costumes	ending	soundtrack	twist

1 I was totally confused by the .... – why did they finish it off like that?
2 The .... were amazing in that film. I'd love to wear something like that.
3 I enjoyed it but the .... was weird. It was set in 1770, but they used punk rock!
4 Is the series .... a true story?
5 Wow, what a ....! I didn't see that coming!

11 Choose the correct words to complete the tips.

If you want to [1]**transform** / **expand** your lifestyle, follow our top tips!

If you do a [2]**sedentary** / **active** job, you need to make sure you build exercise into your day. If you can do a [3]**sedentary** / **regular** workout, even better! It can be difficult to [4]**stay** / **do** in shape when you work [5]**active** / **long** hours, but exercising when you can makes all the difference.

Try to [6]**expand** / **transform** your horizons: sign up for a new activity like high-intensity pool training.

Change what you eat: make sure you [7]**cut down on** / **vary** your diet and [8]**expand** / **cut down** on fatty and sugary foods.

[9]**Keep** / **Work** mentally active, too. Do puzzles, dance – anything to help your brain stay sharp.

Finally, [10]**stay in** / **keep up** the progress! Once you see the rewards of your efforts, you'll be keen to remain your best self.

12 Complete the definitions with the words in the box.

allergies	antibiotics	asthma	food poisoning	medication

1 ....: medical conditions that make you ill when you eat, breathe or touch something.
2 ....: a stomach illness caused by eating food that contains harmful bacteria.
3 ....: an illness that makes it difficult to breathe.
4 ....: drugs that are used to kill bacteria and cure infections.
5 ....: a drug given to someone who is ill.

13 Choose the correct word or phrase to complete the sentences.

1 I'm such a .... sleeper that I don't even wake up with a really loud alarm.
a light **b** heavy **c** weak
2 My wife's .... and she disturbs me when she puts the light on when she can't sleep.
a an insomniac **b** a deep sleeper **c** a snorer
3 I usually .... pretty quickly at night but wake up a few hours later.
a deep sleep **b** drop off **c** nap
4 My dad always has a .... after lunch. Eating seems to make him tired.
a nap **b** lie-in **c** nightmare
5 I love having a .... at the weekends, but I get up early the rest of the week.
a deep sleep **b** snore **c** lie-in
6 My daughter woke me up at 1 a.m. She'd had a .... and couldn't go back to sleep.
a nightmare **b** lie-in **c** snore

14 Complete the sentences with the words in the box.

aerobic	flexibility	moderate	stamina	vigorous

1 It's better to do a small amount of .... exercise every day than to do a lot of exercise on one occasion and then do nothing for weeks.
2 You really only need to do 20 minutes of .... exercise a day, such as a gentle walk.
3 I'm currently building my .... to do a marathon next month.
4 I really enjoy .... exercise like dancing and running.
5 I really need to improve my .... – I can barely touch my toes.

15 Choose the correct words to complete the sentences.

1 There's no real **incentive** / **discipline** for me to do more exercise. I'm fit enough.
2 I'll admit that winning is my main **motivation** / **confidence** when it comes to competitive sport.
3 I think playing in a team really boosted my **confidence** / **challenge**.
4 You need a high level of **benefit** / **discipline** to become a good gymnast or dancer.
5 I like a **challenge** / **motivation**, so I'm going to do an ultra-marathon next year.

16 Complete the sentences with the words *time*, *future*, *moment* or *opportunity*.

1 The .... of the giant panda no longer seems to be under threat.
2 It's .... to get real about online security. We have to take it more seriously.
3 Action is finally being taken to improve air quality – and not a .... too soon.
4 We have a small window of .... in which to slow the rate of global warming.
5 .... is running out for endangered species.

GRAMMAR

present perfect simple and continuous

1 **Use the prompts to write present perfect simple or present perfect continuous sentences.**

1 How long / you / learn the violin?
2 You / ever / go / to Russia?
3 I / go to bed / much later / recently
4 I / wait / here / last two and a half hours!
5 Ali / see / the *James Bond* film / three times

infinitive and *-ing* forms

2 **Rewrite the sentences using the correct form of the verbs in brackets.**

1 I used to buy groceries on the way home from work.
I stopped .... (buy) food on the way home.
2 Ask Sheila if she wants to come to the party.
Remember .... (invite) Sheila to the party.
3 I'll always remember waking up on that beach in Hawaii.
I'll never forget .... (wake) up on that beach in Hawaii.
4 You need to practise every day to learn anything.
The way to learn anything is by .... (practise) every day.
5 I'm travelling around Southeast Asia on my gap year.
My plan is .... (travel) around Southeast Asia on my gap year.

future probability

3 **Complete the sentences with the words in the box.**

certain to	due to	going to
might	unlikely to	'll

1 I .... never go travelling on my own because I'm simply not brave enough.
2 I'm .... see Connie today, so could you give her this birthday card, please?
3 We .... go to Japan this year but we haven't made our minds up yet.
4 They are not .... make it to the airport on time if they don't hurry up.
5 She's .... pass her exam on Monday. There's no doubt about it!

relative clauses

4 **Complete the sentences with a relative pronoun or '–' if the pronoun can be omitted.**

1 Is Bearded Theory the festival .... we first met? I can't remember.
2 The guy .... we spoke to when we first arrived wasn't very helpful.
3 Remember that group .... parents came to the festival with them? How embarrassing!
4 You know that orchestra .... played last night? What was their name again?
5 Look, that's the festival .... I was telling you about the other day.

cleft sentences

5 **Complete the text messages with *what* or *it*. Use the correct form of *be* if necessary.**

LEX
Hey, Jen – I loved your flash mob in town today.

JEN
Haha! Thanks, Lex. 1 .... our leader, Carlo's idea to organise it. We thought it might be a good way to advertise the dance group. 2 .... interesting is that the police didn't try to stop it. They seemed to actually quite enjoy it!

LEX
3 .... I liked about it 4 .... the dance off! I still can't believe you didn't win!

JEN
5 .... my last move that let me down! Haha! I did fall off a bench after all!

STU
Well, what's next? That's 6 .... I want to know!

future continuous and future perfect

6 **Choose the correct words to complete the sentences.**

1 We'll **have finished** / **be finishing** dinner by the time you get back, but I'll leave some in the fridge for you.
2 At this rate, I'll still **have worked** / **be working** on this project well into the new year.
3 She might **have finished** / **be finishing** with it by now. Why don't you go and ask her?
4 Call me later. I'll **have spoken** / **be speaking** to Jacob by then, so I should know more.
5 I'll **have finalised** / **be finalising** the contract by mid-afternoon, so I'll send it across after that.

VOCABULARY

personality adjectives

7 **Complete the sentences with the adjectives in the box.**

adventurous	ambitious	argumentative
curious	stubborn	

1 I must admit, I am quite .... Once I've made up my mind, I rarely change it.
2 Young children are so .... about the world. They want to know everything!
3 I'd say I'm pretty .... I've flown in a helicopter, climbed a mountain – I've even rafted through the Amazon!
4 My mum was a pretty .... businesswoman. She'd become a CEO by her mid-forties.
5 Those two are so .... They're always falling out with each other.

suffixes

8 **Complete the job advert with the adjective form of the words in brackets.**

Food Taster

We're looking for people to taste test our new range of vegan products. This is a very [1] .... (practice) job, and you don't need to be [2] .... (experience) in the role as on-the-job training is provided.

Our workplace is fairly [3] .... (relax) and we're looking for people who are [4] .... (rely) and [5] .... (optimist). In return for your tasting expertise, we offer [6] .... (real) rates of pay and excellent benefits.

science and technology

9 **Match the definitions with the words in the box. There are three words you don't need.**

analyse findings predict remotely researcher smart tech industry virtual reality

1 images and sounds created by a computer that seem real to the user ....
2 controlled by computers, so it appears to act in an intelligent way ....
3 information discovered as a result of a study ....
4 to examine something carefully to understand or explain it ....
5 from a distance ....

health and lifestyle

10 **Complete the phrases with the words in the box.**

do expand keep (×2) stay transform

1 .... your lifestyle
2 .... mentally active
3 .... in shape
4 .... regular workouts
5 .... your horizons
6 .... up your progress

lifestyle adjectives

11 **Choose the correct words to complete the sentences.**

1 I suppose my job is pretty **unique** / **tedious** in that I can be based anywhere in the world.
2 He lives in quite a **unique** / **modest** house, considering he's worth millions.
3 I've been told I'm full of crazy ideas, but I think I'm very **modest** / **ordinary**!
4 This project is so **tedious** / **ordinary**. I can't wait till it's finished.
5 Conditions at sea can be pretty **modest** / **harsh** and it's not fun being caught in a storm.

festivals; the environment

12 **Complete the information about a festival.**

acts attracts carbon footprint festival-goers organisers renewable sustainable venues

A Greener Festival is a not-for-profit organisation which helps festival [1] .... around the world to make their events more sustainable and reduce their [2] .... This lessens their environmental impact and [3] .... those keen to make a difference, including not only [4] .... but the musicians themselves. The organisation's Woodstock Principles, launched on Earth Day 2008, are a set of ten ideas which encourage anyone in the music industry to hold more environmentally-friendly events. These principles include things like using [5] .... energy and reducing waste at [6] ...., as well as selling greener merchandise. It also encourages fans and [7] .... alike to adopt [8] .... practices.

How to ...

13 **Complete the conversation with one word in each gap.**

Pippa: I'm absolutely passionate [1] .... reading. I'm not a big [2] .... of science fiction or fantasy, but I'll read anything else. You?
Max: I'm [3] .... keen on sci-fi either. I've got really [4] .... crime recently.
Pippa: Me too! [5] .... I love about it is trying to guess who did it.
Max: Well, I've just finished a great Harlan Coben mystery. I'd [6] .... happy to lend it you.

14 **Complete the text with the words in the box.**

fact impression sure thought way

Look our new neighbours! I'd have [1] .... they'd stay in more now they've got children. I get the [2] .... they've got a lot of money. I'm not 100 percent [3] .... but I think they've even got a live-in nanny to look after the kids. There's no [4] .... I'd have let someone else bring our kids up! I know for a [5] .... I'd have done a better job myself!

15 **Complete the conversation with one word in each gap.**

Emir: Do you watch much TV?
Burcu: I use streaming services like Netflix, Amazon Prime and .... on.
Emir: I've just finished a good Scandi noir series.
Burcu: What *is* Scandi noir? Is it sort .... dark crime or something?
Emir: Crime stories set in Scandinavian countries. Sometimes weird .... happens. It's good. I like the scenery .... everything. I read the subtitles. I find it .... of interesting listening to the languages.
Burcu: Are there many?
Emir: Languages? Maybe – five .... so.

UNIT 1

Audio 1.01

1 She's never been to Poland.
2 How long have you been studying in Manchester?
3 What's he been up to this week?
4 I've been trying to book flights to Mexico all morning.
5 She's been waiting here for the last four hours.

Audio 1.02

Presenter: Now, here to tell us all about her latest book, *Who Am I? An exploration of identity,* is author and psychologist, Meg Harper. Meg, welcome to the show.
Meg: Thanks for having me.
Presenter: So, Meg – first things first, what does 'identity' really mean?
Meg: Well, that's actually a pretty big question. But essentially, identity is based on four main areas – your personality traits, so whether you're curious or argumentative, stubborn or outgoing; your likes and dislikes, from your taste in music to your favourite food; your moral code, so what you consider to be right and wrong; and the things that motivate you – you know, what gets you out of bed in the morning. Anyone with a strong sense of self would be able to describe these aspects of their identity fairly easily.
Presenter: And is that important? Do we need to have a clear sense of self?
Meg: Yeah, I think it's really important. Your sense of self affects all aspects of your life, from the job you choose to the relationships you form. If you're not sure who you are, it can be difficult to know what you want and you might struggle to make important decisions. Knowing exactly who you are also means you know what you like about yourself and what you need to work on, which can only be a good thing.
Presenter: OK, so where does our identity come from?
Meg: Well, a lot of it seems to come from our parents. They give us a clear sense of what's right and wrong. Both explicitly … so they tell us … And, perhaps more importantly, through their actions.
Presenter: So, they need to obey the rules themselves?
Meg: Exactly. They're effectively a model for how to act. You know, if we see them working hard, we're more likely to have a strong work ethic ourselves when we grow up. If they often get angry or act aggressively towards people, we may think that's an acceptable way to behave, too.
Presenter: Right. And is that it then – whatever we picked up in childhood we're stuck with?
Meg: No, not at all. It isn't something that's fixed. Your identity continues to develop throughout your life. Certainly, as teenagers we often begin to question what we've been taught, to rebel against the values and behaviours modelled by our parents. And as we grow up, we form new relationships and have new experiences – all of which feeds into our sense of who we are.
Presenter: OK, so finally – what would you say to anyone who is feeling a bit lost and doesn't know who they are?
Meg: Don't worry, you'll get there in the end! Explore and experiment, find out what you like doing and who you identify with.

Audio 1.03

Explore and experiment, find out what you like doing and who you identify with.

Audio 1.04

1 My short-term memory is better than my long-term memory.
2 I've got perfect recall when it comes to phone numbers!
3 This song brings back a lot of childhood memories.

Audio 1.05

Olivia: Shall we go backpacking this summer? It'd be great for the three of us to go on an adventure together!
Amy: Backpacking's not really my kind of thing. I'd much rather stay in a hotel.
Chloe: I'd be happy to go backpacking, but if Amy's not sure, let's just do something else.
Amy: Sorry, it's just that I'm not a big fan of camping. Or sharing rooms in hostels for that matter!
Olivia: Well, we don't have to stay in budget accommodation. How about if we go to lots of different places, but stay in some decent hotels?
Amy: OK. Cool. So, where do you want to go?
Chloe: Well, I'd love to go to Thailand. The beaches there look amazing!
Olivia: Hmmm … I'd be happy to do a bit of sunbathing, but I don't want to do it all day! I want to actually go and *do* stuff as well. I'd much rather go to Japan, then we can visit all the old buildings and eat lots of sushi!
Amy: Isn't Japan really expensive though? How about travelling around Europe instead? Does that sound like a plan?
Olivia: Perfect!
Chloe: Sure!

Audio 1.06

1 I'm quite fond of boat trips, actually. They're a great way to see the city.
2 The kids aren't keen on trying unusual foods.
3 Dan's terrified of driving in foreign countries and so am I!
4 I'm not really into visiting museums. I find a lot of them really boring.
5 I always feel nervous about getting lost when I'm in a new city.
6 Katie's quite passionate about culture and the arts.

Audio 1.07

Hi, I'm Jack. I'm passionate about learning languages and I've been studying them for a few years now. The thing I love about languages is that they give you lots of insight into new cultures. I can't stand hearing people shouting loudly at waiters in English when they're in another country. I'd rather give it a go and get it wrong than not try at all. I'm quite ambitious when it comes to learning languages and I can speak three pretty fluently now!

Audio 1.08

Good morning, everyone. Today I'll be talking about the five main personality traits, which are openness, conscientiousness, extroversion, agreeableness and neuroticism.
Now, whilst you may not recognise some of these big words, these five traits are, according to psychologists, the most commonly studied characteristics of personality, and we all score more highly on some traits and lower on others. There is no perfect combination, so you won't need to worry about that when we do a little personality test later on!
Let's start with openness. This personality trait is to do with your interest in the world. If you're keen to get

involved with activities you've never tried before, or enjoy discussing concepts you've never heard of, you're an open person. Whereas open people tend to be comfortable with unfamiliar situations, and feel naturally curious, people who are less open may prefer routines and familiar ideas instead.
Let's move on to conscientiousness. If you're usually punctual, do what you say you'll do, and take responsibility for your actions, then you're a conscientious person. To put that in an educational context, you're the student who hands in work on time, does the recommended reading and attends all your lectures, whereas in your social life, you'll never leave anyone waiting and people will know they can depend on you.
You'll probably be familiar with the term 'extrovert' and 'introvert'. If you're an extrovert, you might be very enthusiastic and love spending time with people. It's likely that no one would ever call you shy and you're the first one up on the dance floor at parties, while other people are only just warming up!
Would you describe yourself as a kind person who trusts other people and would do anything to lend a hand? If so, you may well have a high level of agreeableness. You will be empathetic, which means you'll get other people's feelings, and you will demonstrate characteristics that show you to be pro-social, in other words, you show concern for others.
Finally, let's turn to neuroticism. People often use this term incorrectly, to suggest that a neurotic person is unpredictable and too emotional. This isn't exactly accurate, though someone who demonstrates high neuroticism will probably experience more negative emotions, such as depression or self-doubt. That doesn't mean you aren't still a great person!
To sum up, everyone has all five traits to a greater or lesser degree! Thank you.

Audio 1.09

To sum up, everyone has all five traits to a greater or lesser degree!

UNIT 2

Audio 2.01

1 VR is certain to come down in price eventually.
2 Robert's due to start his new job on Monday.
3 Are you going to bring your headset with you?
4 You're unlikely to catch anything out in the open.
5 Joseph is going to study law at university.
6 VR is likely to be in every household by 2030.

Audio 2.02

1 There's a lack of attractive green spaces in my town.
2 Only a handful of people I know live in the countryside.
3 I spend a good deal of time outdoors.
4 Several of the beaches nearby are quite good.
5 Young people who like gardening are in a minority.

Audio 2.03

Hello and welcome to this month's edition of *Soundbites*. I'm your host, Adam Byrne.
Now, when I was growing up, gardening was something that your parents did at the weekend. The thought of helping pull up weeds or mow the lawn never crossed my mind. In fact, it probably would've felt like a punishment! But these days, more and more young people are taking up gardening. A recent survey suggests that over eighty percent of 18–34-year-olds think gardening is 'cool', with many spending up to two hours a week looking after their plants. So, what do they get out of it? I spoke to three young gardeners to find out.

Audio 2.04

1: So, I used to have very little interest in gardening, even though my mum was always out there digging and chopping things down and that.
Anyway, at the time, I was feeling pretty stressed – I'd just started uni and was feeling a bit overwhelmed. Then I read that gardening was a great way of being mindful. You know, focusing on your surroundings as a way of feeling calm and relaxed. So, I started helping mum out in the garden whenever I was home from uni and it worked. I'm not sure whether it's because of the garden itself, or just because I can leave my desk for a while. But it really helps me get away from it all.

2: I live in a high-rise apartment block, so I love getting out into green open spaces whenever I can. But I had absolutely zero interest in gardening till someone here started a rooftop community garden. Over time, I saw how things started growing and became fascinated. I asked if I could get involved and since then I go up there every weekend. I've learned tons about planting and looking after stuff, how much sunlight or water things need, what to do in different seasons, all that kind of thing. We're planning a vegetable plot at the moment, where residents will get free food when it's ready – I can't wait!

3: I'm an outdoors kind of girl and, growing up on the coast, I always loved exploring the beaches, surfing, that kind of thing.
Anyway, I was out walking one day along this amazing stretch of coastline and I came across this … kind of, bright, pink flower growing straight out of the cliff face. I remember being amazed that something so beautiful could grow in such a wild, remote place. Anyway, I took a photo and looked it up when I got home. Then I started reading about all of the other plants that are native to this area and was just kind of hooked from there. I'm so glad I started studying flowers. Now I grow all sorts of things on my balcony overlooking the sea.

Audio 2.05

Now I grow all sorts of things on my balcony overlooking the sea.

Audio 2.06

1 Man: What do you think life on a tiny island would be like?
Woman: I suppose it depends on how remote it is. Like, if you can hop on a boat and get to the mainland in a few minutes, I'd have thought it wouldn't feel so small.
Man: I reckon you could easily get cut off though. You know, if the sea's rough and ferries are cancelled.
Woman: Maybe.

2 Man: Do you think we'll get used to life on the mainland quickly? I mean, we've lived on the island all our lives.
Woman: I bet we'll settle in in no time! I know for a fact that we're going to meet loads of great people at uni. We'll forget all about this little place!
Man: There's no way I'll forget home so easily! I love it here!

3 Woman: I can't imagine what life will be like round here in the future.
Man: I doubt there'll be anyone here in a hundred years' time! Most people will have moved to the cities for work.
Woman: Hmmm … I'd imagine the farmers will stay.
Man: I get the impression that once the current farming generation retires, there'll be no one to take over.

Audio 2.07

1 There's no way I'd ever consider travelling solo round the world.
2 I know for a fact that I'd feel like I was in prison on a tiny boat.
3 He's obviously not happy where he is at the moment.
4 You're clearly not someone who wants a conventional lifestyle.
5 Tom's bound to live a life of adventure – he can't keep still!

Audio 2.08 and 2.09

Oli: I'd imagine Kwame's feeling nervous about the play tomorrow.
Cara: It's the first night, right? I get the impression that he's feeling pretty confident, actually.
Oli: Oh, yeah?
Cara: Yes – I know for a fact that he's learned his lines off by heart.
Oli: Well, I'd guess you have to, really. There's no way I could be an actor.
Cara: Why not? I'm one hundred per cent sure that you'd be brilliant at it!
Oli: No, I'd be bound to get stage fright!

UNIT 3

Audio 3.01

1 Glastonbury Festival, which has been running since 1970, attracts over 200,000 visitors.
2 The band, who had never played to such a large crowd before, felt very nervous.
3 The headline act, which will perform this evening, is expected to draw a huge crowd.
4 Billie Eilish, who has sold over 5 million records worldwide, will be on stage at nine.
5 The orchestra, which is bigger than ever, will play on the Sticks stage this afternoon.
6 Woodstock, which took place over three days in 1969, was a turning point in music.

Audio 3.02

1 What I like watching are the less well-known acts.
2 It was Max who left the car unlocked, not me.
3 What sounds better to me is finishing on a minor chord.
4 It's you who likes Italian opera – that's why I got the tickets!

Audio 3.03

Alex: Well, that's the first and last time I'm acting on stage! I mean, it was like, a total disaster!
Katy: Oh, no. What happened? Did you mess up your lines?
Alex: No, I'd practised, like, a thousand times! But my partner did and it all got really confusing. She kept coming out with the wrong lines and sometimes forgot what she was supposed to be saying altogether!
Katy: Oops! That happened to me once. I mean, I was the person forgetting the lines. So embarrassing. The play ran for a week and every time I had to go on stage, I could hardly stand up, I was shaking so much. I was just so scared I'd mess up – and I did, every time! I could tell the other guys were frustrated with me, but they were nice enough not to give me a hard time about it. I mean, it wasn't exactly a professional performance. It was just awful, though. Every day I had to go on stage, it was like the worst day of my life!
Alex: Poor you. I guess I should be kinder about my partner – I suppose she had stage fright.
Katy: Yeah – I mean, you feel as if you're going to die of fright. And I knew my lines, they just wouldn't come out of my mouth. It's like I had a total block.
Alex: Hmm … well that does sound awful. But anyway, on top of that, my costume fell to pieces! I mean, it literally fell off on stage!
Katy: Noooo! I helped to make those costumes! How embarrassing!
Alex: Well, it wasn't too bad. It was only the outer layer. And I think someone else made mine, actually. But then, some of the scenery fell over. There was this tree thing in one corner of the stage and bang! It fell over, just like that.
Katy: No way!
Alex: Yes, way! We had to just leave it there until the interval and the props guys sorted it out then. Oh, and listen to this!
Katy: Go on.
Alex: The lighting failed at one point. Like, there was no light whatsoever on stage. We were in the middle of a scene and the lights just went out.
Katy: I bet your time on stage seemed to go on forever! How did the audience react?
Alex: Actually, some of them got up and left which wasn't very nice to see – but totally understandable. I'd have wanted my money back. But the rest were so kind and just pretended the disasters weren't happening.
Katy: That's the good thing about audiences – they do want you to do well.
Alex: Yeah, they were very kind!

Audio 3.04

1 It was like, a total disaster!
2 I'd practised, like, a thousand times!
3 I could hardly stand up, I was shaking so much.
4 It was like the worst day of my life!
5 You feel as if you're going to die of fright.
6 I bet your time on stage seemed to go on forever!

Audio 3.05

It was still a relief to get off stage at the end of the night!

Audio 3.06

Woman: Have you seen *Squid Game*?
Man: No! Isn't it sort of a horror show?
Woman: Something like that. I'd call it a dramatic thriller, actually. Though there are some bits that aren't that nice to watch.
Man: Hmm, I'm not into that kind of thing.
Woman: Well, I definitely wouldn't recommend it for kids.
Man: Isn't it about adults who have to play games to win loads of money?
Woman: Yeah – they compete in Korean children's games and run around and stuff. But the games are deadly!
Man: I think I'll leave that one to you!

Audio 3.07

1 Woman: Who's that guy who played the thief in *Lupin*?
Man: It's what's his name – oh, you know!

2 Man: When was the *Great Gatsby* supposed to be set? I loved the costumes.
Woman: Around the 1920s, I think.

3 Man: How old do you think the actor in *Maid* is?
Woman: I'd say she's young-ish … maybe late 20s?

4 Woman: Did you enjoy watching *the Originals*?
Man: It was OK. It's sort of for a younger audience, really.

5 Man: Is *Money Heist* a dark story?
Woman: I suppose it is, a bit. But I like that kind of thing.

Audio 3.08

1 I love getting caught up in a good mystery series.
2 I like the film. It's sort of a combination of action and thriller.
3 I love dramas that are based on real events.
4 *The Crystal Maze*? Oh, that's where they run around and find crystals or something like that, isn't it?

Audio 3.09 and 3.10

Peter: Have you seen that TV programme, *The Crown*?
Alex: Yeah. I've watched the first series.
Peter: What's it about?
Alex: It's about the British Royal Family. Each series concentrates on a different period of time and the events that took place then. It's a bit slow in places for me, but it's interesting enough.
Peter: Does it show real events and stuff? Or is it all made up?
Alex: It's based on real things that happened, but I think they sort of use a bit of artistic licence – you know, they don't really know what people said or anything so they have to make that up.

Audio 3.11

Hello and welcome to ClickBeat – the show in which my panel and I discuss all things music. Now, today we're focusing on a genre that really does divide opinion – jazz. What is it about this style of music that some people love and others seem to hate? Well, here to help us answer that question is jazz musician Elijah Kegan and music critic Bethany Cartwright. Elijah, Bethany – welcome to the show.

Audio 3.12

Presenter: So, Bethany – what is it about jazz that divides opinion so much?
Bethany: I think partly because it's unpredictable, and it can be difficult to make sense of if you aren't a trained musician. That's because jazz musicians often improvise. In other words, they make music up as they go along, so as a listener, you don't know where it's going next. That can be confusing, as time signatures keep changing. What I mean by that is that you might start out counting one, two, three, four and then find the rhythm's changed to one, two, three, four, five. Counting five beats or seven beats or whatever is very different to most of the music we listen to. It can be tricky to keep track of what's happening. It can create feelings of discomfort, and when we're made to feel uncomfortable by something, we're more likely not to enjoy it.
Presenter: Interesting. Elijah, what do you think?
Elijah: Obviously, I'm a big fan of jazz! I couldn't live without it. Some jazz is very accessible. You'll recognise lots of jazz tunes and tap your feet to them. There's this technique in jazz known as 'noodling'. That's when the music diverts away from the main tune and it can sound quite messy and noisy – though there *is* structure and tune there if you listen for it. I think mainly it's down to the sound – when you have, say, a saxophone involved, it can be quite high pitched and sound like it's screaming. I think that's why some people can't stand it.
Presenter: What do you both think could help people to enjoy jazz more? Or, do they really need to?
Elijah: I do think they're missing out, personally. It's got an interesting history. It's very creative and there are some great tunes and beats – like those ones that get your feet tapping. You don't have to listen to the 'hard core' stuff that serious jazz fans listen to.
Bethany: Elijah's right. There's lots of more sort of basic, structured jazz out there which is a good introduction to the genre. No one *has* to listen to anything they don't want to – but when you give things a go, you often develop new passions for things and it opens your mind.
Presenter: All right, well I think it's time we listened to some, don't you? Coming up next is Duke Ellington's …

Audio 3.13

All right, well I think it's time we listened to some, don't you?

UNIT 4

Audio 4.01

1 By this time next week, I'll have finished this project.
2 Hopefully, I'll have cut out meat entirely by then.
3 With any luck, we'll have bought a house by then.
4 Come round at 7 p.m. – we'll have eaten dinner by then.
5 By this time next week, you'll have graduated from university!

Audio 4.02

1 It was thought that eating cheese before bedtime gives you nightmares.
2 It's been suggested that using your phone in bed makes it harder to drop off.
3 It's believed that up to fifteen percent of the population are sleepwalkers.
4 It's estimated that most people sleep for fewer than seven hours a night.

Audio 4.03

Presenter: Welcome back to the show. Today, we're taking tips from good sleepers across the country with the aim of tackling insomnia! Next on the line is Rob from Lancashire. Rob – what do you do to help you drop off?

Audio 4.04

Presenter: Rob – what do you do to help you drop off?
Rob: Well, I used to use this sleep tracker – in fact, I got a bit obsessed with it. I was told exactly how much deep sleep I was getting, when I was awake and what my total hours' sleep was. I'd check it every morning and I reckon I got less sleep because I was so concerned about whether or not I was getting enough of the 'right' kind! You can't change things, so it's all a bit pointless. My advice is to forget the tracker and focus on techniques for chilling out – it worked for me!
Presenter: Thanks, Rob! Next on the line is Jenna, from Birmingham. Jenna what works for you?
Jenna: I've been an insomniac since I finished university. I think it started with getting all anxious. I kept thinking, 'What will I be doing this time next year? Will I have found a job?', that kind of thing. I'd be so exhausted that I'd need naps during the day – and then the whole vicious circle started again once I got into bed. So, I did a bit of research and discovered an article that said you should stop thinking of yourself as a bad sleeper. I guess it's some kind of reverse psychology. Anyway, I started saying more positive things to myself. It took practice to get anywhere near believing it, but eventually it sank in and now I sleep much better.
Presenter: Great advice, Jenna. I'm sure some of our listeners can relate to that. OK, now let's talk to Álvaro. Álvaro, good morning! What do you do to tackle insomnia?

Álvaro: OK, well, this one might sound a bit weird but I read about it online.
Presenter: Go on!
Álvaro: Nuts! I mean, eating nuts – they make you sleepy! I don't mean right before you go to bed but just eating them on a regular basis. They've got loads of nutrients in them that are associated with sleep, apparently, and it's been recognised that they do something to brainwave frequencies – whatever that means. Anyway, it helps me. The ones that work best are peanuts.
Presenter: Very interesting! Thank you. We've just got time for one last call … Sonya from Edinburgh. Sonya – what's your tip?
Sonya: I stare into the darkness when I'm in bed rather than shutting my eyes and willing myself to go to sleep. Levels of the sleep hormone are increased that way, apparently. It kind of works, weirdly! I also heard that you should try to stay awake as long as you can if you're having problems dropping off. It has some sort of opposite effect – I've not tried that yet, though!
Presenter: OK, thanks Sonya. Well, that's about it for today's show.

Audio 4.05

Thanks to all of our callers for their advice!

Audio 4.06

Amy: So, have you ever done micro-HIIT training?
Ollie: Is that the one where you push yourself really hard for like, three minutes?
Amy: Yeah, that's right! It sounds ridiculously difficult! Sounds like too much effort to me!
Ollie: I know what you mean, but it's supposed to be really good for you and the best thing is it doesn't take very long!
Amy: Well, that's true.
Ollie: The other thing I was reading about was Everesting. Have you ever heard of that?
Amy: No, what's that? Climbing Everest?!
Ollie: Actually, it's cycling. You cycle up a hill – and back down again – until you've cycled a distance the height of Mount Everest – nearly nine kilometres. It's not that far but you do it in one go. I don't think that'd be too hard.
Amy: I completely disagree. You'd get tired quickly going uphill, I think. You're not an experienced cyclist!
Ollie: I see your point, but I'd soon get fitter.
Amy: That's a fair point.
Ollie: On the other hand, I could probably do with finding something more relaxing and low-impact.
Amy: I couldn't agree more! You're under so much pressure at work. How about yogalates? It's a combination of yoga and pilates. You'd increase your strength and de-stress at the same time.
Ollie: That's a good point. And I could do it from home, online. Anyway, what about you? You're more into walking, right?
Amy: I was but I've got really into this virtual training app and I've started running. I love it!

Audio 4.07

1 I agree up to a point, but don't you think the government should play a role, too?

2 I take your point, but that's what footballers expect to get paid.

3 That's a fair point, but don't you think they get enough exercise at school?

Audio 4.08 and 4.09

Marla: Let's do something. It would be a shame to stay in on a day like this.
Dan: I couldn't agree more. What shall we do? Want to try bouldering with me? Come on …
Marla: Climbing over massive rocks all day? No, thanks. It sounds exhausting.
Dan: I know what you mean, but you did say you want to improve your strength a bit …
Marla: That's a fair point, but I've got work tomorrow and I don't want to be worn out.
Dan: You go to the gym all the time – you'll be fine!
Marla: I completely disagree! Last time we went jogging it took me a week to recover!
Dan: All right, I take your point. You do need a lot of stamina. But on the other hand, if you stay here all day, you'll never get fitter!

UNIT 1

Lesson 1A

VOCABULARY

1A **1** b **2** a **3** a **4** c **5** b **6** c

1B
1 argumentative
2 rebellious
3 cheerful
4 outgoing
5 ambitious
6 adventurous
7 curious
8 stubborn

2
1 helpful
2 artistic
3 talented
4 emotional
5 realistic
6 likeable
7 experienced

GRAMMAR

3A
1 been calling
2 had
3 been having
4 visited
5 been studying
6 raised

3B
1 've/have (always) been
2 've/have been working
3 've/have had
4 has helped
5 've/have been practising
6 's/has been

3C
1 I've seen that new Wes Anderson film five times now.
2 You've been working on that report all morning!
3 Have you been anywhere interesting recently?
4 Ben's never tried horse-riding because he's scared of horses!
5 He's taken a year off to go travelling.
6 I've been looking for you for the last half an hour!

PRONUNCIATION

4A
1 She's never been
2 have you been
3 he been
4 I've been
5 She's been

LISTENING

5A The correct order is: c, e, d, a, b.

5B
1 personality traits
2 make important decisions
3 a model
4 fixed
5 feed into

5C Explore and experiment, find out what you like doing and who you identify with.

WRITING

6A
1 adventurous
2 risk-taker
3 indoor activities
4 music teacher
5 curious
6 extreme

6B Present perfect simple: I've actually changed, I've always been, I've taken up, I've changed, I've outgrown, I've changed, I've always had
Present perfect continuous: I've been channelling, I've been working

6C Sample answer: Have I changed as I've got older? I don't think my personality's all that different and it doesn't seem to change much in my work or in my personal life. I'm neither outgoing nor shy, though I can be more or less of those things depending on who I'm with.
I've had the same hobbies since I was a kid. I still love nothing more than dancing and playing music. Recently, I've taken up swimming, too, though I haven't been attending classes lately as I've injured my shoulder.
As for values, I think I've become more open-minded and judge other people less than I used to. I'd like to think people see me that way, too. I'm more likely to stand up for myself and others, as well.

Lesson 1B

VOCABULARY

1
1 remember every detail
2 short-term
3 heart
4 brought back memories
5 childhood
6 got

2A **1** c **2** b **3** f **4** e **5** a **6** d

2B
1 on the tip of my tongue
2 rings a bell
3 memory is playing tricks on me
4 refresh my memory
5 in one ear and out the other
6 slipped my mind

PRONUNCIATION

3A
1 short-term memory
2 perfect recall
3 childhood memories

GRAMMAR

4A
1 to meet
2 to set
3 getting up
4 going
5 to have
6 to lock

4B
1 to climb
2 to improve
3 setting off
4 to make sure
5 having
6 to reach

READING

5A 2, 3, 5, 6

5B **1** help us recall past events, learn from our mistakes, creating our identities
2 we wish that what we are saying is true, or we want our listener to think in a particular way ..., we might want to make them laugh or feel sorry for us
3 false memories
4 the 'audience-tuning' effect
5 fill in the gaps

5C **1** b **2** c **3** b

Lesson 1C

VOCABULARY

1A **1** about
2 of
3 of
4 by
5 on
6 into
7 of
8 about

1B **1** passionate about
2 nervous about
3 keen on
4 terrified of
5 fed up of
6 really into

HOW TO ...

2A Going on holiday / going backpacking together; Yes, they do.

2B **1** my kind of thing
2 not a big fan of
3 How about if we
4 I'd love to
5 don't want to
6 sound like a plan

PRONUNCIATION

3A and **3B**
1 I'm quite <u>fond</u> of boat trips, actually. They're a great way to see the city.
2 The kids aren't <u>keen</u> on trying unusual foods.
3 Dan's <u>ter</u>rified of driving in foreign countries and so am I!
4 I'm not <u>real</u>ly into visiting museums. I find a lot of them really boring.
5 I always feel <u>ner</u>vous about getting lost when I'm in a new city.
6 Katie's quite <u>pass</u>ionate about culture and the arts.

SPEAKING

4A **1** e **2** c **3** d **4** f **5** b **6** a

Lesson 1D

GRAMMAR

1A **1** d **2** a **3** f **4** e **5** b **6** c

1B **1** confident with friends, intimidated by people at work
2 to see you, too much work to do
3 meeting new people, not very sociable
4 my parents, walking home
5 mowed the lawn, cleaned the house
6 self-esteem, very confident

LISTENING

2A **1** e **2** c **3** b **4** a **5** d

2B **1** perfect combination
2 (usually) punctual
3 educational context
4 shy
5 feelings
6 negative emotions

2C To sum up, everyone has all five traits to a greater or lesser degree!

UNIT 2

Lesson 2A

VOCABULARY

1 **1** Smart
2 analyse
3 remotely
4 predicted
5 findings
6 Researchers
7 tech industry
8 virtual reality

2 **1** b **2** a **3** c **4** a **5** c **6** b

GRAMMAR

3A **1** definitely won't
2 unlikely
3 certain to
4 due to
5 may not
6 could

3B **1** is unlikely to
2 is going to
3 I'll ever attend / I'd ever attend
4 is certain to / will certainly
5 due to hand in
6 might find

PRONUNCIATION

4A **1** certain to
2 due to
3 going to
4 unlikely to
5 is going to
6 likely to

READING

5A **1** a 2 b 3 b 4 a 5 a 6 b

5B **1** T
2 T
3 T
4 F (She is amazed by it.)
5 F (She has not presented at a conference yet.)
6 T

Lesson 2B

VOCABULARY

1A **1** b **2** f **3** a **4** c **5** e **6** d

1B **1** woodland
2 river bank
3 open spaces
4 tracks
5 scenery
6 sunlight

GRAMMAR

2A **1** few
2 No
3 minority
4 little
5 a handful of
6 a few

2B **1** a handful of
2 A few
3 Every/Each
4 no / not any
5 lack
6 little
7 deal
8 few

PRONUNCIATION

3A **1** There's a lack‿of attractive green spaces in my town.
2 Only a handful‿of people I know live in the countryside.
3 I spend a good‿deal‿of my time outdoors.
4 Several‿of‿the beaches nearby are quite good.
5 Young people who like gardening are‿in‿a minority.

LISTENING

4A c

4B **a** 3 **b** 2 **c** 1 **d** 2 **e** 3 **f** 1

4C **1** T
2 F (She wasn't sure whether it was because of the garden or getting away from her desk.)
3 T
4 F (He became interested over time.)
5 T
6 T
7 F (She has a lot of new knowledge about plants.)

4D Now I grow all sorts of things on my balcony overlooking the sea.

WRITING

5A c

5B **1** Despite
2 While/Although
3 Although/While
4 However
5 However
6 despite

5C **1** **Although** ~~despite~~ I love living in the city, …
2 **However**, ~~Although~~ I'm starting to find it a little small.
3 **Although/While** ~~Despite~~ many people I know prefer renting, …
4 **Although/While** ~~However~~ there can be a great sense of community in villages …
5 **Despite** ~~Although~~ the fact that public transport is so good in the city,
6 **However**, ~~Despite~~ I'll admit it can be boring at times.

5E Sample answer:
Some people prefer to spend most of their time indoors, while others prefer to be outdoors. So, which is most beneficial for our well-being?
Let's first consider mental well-being. Although there's much to be said for snuggling down to binge-watch the latest hit TV series, or talking about our worries over coffee with friends, it's just as important to get mood-boosting fresh air in our lungs and sunlight on our faces.
Despite warnings, when it comes to physical well-being, many of us still don't get moving as much as we should. However, it isn't difficult to build in a few minutes' walk a day, even if sports aren't our thing. Of course, the more exercise we do, the healthier our bodies become.
While indoor and outdoor activities are both advantageous for our well-being, I believe it is a combination of the two that benefits us most.

Lesson 2C

VOCABULARY

1 **1** unique
2 ordinary
3 harsh
4 rewarding
5 exhausting
6 tedious
7 modest

HOW TO …

2A what living on a tiny/small island is like; how going to live on the mainland will affect them; whether anyone will be living in the area in 100 years' time

2B **1** c **2** h **3** a **4** e **5** g **6** b **7** f **8** d

PRONUNCIATION

3 **1** way
2 fact
3 not
4 clearly
5 bound

SPEAKING

4A and **4B**
1 imagine
2 impression
3 fact
4 way
5 sure
6 bound

Lesson 2D

VOCABULARY

1 **1** finest
2 magnificent
3 mighty
4 precious
5 finest
6 astonishing

READING

2A **1** Yes
2 No (only in theory)

2B **1** incredible
2 (our) mistakes
3 space-time
4 face creams
5 (mathematical) calculations
6 laws of physics
7 dark matter
8 wormholes

2C b

REVIEW 1–2

GRAMMAR

1 **1** been learning
2 emailed
3 been
4 had
5 been working

2 **1** to repair
2 to save
3 to go
4 to get
5 going
6 to say
7 to retrain
8 to do
9 seeing

3 Suggested answers
1 Whereas/While/Whilst I enjoy writing stories, I don't have a brilliant imagination.
2 While/Whilst I'm actually quite shy, I love performing on stage.
3 Whereas/While/Whilst I can organise other people, I can't organise myself.
4 Whereas/While/Whilst I'm happy to listen to people's problems, I don't like giving advice. / I'm happy to listen to people's problems, whereas/while/whilst I don't like giving advice.
5 Whereas/While/Whilst I've never enjoyed playing football, I've always enjoyed watching it. / I've never enjoyed playing football, whereas/while/whilst I've always enjoyed watching it.

4 **1** to leave
2 going to happen
3 might not be
4 won't enjoy
5 will be able
6 will also be
7 won't need
8 be able
9 to meet
10 will give

5 **1** a little
2 lack of
3 aren't any
4 majority
5 Very few

VOCABULARY

6 **1** rebellious
2 argumentative
3 curious
4 adventurous
5 stubborn

7 **1** experienced
2 optimistic
3 reliable
4 emotional
5 practical

8 **1** recall
2 detail
3 memory
4 short-term
5 by heart

9 **1** rings a bell
2 go in one ear and out the other
3 playing tricks on me
4 on the tip of my tongue
5 refresh my memory

10 **1** up
2 of
3 into
4 about
5 on

11 **1** a **2** c **3** b **4** a **5** c

12 **1** research
2 predicted
3 analysis
4 researcher
5 scientific
6 remotely

13 **1** sunlight
2 river bank
3 deserted
4 woodland
5 scenery

14 **1** tedious
2 unique
3 modest
4 harsh
5 rewarding

15 **1** a **2** b **3** a **4** a **5** b

UNIT 3

Lesson 3A

VOCABULARY

1 **1** attending
2 line-up
3 acts
4 atmosphere
5 organisers
6 venue
7 attracts
8 festival-goers

2 **1** footprint
2 resources
3 recycling
4 emissions
5 renewable
6 power

GRAMMAR

3A **1** c **2** a **3** c **4** b

3B sentences 1 and 3

PRONUNCIATION

4A **1** Glastonbury Festival, which has been running since 1970, attracts over 200,000 visitors.
2 The band, who had never played to such a large crowd before, felt very nervous.
3 The headline act, which will perform this evening, is expected to draw a huge crowd.
4 Billie Eilish, who has sold over 5 million records worldwide, will be on stage at nine.
5 The orchestra, which is bigger than ever, will play on the Sticks stage this afternoon.
6 Woodstock, which took place over three days in 1969, was a turning point in music.

READING

5A green festivals, product quality, renewable energy, sustainable products, transport

5B **1** environmental policies
2 refill stations
3 go plastic-free
4 wind it up

WRITING

6A **1** to ask them to clean up after the festival

6B **1** f **2** a **3** e **4** b **5** c **6** d

6D See Ex 6A for a sample answer.

7A Sample answer:
In most towns and cities, people pay taxes and local governments use these taxes to maintain the local environment. While it would be good for people to look after their local environment, it would not work in practice.
The first reason is most people do not have time to tidy public gardens or clean up litter from the streets. People lead busy lives and do not have time for additional duties.
Also, some of these duties require skills or knowledge that most people do not have. Take looking after local woodland, for example. Most people would be unable to do that well.
Although people would probably look after their environment better if they had to do it themselves, I believe it is better for local governments to do this, by employing the right people with the right skills.

Lesson 3B

VOCABULARY

1A **1** b **2** a **3** c **4** c **5** a

1B **1** carry on
2 fall back on
3 came up with
4 put you off
5 ended up
6 put up with

2 **1** speak up
2 get your message across
3 spell out
4 coming back to
5 bring up
6 came across
7 pointed out that
8 move on from

GRAMMAR

3A **1** d **2** a **3** h **4** b **5** f **6** g **7** e **8** c

3B **1** b **2** c **3** a **4** c

PRONUNCIATION

4A **1** What I like watching are the less well-known acts.
2 It was Max who left the car unlocked, not me.
3 What sounds better to me is finishing on a minor chord.
4 It's you who likes Italian opera – that's why I got the tickets!

LISTENING

5A D, A, E, B, C

5B **1** F (She got confused.)
2 T
3 T
4 F (They had to leave it until the interval.)
5 F (Alex would have understood if they had.)
6 T

5C **1** disaster
2 thousand
3 shaking
4 worst
5 fright
6 forever

5D It was still a relief to get off stage at the end of the night.

Lesson 3C

VOCABULARY

1A **1** based
2 cast
3 set
4 scenes
5 ending
6 twist
7 costumes
8 soundtrack

1B **1** subtitles
2 set
3 twist
4 cast
5 scene
6 based

HOW TO ...

2A and stuff, bits, something like that, sort of, that kind of thing

2B **1** c **2** e **3** a **4** b **5** d

PRONUNCIATION

3A **1** getting caught up
2 sort of
3 based on
4 something like that

SPEAKING

4A **1** about
2 bit
3 and
4 of
5 or

Lesson 3D

GRAMMAR

1A **1** didn't
2 don't
3 did
4 do
5 Do
6 did

1B **1** do
2 doesn't
3 did
4 did
5 don't
6 do
7 do
8 does

LISTENING

2A **1** jazz (music)
2 a jazz musician
3 a music critic

2B **1** c **2** b **3** a

2C **1** improvise / make music up
2 uncomfortable
3 technique
4 messy and noisy
5 interesting history
6 good introduction

2D All right, well I think it's time we listened to some, don't you?

UNIT 4

Lesson 4A

VOCABULARY

1 **1** keep/stay
2 cut
3 expand
4 stay/keep
5 doing
6 did
7 worked
8 transformed
9 vary
10 keep

2A illness: allergies, asthma, food poisoning, run-down
treatment: antibiotics, first aid, medication, vaccine

2B **1** food poisoning
2 allergies
3 first aid
4 antibiotics/medication
5 vaccines/medication/antibiotics
6 run-down

GRAMMAR

3A **1** a **2** a **3** c **4** b

3B **1** have been
2 be celebrating
3 be having
4 be setting up
5 be going
6 have improved
7 have done
8 be writing

PRONUNCIATION

4A **1** I'll have finished
2 I'll have cut out
3 we'll have bought
4 we'll have eaten
5 you'll have graduated

READING

5A b

5B **1** T **2** F **3** T **4** F **5** F **6** T

5C **1** cell damage
2 (their) (hard-earned) cash
3 (another/a) marketing trick
4 ice cream

Lesson 4B

VOCABULARY

1A **1** exhausted
2 oversleep
3 dropping off
4 nightmare
5 snore
6 keep
7 sleeper
8 deep

1B **1** a **2** a **3** b **4** a **5** b **6** c

GRAMMAR

2A **1** d **2** a **3** e **4** c **5** b

2 **1** is suggested/has been suggested
2 is (generally) accepted
3 is (also) suspected
4 was (once) assumed
5 is now not/is not now considered
6 is defined/has been defined
7 is (more easily) understood
8 is observed/has been observed
9 was noticed
10 wasn't/hasn't been discovered

PRONUNCIATION

3B **1** It was thought that eating cheese before bedtime gives you nightmares.
2 It's been suggested that using your phone in bed makes it harder to drop off.
3 It's believed that up to fifteen percent of the population are sleepwalkers.
4 It's estimated that most people sleep for fewer than seven hours a night.

LISTENING

4A a phone-in show

4B **1** c **2** a **3** c **4** c **5** b

4C Thanks to all of our callers for their advice.

WRITING

5A nightmares, sleep positions, lack of sleep, sleep and disability, dreams, sleep behaviour and conditions

5B **1** a **2** d **3** e **4** c **5** b

5D Sample answer:
Some people fall asleep in seconds and wake up full of energy the next morning. Others take hours to get to sleep, wake up during the night and struggle to wake up the next day. Me? I'm a combination of the two.
It's quite common for me, when I'm tired, to drop off within seconds. I can fall asleep on the sofa, on the train and even on my balcony. But at night, I can wake up an hour or two before my alarm goes off and then not get back to sleep.
So, what do I do? I try to relax, but my mind usually has other ideas. I try to focus on my breathing, but for some reason that just makes me feel anxious. I try every sleep position possible, but I can never quite find the right one. In the end, I usually just get up and start my day. I feel exhausted, but I can always have a nap later.

Lesson 4C

VOCABULARY

1
1 stamina
2 aerobic
3 Strength
4 low-impact
5 moderate
6 High-impact

2
1 challenge
2 encouragement
3 incentive
4 benefit
5 discipline
6 confidence

HOW TO ...

3A Different kinds of exercise.

3B **1** PA **2** A **3** D **4** A **5** A **6** A

PRONUNCIATION

4A The main stress is on *point* in all three sentences.

SPEAKING

5A
1 couldn't agree
2 you mean
3 point
4 disagree
5 your point
6 other hand

Lesson 4D

VOCABULARY

1
1 Time is running out
2 just in time
3 window of opportunity
4 not a moment too soon
5 is still under threat
6 It's time to move on from
7 under threat
8 time

READING

2A to provide a balanced argument

2B **1** T **2** T **3** F **4** T **5** T **6** F **7** T **8** F

REVIEW 3–4

GRAMMAR

1
1 the theatre where Nick
2 the girl we met at
3 the guy whose car
4 which opened last year
5 the hotel we stayed

2 **1** b **2** d **3** f **4** e **5** a **6** c

3
1 do
2 did
3 do
4 don't
5 does
6 did
7 does

4
1 be hearing
2 will have got used to
3 have fallen
4 will have shrunk
5 will have risen
6 will have increased
7 will have started
8 will have done

5 **1** a **2** c **3** b **4** c

VOCABULARY

6
1 line-up
2 atmosphere
3 organisers
4 attended
5 attracting
6 festival-goers
7 act
8 venue

7
1 footprint
2 recycling
3 emissions
4 resources
5 power

8
1 come up with
2 fall back on
3 live up to
4 messed up (all my lines) / messed (all my lines) up
5 putting (me off)

9
1 across
2 on to
3 up
4 back
5 out

10
1 ending
2 costumes
3 soundtrack
4 based on
5 twist